Canada's
Other
Red
Scare

Rethinking Canada in the World
Series editors: Ian McKay and Sean Mills

Supported by the Wilson Institute for Canadian History at McMaster University, this series is committed to books that rethink Canadian history from transnational and global perspectives. It enlarges approaches to the study of Canada in the world by exploring how Canadian history has long been a dynamic product of global currents and forces. The series will also reinvigorate understanding of Canada's role as an international actor and how Canadians have contributed to intellectual, political, cultural, social, and material exchanges around the world.

Volumes included in the series explore the ideas, movements, people, and institutions that have transcended political boundaries and territories to shape Canadian society and the state. These include both state and non-state actors, and phenomena such as international migration, diaspora politics, religious movements, evolving conceptions of human rights and civil society, popular culture, technology, epidemics, wars, and global finance and trade.

The series charts a new direction by exploring networks of transmission and exchange from a standpoint that is not solely national or international, expanding the history of Canada's engagement with the world.

http://wilson.humanities.mcmaster.ca

Canada's Other Red Scare

Indigenous Protest and Colonial Encounters during the Global Sixties

SCOTT RUTHERFORD

MCGILL-QUEEN'S UNIVERSITY PRESS

Montreal & Kingston · London · Chicago

ISBN 978-0-2280-0405-9 (cloth)
ISBN 978-0-2280-0406-6 (paper)
ISBN 978-0-2280-0511-7 (ePDF)
ISBN 978-0-2280-0512-4 (ePUB)

Legal deposit fourth quarter 2020
Bibliothèque nationale du Québec

Printed in Canada on acid-free paper that is 100% ancient forest free
(100% post-consumer recycled), processed chlorine free

This book has been published with the help of a grant from the Canadian Federation for the Humanities and Social Sciences, through the
Awards to Scholarly Publications Program, using funds provided by
the Social Sciences and Humanities Research Council of Canada.

We acknowledge the support of the Canada Council for the Arts.

Nous remercions le Conseil des arts du Canada de son soutien.

Library and Archives Canada Cataloguing in Publication

Title: Canada's other red scare : Indigenous protest and colonial
    encounters during the global sixties / Scott Rutherford.
Names: Rutherford, Scott, 1979- author.
Series: Rethinking Canada in the world ; 6.
Description: Series statement: Rethinking Canada in the world ; 6 |
    Includes bibliographical references and index.
Identifiers: Canadiana (print) 20200329383 | Canadiana (ebook)
    20200329553 | ISBN 9780228004066 (softcover) | ISBN 9780228004059
    (hardcover) | ISBN 9780228005117 (PDF) | ISBN 9780228005124 (EPUB)
Subjects: LCSH: Protest movements—Ontario—Kenora—History—
    20th century. | LCSH: Civil rights demonstrations—Ontario—
    Kenora—History—20th century. | LCSH: Indigenous peoples—
    Ontario—Kenora—Social conditions—20th century. | LCSH: Kenora
    (Ont.)—Race relations—History—20th century. | LCSH: Kenora
    (Ont.)—Ethnic relations—History—20th century.
Classification: LCC FC3099.K46 Z7 2020 | DDC 971.3/11200497—dc23

Contents

Acknowledgments

This project began as a doctoral dissertation a decade and a half ago. In the time it has taken to get from then to now, I have benefitted tremendously from the generosity, kindness, sage advice, and patience of so many people that I won't be able to name most of them here.

In the first phase of this book's life as a dissertation, my research was aided by a Social Sciences and Humanities Research Council graduate scholarship. In the second phase, I received a stipend from the Fund for Scholarly Research and Creative Work and Professional Development at Queen's University for adjunct instructors. It allowed me to write last summer while only doing minimal teaching related work.

I was honoured to work with such a supportive team at McGill-Queen's University Press which included Jonathan Crago, Kathleen Fraser, Susan Glickman, and three anonymous readers. Susan's skills as an editor were especially appreciated. Francine Berish at Queen's University Library was extremely patient in helping me create the map used in this book just as the university was closing for its winter break. An earlier verision of chapter 1 was published in *American Indian Quarterly*, while an earlier version of chapter 5 appeared in Dan Berger (ed.), *Hidden Histories of the 1970s*. All errors in this book are mine alone.

Over the years, archivists and librarians in numerous institutions across North America aided my research significantly. Special thanks to Don Colborne who, when this project was still in its very early days, lent me boxes of his papers from several key moments which shape this book. I deeply regret that I was not able to return them before they were destroyed in a fire at my parents' house in Kenora in 2012. It was a fire that also, tragically, took my father's life.

Dad, I miss you.

This book was on pause for a while as life took several unexpected turns, as it does for most of us. I have been lucky to have the support of friends and family in many different parts of the world, but especially in Kenora, Winnipeg, Toronto, Hamilton, Havana, Brampton, Montreal, and in Kingston, where I have lived longer than I ever expected to. David Austin and Sean Mills both deserve special thanks. They have been friends for many years. We don't see each other as much as we used to, but conversations with them shaped this book from start to finish.

In 2016, Barrington Walker and Georgina Riel offered me a desk in their air-conditioned basement as an escape from another humid Kingston summer. I'm not sure how much writing Barrington and I accomplished over those months, but his and Georgina's guidance and friendship came at an especially important moment.

Karen Dubinsky has taken on many different roles over the lifespan of this book. First as a PhD supervisor, then as a collaborator on several books, conferences, and most recently a seminar series. And always as a friend. She has been a constant champion of mine both as a scholar and a teacher. She has figuratively and literally (I'm sure) kicked down doors on my behalf. "Thank you" will never be enough.

My mother Janet, my sister Jessica, and my partner Sayyida Jaffer have all been equally important people along this journey. I have leaned on them tremendously in my attempt to make sense of the worlds of the past and present. Sayyida's unwavering belief in our ability to create a just and equitable future is the ideal I strive to live up to.

"Louis Cameron (occupation of park in Kenora)," 1 August 1974, Photographer Frank Chalmers. University of Manitoba Archives and Special Collections, *Winnipeg Tribune* fonds, PC 18 (A.81-12), Box 46, Item 18-2933-018.

"Police Keep Eye on Indians," August 1974. University of Manitoba Archives & Special Collections, *Winnipeg Tribune* fonds, PC 18 (A.81-12), Box 46, Item 18-2931-19.

Opposite "Louis Cameron (occupation of park in Kenora)," 1 August 1974, Photographer Frank Chalmers. University of Manitoba Archives and Special Collections, *Winnipeg Tribune* fonds, PC 18 (A.81-12), Box 46, Item 18-2933-016.

"Kenora" 22 August 1974, University of Manitoba Archives and Special Collections, *Winnipeg Tribune* fonds, P C 18 (A.81-12), Box 46, Item 18-2931-23.

Opposite "Anicinabe Park," 14 August 1974, Photographer Frank Chalmers. University of Manitoba Archives and Special Collections, *Winnipeg Tribune* fonds, P C 18 (A.81-12), Box 46, Item 18-3615-001.

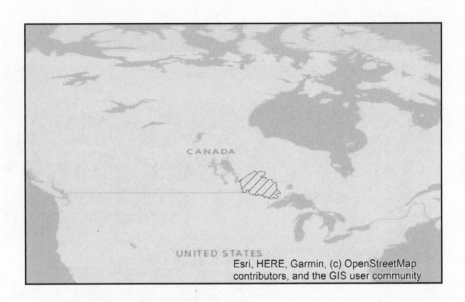

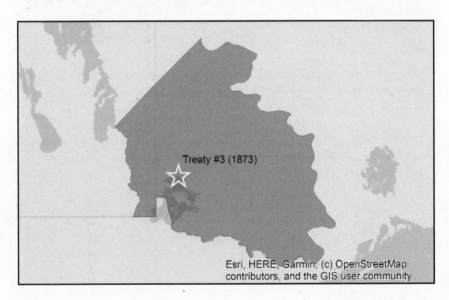

Treaty #3 (1873)

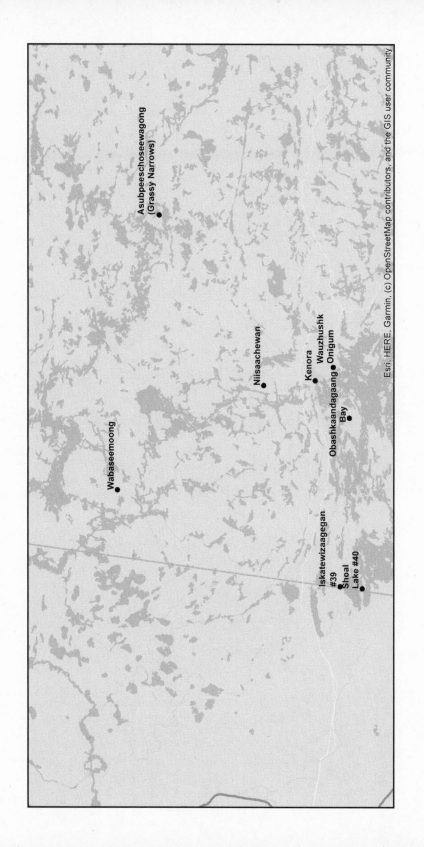

Asubpeeschoseewagong
(Grassy Narrows)

Niisaachewan

Wabaseemoong

Kenora
Wauzhushk
Onigum
Obashkaandagaang Bay

Iskatewizaagegan
#39
Shoal
Lake #40

Canada's
Other
Red
Scare

The Town with a Bad Name

I grew up as a white settler in "a town with a bad name," as a reporter for *Akwesasne Notes* once called Kenora, Ontario, in the fall of 1974. It had earned this bad name, according to the reporter, because the town "had the reputation as one of the worst Indian scenes in Canada"[1] owing to the daily discrimination and hostility Indigenous peoples in the area faced.[2] This probably was not a startling revelation to the magazine's readers in 1974 as, since at least the early 1960s, Indigenous peoples in the Treaty #3 territory had made very public protests against such treatment which we now understand as settler-colonial. A "settler-colonial relationship," Glen Sean Coulthard writes, "is one characterized by a particular form of *domination*; that is, it is a relationship where power – in this case, interrelated discursive and non-discursive facets of economic, gendered, racial, and state power – has been structured into a relatively secure or sedimented set of hierarchical social relations that continue to facilitate the *dispossession* of Indigenous peoples of their lands and self-determining authority."[3] This book pays attention to how the manifestations of settler-colonialism took shape through the construction and deployment of racist stereotypes, employment discrimination, the rise in violent deaths amongst Anishinaabe peoples, mercury poisoning, land dispossession, and other forms of dehumanization.

Over this same ten-year period, from 1965 until 1974, Indigenous peoples in the territory covered by Treaty #3 were insisting in very public demonstrations that other people, from government officials to restaurant owners to their neighbours, begin paying attention to these everyday forms of dehumanization and dispossession. Their actions included sensational moments such as marches, government office sit-ins, an armed land occupation, and a cross-country caravan, as well as more muted, but no less important, activities such as organizing a series of lectures in a high school, educational campaigns, letters to government officials, and work on grassroots committees. This book pays attention to both sets of activities to demonstrate how, as historians Mary Jane Logan McCallum and Adele Perry put it, "Indigenous humanity is powerfully asserted in everyday acts that illuminate colonial practices."[4] This book picks up the narrative in November 1965 on a night which saw at least 400 Indigenous men and women who had come from nearby communities and white allies march down Main Street demanding action from all levels of government on a long list of grievances.[5] The book continues through the summer of 1974 when 150 young men and women, calling themselves the Ojibway Warrior Society, armed themselves and occupied a small park on the town's south side. In doing so they forwarded new notions of recognition, humanity, and autonomy that drew both from past forms of Indigenous resistance and from broader global anti-colonial movements. It ends with the Native People's Caravan in the fall of 1974. I pay attention to these moments of Indigenous resistances amongst others of the area to challenge the idea that Indigenous histories in twentieth-century Canada are only stories of "loss."[6]

In writing about Thunder Bay, Northwestern Ontario's most populous city, Tanya Talaga recently said it has historically been a city of "two faces": a "white face" and a "red face."[7] She could easily have been talking about any town across the region, including Kenora, where I grew up in the 1980s and 1990s as a son whose father worked as a railroader and mother as a billing-clerk for local doctors. My European ancestors have lived in the area since at least the late 1800s. The amalgamated city of Kenora now has around 15,000 residents – in the summer that figure jumps dramatically because of its location on the northern shores of Lake of the Woods, famous for fishing, boating, pulp and paper milling and, now, big expensive cottages that most people in Kenora cannot afford. I am familiar with many of the places mentioned in this book, but I do not remember as a kid or young adult learning much about their importance as both sites of settler-colonial encounter or of the Indigenous resistance that produced some of the most dramatic images coming from Canada during the "global sixties." The local history I knew best before leaving home for university was, for example, how Kenora got its name. It was known as "Rat Portage" until in 1905, when a local businessman refused to put the name "Rat" on his merchandise. A new name was created from the first two letters of three local communities: KE (Keewatin) – NO (Norman) – RA (Rat Portage). I also knew that in the 1870s and 1880s, it was part a boundary dispute between Ontario and Manitoba. Hockey history has always been prominent in Northwestern Ontario; the Kenora Thistles hockey team that won the 1907 Stanley Cup is revered and its name passed on to all levels of rep hockey teams. I knew Kenora's long railroad history as well which, as one former railroader once proudly told me, helped transport troops to put down the "Riel Rebellion" in 1885. (This last story was repeated, with much less reverence, by the Ojibway Warrior during the Anicinabe Park takeover in 1974.) Like other small towns, it had bank-robbers as well as whiskey smugglers. This type of popular civic history is reframed nostalgically and reinscribed in our consciousness through tourism, craft industries, and life-style branding, all of which have grown in importance in a place where work in the natural resource industries has, for the most part, disappeared.

I wish these civic pride lessons had been problematized with more honest and historically informed discussions challenging the sense of naturalized superiority of white faces in my "two-faced" town. Learning that history is both a contested process and a silence-producing affair helps me recognize my own complicity in the discursive and material practices that, in Coulthard's words, come to shape settler-colonial dispossession. Could a more honest accounting have equipped me with better tools to question the stories generations of white settlers repeat, around the dinner table, on the lake, in restaurants and hockey arenas? Settler-colonialism is not an event – that is, something best thought of as part of the past – but rather a process that continues to reassert its authority to dispossess in the present.

What I might tell a younger me growing up in Kenora was that I was a settler growing up on land governed by a treaty relationship between the Crown and Anishinaabe nations.[8] Treaty #3 was signed on 3 October

1873, after nearly four years of negotiating between Anishinaabe nations and Canadian officials. It was part of a late nineteenth-century series of treaties known popularly as "the numbered treaties" which were signed across Western Canada to facilitate dispossession of Indigenous land for the expansion of European settlement across Northwestern Ontario and what became the Prairie provinces.[9] The lakes and rivers of Northwestern Ontario were significant routes for connecting the dominion of Canada to what had been Hudson's Bay Company territory. The Anishinaabe and Métis living here had skills that guided Europeans through the territory and were able to draw out more concessions from the crown than the latter wanted to give.[10] So Indigenous negotiators in Rainy River and Lake of the Woods had somewhat more power to assert their agency than those who had signed numbered treaties before them. These negotiators also knew that American Indians in the northern United States had successfully held out for more concessions from that government. This leads Gerald Friesen to suggest that though they had more autonomy before signing the treaty, the Indigenous peoples of what would become Northwestern Ontario and southeastern Manitoba negotiated "as firmly as they could, won concessions where possible, and produced a settlement that had positive as well as negative features for their group."[11]

However, the relationship that Treaty #3 formalized between Indigenous peoples and the crown in October 1873 remains contested and continues to facilitate further dispossession. Brittany Luby, for example, writes that one crucial site of tension is that oral and written sources both show that Anishinaabe negotiators did not believe they were ceding all title to lands in Northwestern Ontario and Southeastern Manitoba in the treaty.[12] They believed they were agreeing to a conditional "land sharing agreement" in exchange for reserve lands, cash, farming assistance, and allowances for hunting and fishing. As Luby puts it, the Canadian government "did not understand it the same way." For them, the treaty opened up the area for colonization, agriculture, and timber extraction.[13] This was one of numerous discrepancies. Treaty #3 also established two types of land reserved for "Indians": wild land and farming land. Considerable disagreement emerged around the location of reserves.[14] Indigenous peoples wanted fertile land along Rainy River and Lake of the Woods, whereas the Canadian government wanted to save those places for white settlers, of which there were already thousands by the 1870s and many more to come. Indigenous oral and written sources also include no mention of the limitations on fishing and hunting rights that are included in the Canadian government version of the treaty.[15]

That Treaty #3 negotiators believed they relinquished nothing in 1873 still matters today. Activists organizing around ongoing mercury poisoning and anti-clear-cutting have cited this contested meaning of the treaty.[16] It was also a contested history that the Ojibway Warrior Society pointed to when they organized some of Canada's first "Red Power" protests in 1973 and 1974 advocating Indigenous liberation and Ojibwe nationhood. As was stated to the press at the time, "when we signed treaties, the treaties were a different kind of law – an aboriginal law, a hereditary law."[17] Luby reminds us that a treaty was something the Canadian government understood as diplomacy rather than as sacred covenant. "What is clear" she writes, "is that Anishinaabe negotiators conducted ceremonies that both sanctified and guaranteed treaty in Anishinaabe legal traditions."[18] None of this is to say that when Treaty #3 – or any of the numbered treaties – was signed each party was negotiating from a place of equal power. Far from it. The threat of violence always loomed over the heads of Anishinaabe negotiators during the treaty process. James Daschuk, for example, points to policies of starvation and the onset of disease in Western Canada as key factors that gave the crown a distinct advantage in treaty-making processes during the period. As Daschuk notes, Prime Minister John A. Macdonald's "plan to starve uncooperative Indians onto reserve and into submission might have been cruel, but it was certainly effective."[19] Barrington Walker argues that the Canadian government's Indian policy, most notably the Indian Act (which ended up defining who was and was not an "Indian" as well as leading to the residential school system) drew from hegemonic notions of racial naturalism and racial historicism in efforts to construct a racially homogenous country. In other words, a white country. "Taken together," Walker writes, "these instances – alongside many others – point to a broad web of interlocking attitudes, outlooks, techniques, and modes of racial governance in the colonial early Confederation eras that created much of the foundation of modern Canada."[20]

The place where I grew up has always been contested space, though I didn't believe it back then. I knew Main Street not as the site of Canada's

"First Civil Rights March" but as the street where my grandfather managed a Woolworths. I knew Beaver Brae only as my old high school rather than the place where renowned scholars of the late 1960s in North America gathered to debate the impact of "cross cultural difference" in the spring of 1967. I knew Anicinabe Park not as a site of Red Power protest, but as a spot to swim. How would knowing these histories have denaturalized the assumption I had, because of the way I'd understood history, that white folks had been the only active subjects in the place I grew up? This book supports historian Frederick Cooper's contention that colonization is not only "a terrain where concepts were imposed … but also engaged and contested."[21] How do I think about settler-colonialism when its logics and acts of dispossession are held up like a mirror?

In *Silencing the Past*, Michel-Rolph Trouillot asks what makes history thinkable? He writes that "When reality does not coincide with deeply held beliefs, human beings tend to phrase interpretations that force reality within the scope of these beliefs. They devise formulas to repress the unthinkable and to bring it back within the realm of accepted discourse."[22] Trouillot is speaking specifically about the Haitian Revolution when enslaved Africans acted on their visions of freedom. It was a set of events that Trouillot says "entered history being unthinkable even as it happened," because when people are confronted with moments that defy expectation we are prone to interpret them with "ready-made" categories – categories that were, in Trouillot's example, "incompatible with the idea of a slave revolution."[23] As Trouillot asks, "if some events cannot be accepted even as they occur, how can they be assessed later? … [h]ow does one write history of the impossible?" Many settler people – from government officials to reporters and local residents – living through the moments covered by this book saw Indigenous peoples asserting their humanity in ways that challenged the"ready-made categories" that racial regimes had created: ways that made history impossible even as it was happening, which is often, as we will see, why the ubiquitous figure of the"outsider" was often blamed when Indigenous protest took place locally. They were defying the hegemonic settler-colonial notions of what it was to be an "Indian." Such defiance is also what this book is about.

Racism makes people unthinkable as active historical subjects. Why settlers are so deeply invested in racial hierarchies was a question that

Louis Cameron thought about a lot. Cameron was an Anishinaabe man from Wabaseemoong Independent Nation (Whitedog) and one of the key theorists of Indigenous resistance in this book. In the aftermath of the 1974 Anicinabe Park occupation, he gave numerous wide-ranging interviews. In one, he suggested that settler attitudes towards Indigenous peoples were informed by certain types of insecurities the former held. He said he had sympathy for the way that Kenora's economy was controlled from "Toronto or the U.S. So these people have no material foundation" and those with small businesses just "hang onto them with their entire life."[24] In their economic history of Northwestern Ontario, Robert Wightman and Nancy M. Wightman show that in post-1945 society, towns in Northwestern Ontario relied on a natural resource-based economy. By the 1970s, the over-consumption of natural resources and a global economic recession contributed to a mounting employment crisis in the sector.[25] G.R. Weller suggests that this economic downturn fuelled political frustration expressed through the language of regional alienation. "As a hinterland region," he writes, "northwestern Ontario has material, people and money extracted from it to serve the interests of the metropolis ... [a]ll of the key segments of this region's economy are ... based upon the needs of another region and not of northwestern Ontario."[26] Frustration with such precarity found a convenient target: Indigenous peoples.

"The thing about the North," Tanya Talaga writes, is that "everybody knows everybody else."[27] A popular argument made amongst some actors during the period this book covers is that the types of insecurities Cameron identifies were a root cause of racism and could be changed through greater cultural contact between Indigenous and settler cultures. Scholars such as Jeff Denis are not convinced that this familiarity, or what is called "the contact-theory of change," offers a meaningful pathway to decolonization. What he finds is that contact, friendships, even intermarriage, may reduce crude stereotypes and overt racism, but that the result is frequently just discourse on an individual rather than group level. Opinions about policies may still remain conservative, general opinion may not change and settler-communities still end up opposing "policies to compensate for historical injustices and resent Indigenous peoples who exercise treaty rights or seek substantive equality."[28] The singling out of "the good Indian" as exceptional does not challenge notions of white superiority but reinforces them. This "subtyping," as Denis calls it, can turn into paternalism, with warm attitudes towards one member of a racialized group and a conviction of knowing what's best for the others, all of which maintains "a superior sense of *group* position. Violating the stereotype makes you an exception rather than a rule … While rejecting absolute racial categorizations, this process draws on shared images of what constitutes a 'typical' or 'good' or 'bad' Indian. By viewing characteristics like forward-thinking educated, entrepreneurial, trustworthy, and 'doing good' as fundamentally 'unIndian', whites preserve the negative connotations of the larger 'Indian category' and uphold their sense of group superiority."[29] This "common sense" racial discourse was also critical to the production of difference that shaped both whiteness and the racism witnessed in Kenora from 1965 to 1974. "Good Indians" did not need to lose their "Indianness" entirely. They just needed to abide by the practices governing settler life. In contrast, "bad Indians" were those who took what was offered to them but seemed ungrateful, unable to abide by or unwilling to feign respect for the rules governing the workday. Here, in this world of "good" and "bad," is where some of the socio-economic insecurities begin to look less like the motor of racism and more like one component of a much larger ideological system of dehumanization. From reading Cedric Robinson and others, I have come to understand this experience within a broader ideological process called "racial capitalism." Here race, a socially produced category of difference, and capitalism become co-constitutive. Robinson argues that the production of such racial difference began in Europe when the English colonized Ireland in the late sixteenth century. In other words, there is no such thing as non-racist capitalism because as Robin D.G. Kelley notes, "the first European proletarians were *racial* subjects … and they were victims of dispossession (enclosure), colonialism and slavery *within Europe*."[30]

Numerous important global political, social, and cultural tensions shaped Indigenous protest and colonial encounter in the Kenora area. The broad anti-racist and anti-colonial movements that reshaped the post 1945 world were one set of key global influences. That colonialism was a source of tension for Canada in the postwar period is made clear by the work of Robert Teigrob. He argues, for example, that in this period "the nation remained a settler society dominated by British- and French-stock whites." In addition to continuing racially restrictive immigration policies that had shaped "White Canada" until the mid-1960s, he suggests that many Canadians "continued to defend the practice of colonialism" in the decades following World War II. "The underlying fear," Teigrob suggests, "was that admission of 'weaker southern races' would 'contaminate' the nation's homogenous racial makeup and dilute its British character." [31]

Hoping to expand the global framework of this book and to make better sense of the role that settler-colonialism and anti-colonial activism played in shaping Canada in the 1960s and 1970s, I've turned to David Theo Goldberg. In *The Threat of Race*, he argues that there have been three "significant periods of broad *anti-racist* mobilization: abolitionism through the nineteenth century; anticolonialism and the civil rights movements from roughly the 1920s through the 1960s; and the anti-apartheid and the multicultural movements of the 1970s to the 1990s." [32] For Goldberg, anti-colonial struggle, primarily in Asia and Africa, and the civil rights movements in the United States can be thought of as broad anti-racist mobilization precisely because of their deep historical connections to each other through seeing race as a historical construct. "Colonialism was factored constitutively around racial conception and configuration. How colonizing metropoles and their agents thought about race determined directly the very structures of colonial order and arrangement," Goldberg argues. [33] He goes on to note that "[a]nti-colonial movements get going as a set of movements – just as the civil rights movement in the United States gathers steam, fueled by common cause(s) but then also by the growing *encouragement* of their respective, if relative, successes." [34] Both were efforts to "undo the histories of racially ordered structures, legal enforcements, group-driven exclusions, conceptual colonialism and racially indexed foreshortened lives." [35] This helps demonstrate that while anti-colonial and civil rights-based movements could have different political goals, what they shared was a common desire to dismantle certain racial logics of social order. It also helps to not see a fundamental disconnect between the two, or that civil rights simply shifted to more radical anti-colonial positions. It's a problem that Robin D.G. Kelley suggests in the context of Black Americans has been "told so many times, in books, documentary films, in African American history courses all across the United States, that it has become a kind of common sense."[36] Moreover, he argues, it obscures as much as it reveals about the political and social imagination of Black activists in the United States: it limits Black nationalism to the US domestic sphere; it limits civil rights organizing to the southern states; and it hides radical Black working-class movements that didn't necessarily see themselves as part of the civil rights movement, to name a few areas commonly overlooked.[37] In the context of Indigenous protests in Kenora during this period, I have tried to avoid analyses that portray a "civil rights" type politics in the 1960s giving way to a more radical anti-colonial nationalism in the 1970s. As this book tries to show, there was evidence of a tempered, but present, critique of colonialism, especially land dispossession, in rights and recognition based protests and rights type discourse, especially around economic opportunity, that shaped discourses of anti-colonial nationalism.

Places like Kenora and groups such as the Ojibway Warrior Society or the Indian-White Committee (organizers of a march in 1965) are not likely the first things that come to mind when we think of the "Sixties." We reserve that for university campuses such as Columbia and Berkeley, the Civil Rights Movement of Black Americans, the Vietnam War, and Woodstock in the USA or Women's Liberation. Or we might think of mass demonstrations by leftist students in France and Czechoslovakia in 1968 aimed at tearing down "the system." Alice Echols launched one of the earliest critiques of Sixties historiography when she argued that much of what has shaped Western imagination about the era has been "books by white male new leftists ... Their experiences are presented as universal, as defining the era, whereas the experiences of women and people of color ... are constructed as particularistic."[38] If certain subjects shape popular imagination, one year, 1968, also occupies a privileged place. Van Gosse points out some problems with seeing that year as the supposed apex of the period. It was important because it was a year of political revolt in the Western world and the culmination of much utopic thinking, global protests against US imperialism, and massive social upheaval. On the back side of 1968, the period ends up being seen as a hardening of social and cultural categories, a period of decline, of distancing from such utopic thinking. The declension model suggests an end to the possibility of wide-scale social change in North America as left-wing movements begin to adopt "revolutionary violence," "tarnishing" the idealism of the New Left and signalling the ultimate closure of the period's utopian ambitions.[39] Such models fail to account for the many new forms of radical thought that involved a complex mix of utopic political theory, grassroots organizing and action in places outside of university campuses and Western urban centres after 1968.

While wanting to avoid the declension model, some of the more popular subjects of the Global Sixties, and especially the focus on 1968, this book recognizes that for many actors of the period, especially in the West, issues such as anti-war activism, student politics, and "free love" reshaped their political and social imaginations. But as I and my colleagues suggest in *New World Coming*, "if the period is understood only as the global events of 1968, we cut ourselves off from seeing resistance as a continuing process, and instead see it as isolated events now closed off from the present. We also miss the extraordinary array of different locations, both local and international, where resistance took place."[40] If we focus on the period as part of a process the way Indigenous activists and theorists such as the Métis scholar Howard Adams did, we can analyze the way that Africa, Asia, and the Caribbean transformed Marxism, to take one example, into a political theory useful for colonized peoples in Canada.[41] Moreover, increased immigration from the "Third World," especially Caribbean countries, Black anti-poverty and anti-racist organizing in Halifax, Toronto, and Montreal, the affective linkages New Leftists made to anti-imperialism through organizing Fair Play for Cuba and anti-Vietnam War protests, the anti-colonial activism of Quebec liberation, all fused global struggle with a sense of defining what the Sixties in Canada might look like.[42] In *New World Coming* we argued "that the challenges that citizens made to dominant power structures, cultural systems, and everyday activities ... were conceptualized in a global sphere ... The local and the everyday were read through a larger transnational lens, and resistance was forged at least in part through the interaction of daily experience with an understanding of global developments."[43] This perspective has shaped my approach to understanding Indigenous histories of resistance in this book.

This book is not meant to reduce the broad spectrum of Indigenous political imagination in the period to mimicry of what was happening in the US or across the decolonizing Third World. Rather, it investigates the ways that these global ideas and examples, both through direct contact with actors and the circulation of ideas through media, shaped such moments as the "Indian Rights" march in 1965 or the Native People's Caravan in September 1974. As Anthony Hall demonstrates, such a transnational approach also helps us understand the way that for much of the nineteenth and twentieth centuries, the regulation of Indigenous life in Canada has been connected to politics and culture outside its borders. "The convergence," Hall argues, "points to the importance of picturing local histories and the treatment of Indigenous peoples in the context of larger patterns of empire, ideology, and policy making."[44] In Kenora, the connections between the march in 1965, the occupation in 1974, and other events went beyond how Indigenous actors related to the question of Third World decolonization. My book asks how movements and moments that took place outside Canadian borders (Black American civil rights, Black Power in the Caribbean and the United States, the Cuban Revolution, the American Indian Movement, and even International Development discourse) helped shape a ten-year period of Indigenous protest and settler-colonial conflict in a small town close to the borders of Manitoba, Ontario, and Minnesota. Indigenous protestors and non-Indigenous peoples (whether they were journalists, trade unionists, conservative town councillors, tourists in the Kenora area, federal politicians, or academics,) translated Indigenous activism through such global comparatives. This translation could illuminate and inspire, but also erase local complexities. This can be a reminder (to myself as much as anyone) that while we seek connections across geopolitical borders, there is danger in too broadly collapsing histories. Transnational reading can complicate the reification of history as a national project, but it also requires that we do not ignore the specificities of place.

Appreciating the centrality of anti-colonialism and rights movements globally during the period covered in this book also allows me to better situate the connections of Indigenous activism in Northwestern Ontario to a third global historical moment: the Cold War. This was not only a struggle between two opposing superpowers but one that included decolonizing Third World countries. The very term "Third World" comes out of both a history of empire and a challenge to Cold War ideologies. Gaining prominence after the Bandung conference in 1955 that brought African and Asian leaders together, the term signalled "the global majority" who had shaken off colonialism in the name of national independence. It also, according to Odd Arne Westad, "implied a distinct position in Cold War terms, the refusal to be ruled by the superpowers and their ideologies, the search for alternatives both to capitalism and communism, a 'third way' for newly liberated states."[45] The connection between the Third World and the Cold War impacts histories of Indigenous activism in numerous ways during the period discussed in this book. This is especially true when considering the Canadian state's response to high-profile Indigenous protests. Two key aspects emerged: one was the state blaming "communists" for agitating Indigenous peoples, a tactic meant to deflect attention away from the issues in favour of blaming outside agitators, a topic covered at length in chapter 6. And in chapter 2, I discuss the way that the language of "international development," a Cold War construct in many ways, and methods of making formerly colonized peoples productive for capitalist economies were promoted as models for Indigenous community development and integration in Northwestern Ontario in the 1960s and early 1970s. As David Meren has recently demonstrated, Canadian Indian policy and foreign aid were interconnected in Canada after World War II. He shows that there were "intersecting notions of 'modernization,' liberal-capitalist preoccupations, and racialized understanding of development" which "informed Canadian efforts in both fields." That is, "Canadian encounters with the Global South shaped Indigenous-Canadian relations after 1945."[46]

Situating these histories of Indigenous resistance within a global framework demonstrates the multitude of ways that settler-colonial dispossession shaped day-to-day life locally as it drew power from transnational racial ideologies. The global is also a way for this book to expand our sense of what shaped Indigenous activist imaginaries. Coulthard argues that three watershed moments shaped this period.

"The first," he writes, "was the materialization of widespread First Nation opposition" to the 1969 White Paper (known officially as the Statement of the Government of Canada on Indian Policy). The White Paper, essentially proposed to end the government's commitments as outlined in the Indian Act and to terminate treaty agreements. The response from Indigenous organizations, especially as encapsulated in Harold Cardinal's book *The Unjust Society*, is thought of as a key origin point for Indigenous nationalism in Canada. The second crucial moment was the "partial recognition of Aboriginal 'title' in the Supreme Court of Canada's 1973 *Calder* decision." This set in motion the possibility of the court as an avenue through which Indigenous dispossession might be addressed, as demonstrated by the Ojibway Warrior Society's land claim during the Anicinabe Park occupation. The third event (or "cluster of events," as Coulthard calls them) "emerged following the turbulent decade of energy politics that followed the oil crisis of the early 1970s" and the "aggressive push" of the Canadian government and business to rapidly increase development in "northern Canada."[47] While this factor is not directly related to the events discussed in this book, Indigenous activism about the issue of mercury poisoning, which began in the early 1970s and continues today, was the result of natural resource development in Northwestern Ontario and therefore connects well to Coulthard's third watershed moment. This book supports Coulthard's framework for understanding the emergence of Indigenous anti-colonial nationalism and how it reshaped settler-colonialism and also suggests some other watershed moments derived from considering the histories of Indigenous activism in Northwestern Ontario such as the "Indian Rights" march in 1965, and interactions between Black Power organizers and Indigenous activists in shaping what became Indigenous anti-colonial praxis by the early 1970s.

This book consists of six core chapters and a conclusion, beginning in 1965 and ending in 1974. Each chapter is constructed around a central event. In order, these include the "Indian Rights" march, the Resolving Conflicts Seminar Series, a meeting between black and Indigenous activists in Toronto that helped develop the language of "Red Power," the report on violent deaths in the Treaty #3 area in 1973, the Anicinabe Park occupation in 1974, and the Native Peoples Caravan later that same fall. The book discusses the tensions involved in these moments between Indigenous activists and the broader structural and cultural systems they were intent on changing. Archives are places of power; they collect certain histories and silence others. As Michel-Rolph Trouillot argues, "silences enter the process of historical production at four crucial moments: the moment of fact creation (the making of sources); the moment of fact assembly (the making of *archives*); the moment of fact retrieval (the making of *narratives*); and the moment of retrospective significance (the making of *history* in the final instance)."[48] In my attempt to represent some of the arguments and histories that animated this ten-year period of Indigenous resistance and colonial encounter through local protests, I too have no doubt produced silence. This work centres the perspectives of the main actors and is based primarily on voices accessed through archival documentation, previously published and recorded interviews, and media coverage, both alternative and mainstream. I conducted two interviews (with Jan Carew and Lee Maracle) though others had been planned. Indigenous activist-intellectuals left significant written records of their ideas and movements. Organizations such as the Ontario Human Rights Commission saved a great deal of Indigenous-produced literature from the Indian-White Committee, for example, including minutes of the mayor's committees and the various talks given by some of the march's main public figures. They also collected testimony from many business owners and other settlers that I have used to discuss various colonial encounters. The Canadian Association in Support of Native Peoples collected similar testimonies during the Anicinabe Park occupation and the Native People's Caravan, while the Social Planning Council left extensive minutes and verbatim testimony from the meetings that produced the Violent Death Report in 1973. This was also a period of wide-ranging literature production by Indigenous writers and activist organizations. I've made extensive use of published writings in *Akwesasne Notes* and Grand Council Treaty #3 newsletters and movement literature written by Black and Indigenous activists, as well as memoirs and previously recorded interviews. I have also tried to engage in archival reading not only located in tracing silences but in marking the way government officials actually spoke about Indigenous protestors and how these attitudes often undermined attempts at justice undertaken by Indigenous men and women in the period.

Chapter 1 covers the build-up to and aftermath of the "Indian Rights march" which took place in Kenora in November 1965. In this chapter, I rely on media coverage, archival collections from the Ontario Human Rights Commission, and Indian-White Committee literature to discuss how discourse and practice shaped everyday racism at lunch counters, in hotel bar-rooms, and on the streets of Kenora. I also write about how Indigenous peoples and non-Indigenous peoples responded publicly and collectively to such experiences, resulting in the Indian Rights March. I argue that in the aftermath of the march, which some called "Canada's First Civil Rights March," much of the debate about the meaning of Indigenous protest collided with the "absent" presence of Blackness in Canada as well as constructed meanings about different types of whiteness. In 1965, the easiest way to make sense of the discrimination against Indigenous peoples in Kenora and their public resistance to it was to claim that this town and its residents were more akin to white Southerners in the United States than to fellow Canadians. I also show how some officials continued to deny the extent of racism and were primarily concerned with preserving the town's reputation as a tourist destination.

Chapter 2 takes place in the aftermath of the march, mostly in the spring of 1967. Here I do a close reading of a set of lectures in Kenora that the Indian-White Committee imagined as way to think about racism not as ideology but as cultural ignorance. Focusing on cultural differences, each speaker tried to explain a different facet of Indigenous culture broadly and of "Ojibwa" culture specifically. I argue that what ended up happening was that the speakers used culture as way to talk about how Indigenous peoples related to categories such as citizenship, labour, and progress. There existed disagreement as to whether Anishinaabe culture was a tool of progress or a barrier to a good life. Here socio-economic and political issues were considered through the lens of culture. During this moment, people such as Fred Kelly tried to use culture as a way to further problematize the idea of Canada having "an Indian problem." This was a theme that most speakers during the seminar series discussed. I suggest that these contested understandings of Indigenous culture were not unique to Kenora. They are connected to emerging debates at the time about Canada's role internationally in providing aid to the decolonizing Third World. How officials as well as everyday folks thought about the barriers to progress in the Third World was reflected in discourse about similar issues locally.

Chapter 3 continues this book's efforts to situate colonial encounters in Canada in a transnational framework. In this chapter, I follow the emergence of Indigenous anti-colonial theory in the mid-1960s in three distinct mediums. The first is grassroots organizing and the circulation of ideas through conferences and community newspapers. The second is the interactions between Indigenous thinkers and organizers in Canada and the Black Panther Party in the United States and Black Power figures from the Caribbean. Here I suggest that Indigenous anti-colonial thinking in Canada was a mixture of local experience and globally circulating ideas about national liberation. I also emphasis the significance of travel by Indigenous figures outside of Canada to places like China, Tanzania, and California. Finally, because the politics of decolonization circulated through cultural production, I suggest that the Indigenous cultural production in the late 1960s and 1970s helped construct critical knowledge that Canada was a settler-colonial state. These, however, were contested narratives. The state competed with filmmakers, for example, over the memory of Louis Riel and the Northwest resistance. I believe this is evidence that cultural battles over history were perhaps as important as political battles over policies in the development of Red Power.

Chapter 4 returns to Kenora to situate the articulation of Red Power within local circumstances. I look at three case studies by which to better understand the emergence of anti-colonial movements in Kenora. Those are the Violent Death Report, mercury poisoning, and Jay Treaty Protests at the Ontario-Minnesota border in the aftermath of the Wounded Knee occupation in South Dakota. I trace the various contexts in which Indigenous lives were devalued in Kenora and the resulting forms of grassroots organizing that emerged.

Because "Red Power" in Canada reached its apex after 1968, Indigenous protests are sometimes overlooked in the global histories of the Sixties. In chapter 5, I argue that the forty-day armed occupation of Anicinabe Park in Kenora, Ontario, during the summer of 1974 is one such moment demonstrating intersections between the global and the local. In this event we can observe several crucial links between Indigenous decolonization in Canada and the global forces of anti-colonial liberation that were so dominant in the post–World War II period. The six-week occupation illuminates significantly the intersecting dynamics of locally situated acts of dispossession within broader settler-colonial structures and patterns of systemic discrimination. It also suggests the park occupation offers significant insight into the meaning of "violence" in a settler-Indigenous town such as Kenora.

This final chapter argues that the Canadian state, through surveillance and *agents provocateurs*, actively tried to disrupt these movement in Canada during the mid-1970s, especially when Indigenous activists began to work towards multi-racial and working-class coalitions with Black Power organizers. The chapter uses the Native People's Caravan that went from Vancouver to Kenora and on to Ottawa and ended with the "riot on Parliament Hill" to show how Douglas Durham, an FBI infiltrator of the American Indian Movement, is important to our understanding of how the Canadian state surveilled Indigenous movements in Canada. The chapter ends with an examination of Warren Hart, a controversial yet revealing figure in the transnational history of surveillance of activist movements. Hart, a former FBI *agent provocateur* of the Black Panther Party, was brought to Canada by the RCMP to do similar work here. He disrupted the attempt of Caribbean activist Rosie Douglas to form a coalition with Louis Cameron.

The book ends with a "letter to Louis Cameron." In it I argue for his place as key anti-colonial thinker of period and discuss some of the ramifications he and others faced for the protests they took part in. I also situate Indigenous protests from the period within contemporary developments. This includes how activists still draw from the legacies of the wide range of actions taken by Indigenous actors in the period and the continuing injustices from that period that remain sites of resistance today.

CHAPTER 1

Canada's Alabama?
Race, Racism, and the Indian Rights March in Kenora

Without the grim reminder from the South we might still be oblivious to the inhuman conditions of our North. Of the black Canadians in our midst – Métis, Indian, Eskimo, Negro, we would be saying what Auden wrote of another citizen:

> Was he free? Was he happy?
> The question is absurd;
> Had anything been wrong.
> We should certainly have heard.[1]

James Eayrs, *Toronto Star*, February 1969

I'm all for the Indians; I treat them like any other coloured man. But in this area they are no damned good. Less than one percent will co-operate. Some of the older generation are O.K., but the young ones are no good. But that's the younger generation all over. Look at the South. Look at what's going on in Vietnam.[2]

George Miller, tourist camp operator, Kenora, 1965

On 7 March 1965, close to six hundred Black Americans attempted to march from Selma, Alabama, to Montgomery, Alabama, to force the issues of voting rights and desegregation. Organized by Martin Luther King Jr and the Southern Christian Leadership Conference, the march was one of the many ways Black Americans built the burgeoning civil rights movement in the United States. To make it from one side of the Alabama River to the other, however, they needed to cross the Edmund Pettus bridge where dozens of law enforcement officers and over one hundred white onlookers were waiting. Alabama governor George Wallace had ordered the officers to stop the marchers from getting across the bridge. No amount of persuasion from the delegation worked. When the marchers refused to leave, officers wielding billy-clubs and tear gas moved in on them. The incident has come to be known as "Bloody Sunday."

Television cameras caught much of what happened: images of Black men, women, and children being beaten by police for trying to cross a bridge were broadcast across North America. Historian Jason Sokol writes that the images from Selma "exposed a black disenfranchisement … too flagrant for many Americans to miss."[3] If, according to Mary L. Dudziak, civil rights marchers often "reinforced the idea that their struggle was a quintessentially *American* struggle," moments such as Bloody Sunday also had a global resonance.[4] In Northern Ireland, some students took "the precedent of Martin Luther King's march from Selma to Montgomery in 1965 as the prototype for the long march from Belfast to Derry in 1969."[5] Ann Curthoys recalls that as a student activist in Australia during the 1960s, she and her white comrades often invoked the image of Black American protest and tactics such as "Freedom Rides" to help raise awareness about the plight of local Indigenous peoples.[6] Across Canada there were demonstrations in support of the Selma marchers: in Toronto a sit-in and vigil was held outside the US consulate on University Avenue, while the undergraduate student council at the University of Manitoba in Winnipeg acted in solidarity with Selma demonstrators by sending telegrams to Governor Wallace and to Dr Martin Luther King Jr.[7] The largest of these demonstrations took place in Ottawa, where close to two thousand people protested in front of the US Embassy.[8]

David Churchill suggests that this type of transnational solidarity, caring for people thousands of miles away in a different country, was generally lauded in Canadian media commentary. For example, an editorial "of the normally staid *Globe and Mail*" celebrated the demonstrators' "expressions of anger against racism in in the US."[9] These acts of solidarity were portrayed as expressions of Canadian moral superiority when it came to questions of racial discrimination. Yet such self-congratulatory rhetoric began to crack beside evidence suggesting Canada had its own group of disenfranchised peoples. One writer, for example, argued that the poverty evident on many reserves contradicted narratives that portrayed Canada as "holier than America." The problem of "Indians and Eskimos," rather than the status of Black Americans, was Canada's most pressing social issue, said one reader of the *Toronto Star*.[10] Alternative publications, such as the *Marxist Quarterly*, hoped that the "solidarity" shown towards Selma marchers would inspire new critiques of "Anglo-Saxon superiority attitudes and discrimination in Canada," including "the system of white superiority embodied in the Indian Act."[11] A particularly harsh assessment came from Patricia Clarke, a columnist for the *United Church Observer*, who scolded the "pretty girls" who would rather bring attention to the plight of Black Americans in the Southern United States than turn their attention towards "the slums in Africville" or the shacks lived in by "Indians" in Canada. "Everyone is quick to join sit-ins in Alabama," quipped Clarke. But who, she asked, "is sitting in Kenora restaurants where Indians can't get a meal?"[12]

In the summer of 1965, journalist Ian Adams wrote an exposé of anti-Indigenous discrimination in Kenora that would help publicize the fact that the experiences of Indigenous communities in Northwestern Ontario were not unlike those of Blacks in the Southern United States. Adams revealed that Kenora was a town divided between "Whites" and "Indians." The latter faced persistent discrimination from businesses and potential employers, from waitresses and barkeepers, from the media and the police. It was racially segregated, as demonstrated by the three different types of laundromats in town: one for "whites," one for "Indians," and one for "Indian women with white husbands."[13] The laundromats were shining examples of how *Indian Act* policies produced a culture of racial segregation through the ordering of gender to determine who was and was not a status Indian.[14]

Yet what Adams exposed to Canadian readers was not news to many Indigenous folks in Kenora and nearby Treaty #3 communities. Indeed, for at least a year prior to the *Maclean's* article, a small number of men and women from several First Nations and a few progressive white residents had been meeting in a group called the Indian-White Committee (IWC) to address the discrimination faced by Indigenous peoples in the area. Throughout 1964 and 1965, the IWC began organizing to challenge the racist thinking and practices that underlay social and economic inequalities experienced by Indigenous communities. Their collective response reached an apex in late November 1965 with a march down Main

Street, Kenora, popularly referred to as the "Indian Rights March" and "Canada's First Civil Rights March."

Upon returning from a conference organized by the Indian-Eskimo Association (IEA)[15] in London, Ontario, late in 1964, Fred Green, then chief of Shoal Lake # 39 First Nation (Iskatewizaagegan #39) and an IWC member, said "a seed" had grown in his mind. Green told reporters that seeing Dr Gilbert Clarence Monture, a founding member of the IEA, urge "Indian people to get up and do things made me feel that our Indians of this District should get together and organize."[16] As another person returning from the conference put it, through education and traditional practices, "Indians ... were able to speak out and express their thoughts."[17] Indeed, cultural revival played an important role in Indigenous political expression in this period. Amendments to the Indian Act in 1884 had criminalized many traditional practices, restrictions that J.R. Miller argues were intended to "control Indians politically and alter them culturally."[18] In 1914, it was amended again to, in the words of Allan Downey, "make off-reserve dancing punishable by incarceration and require Indigenous peoples in western Canada to obtain permission to appear in regalia."[19] Abandoning some of these restrictions in 1951 allowed Indigenous peoples to reengage with "traditional rites, crafts, and arts." [20] IWC participants saw cultural revival as an important form of expression, as one member made clear by telling a local journalist that Indigenous women's groups in the region should "be encouraged to be active and revive the handcrafts and other things Indian women used to do in the past."[21] In attending such conferences and making these broad connections, the IWC was participating in a vibrant period of organizing that would concern itself with, in the words of Ken Coates, "human rights, decolonization, and self-determination," [22] though few Indigenous public figures in the Kenora area would adopt such rhetoric until the Red Power protests of the early 1970s.

The IWC also publicly confronted some of the key ideological foundations that informed racist attitudes and practices in Kenora. This was significant, since according to David Austin, "we have to drag ourselves deeper into race and racism in order to emancipate ourselves from it."[23] For him this means that we need to "understand the irrational-rational logic that facilitates its survival."[24] The IWC challenged the idea that there was a scientific basis for racial hierarchies, and refused to describe inequality as "an Indian problem." In the local newspaper, Harry Shankowski, an IWC member, called the racism that Indigenous peoples experienced in Kenora "a problem of human beings," rejecting the notion socio-economic inequality was because Indigenous peoples lacked ability. He argued instead that race was socially constructed and racism in Kenora was a product of white working-class insecurities. Shankowski referenced the southern United States to illustrate his point. "I have heard that in the Southern U.S.A. the poorest white is a racist, simply because, he fears that the Negro if given an equal opportunity might someday be a white man's boss." The same fear, he believed, underlay the situation in Kenora and kept Indigenous peoples from finding steady employment. A way to address such misguided ideas was through education. So throughout 1965, the IWC engaged in a two-pronged approach linking racism and colonialism to poverty in Kenora. On the one hand, they tried to generate enthusiasm for organizing locally, and on the other, they attempted to use public education to challenge the dominant attitudes of the white majority.[25]

At the end of October 1965, the IWC announced plans for a conference. Frederick Kelly, from Ojibways of the Onigaming First Nation, an IWC member and one of the conference co-chairs, wrote a two-page article in Kenora's *Daily Miner and News* explaining the purpose. This would be an opportunity for local Indigenous people to collectively express their views about how to effect change by challenging the racist stereotypes they encountered daily. The event would begin to help reverse the psychological damage done by these negative stereotypes, especially those that led to a lack of steady employment. He suggested that "the Indian's plight is a social problem requiring the attention of every citizen." However, in order to build a new narrative, Kelly argued, it was important for local white residents to come, listen, and lend their support. "Unless a meaningful dialogue is created in the community between the Indian peoples and the whites – between the economically depressed and the affluent, between Indian Society and Culture and the rapidly changing white community, then we cannot expect true progress." Kelly suggested that the conference "will present an opportunity for Indians to express their thoughts and views, it will not be just another session for the whites to appear and present all of the 'answers.'"[26]

Kelly hoped that white residents in Kenora would come to the conference not to offer answers, but to listen. What happened instead was that few white people bothered to show up. "The Indian White Committee was given the ball," Kelly told reporters afterwards, "we wanted an audience to hear grievances, but no one was there."[27] In response, Peter Seymour, a longtime Anishinaabe rights advocate in Treaty #3, Kelly, and Alan Borovoy (then an officer with the Ontario's Labour Committee for Human Rights), in addition to other members of the IWC, began visiting local reserves, churches, and community centres for a different type of action, one that would not as easily be ignored.[28] "Sometimes," Borovoy claimed, "injustices are too well entrenched and the facts to well known for surveys to work."[29]

As day gave way to night on the evening of 22 November 1965, nearly four hundred Indigenous men and women, along with dozens of white supporters, gathered at the Indian Friendship Centre in Kenora. As the frigid winter air pressed against their bodies, they linked arm-in-arm four persons across and began what would be a half-kilometre trek north up Main Street. Their path took them past the Kenricia hotel, the Woolworth's department store, and Fife's hardware. The sight of these respectable actors wearing winter coats over suits and dresses challenged some of the common stereotypes that marked Indigenous life in early 1960s Canada.[30] The marchers encountered a police presence, as rumours of the likelihood of a violent confrontation between marchers and townspeople had swirled in the lead-up to the night. John Barbarash, then the host of Indian Magazine on CBC radio, recalls: "Here were all of these policemen ... and townspeople and so forth expecting violence." What onlookers saw was a marching procession carrying placards who "filed very graciously into this hall."[31] Once they were seated inside the Legion Hall where town council was meeting, everyone's eyes turned to the two people who would explain the purpose of the march. Peter Seymour and Fred Kelly faced the mayor and his councillors using words that immediately reimagined Kenora as an Indigenous space.[32] They informed town council that they were not there as "subjects" but instead as "neighbours."

And, as neighbours, their problems were not "Indian problems," but community issues requiring shared solutions.[33]

Having made that point, they began clearly outlining the unrelenting economic and social inequities Indigenous peoples faced both in town and on reserves. Audience members learned that "in some cases, even where flush toilets have been introduced to the reserve, they serve not the Indian but the white residents." While this example spoke to a culture of segregation, other amenities were completely missing on reserve. This included not having telephone service, which, town council learned, resulted in a woman losing her child soon after giving birth because the family could not notify the hospital of medical complications.[34]

From a lack of basic services on reserves the speakers moved on to sharing how economic disenfranchisement marked Indigenous peoples who either lived in Kenora or travelled there for work. The delegation used employment statistics to illustrate that out of three thousand status Indians in Kenora, only twelve were employed full-time. Of this dozen, only a couple of men had lucrative unionized jobs at the pulp and paper mill. The IWC also focused on Kenora's service economy, calling it essentially "whites only," as young Indigenous men and women were rarely seen in these jobs. Along with these statistics, they shared poignant examples illustrating that when hired, they were often exploited. For example, the delegation recalled how "a young Indian girl complained of her difficulties as a kitchen worker at a nearby tourist establishment." She worked twelve-hour days seven days a week; after paying room and board to her employer, this "left her with a net income of 3 dollars per day."[35] Such exploitation was partially explained by the limited employment opportunities for Indigenous women who, as historian Mary Jane Logan McCallum shows, at the time relied primarily on work in restaurants, tourist camps, and other service industry jobs.[36]

In focusing on employment discrimination, the delegation was again challenging a key tenet of settler-colonial racism: that Indigenous peoples were responsible for their own poverty because they were not interested in entering the labour market. As Logan McCallum argues in her history of Indigenous women and work, the "prevailing ethnographic logic" of the period "presumed Indians had no motivation to work at all" and, moreover, were unable to attend work regularly or show up on time. Such arguments were popularly understood as the reason for Indigenous poverty and government dependence.[37] The IWC flipped such "logic" on its head. They suggested what had created "a welfare cheque solution" and self-destructive behaviours such as alcoholism was not some scientifically predetermined flaw but white racism, which kept Indigenous folk in precarious employment as seasonal workers and made governments regulate their traditional economies, especially trapping. "We live in poverty at home, we cannot get enough jobs outside," they argued. "Many of us who do get jobs suffer degrading exploitation. Even our traditional occupations meet pressing government restrictions ... is there any wonder that so many of our people turn to alcohol? ... Indian people drink for the same reasons that so many other people do – frustration."[38]

The marchers brought with them many grievances but also suggestions for possible solutions. Instead of being sent to jail for minor offences, they suggested better funding for addictions treatment. They advocated for better job training, for the mayor to pressure federal agencies responsible for regulating the trapping season, for immediate installation of phone service on reserves, and for the formation of a "mayor's committee." The Ontario Human Rights Commission (OHRC) had successfully lobbied for a mayor's committee in Amherstburg, Ontario, in an effort to curb anti-Black racism. On that model, the Kenora committee would facilitate dialogue between representatives from reserves, local members of the IWC, and the town council. The marchers ended the demonstration telling the town council that they "cannot and do not expect miracles overnight. But in the words of the late US President John F. Kennedy: 'Let Us Begin.'"[39]

To make sense of the protest scenes coming out of Kenora, media commentators employed geographical analogies. *The Times of London*, for example, was unique in comparing this moment not to the American South but instead to South Africa. The "white population in Canada," they claimed, should be embarrassed that reserves around Kenora were so much like Bantustans in South Africa.[40] South Africa was an outlier for the most part, as many headlines in Canada and elsewhere referred to Black Americans and the southern United States to explain Indigenous protest in Kenora to readers. Press across Canada immediately coined the protest "Canada's First Civil Rights March," and Kenora became "Canada's Alabama" for the presumed similarities to what was happening in the United States. Headlines such as "[A] Canadian Selma, Alabama in the Making," "100 Kenora Indians Plan 'Selma' March" and phrases like "Our 'Mississippi Indians,'" were common and shaped interpretations about the experience of Indigenous peoples and the root causes of those experiences. The *Toronto Star* wrote that comparing the plight of "Indians to the problems of Negroes in Mississippi" was not unreasonable. Those in Kenora "are poor, live in squalor, are under-educated and discriminated against. Resentments are reaching boiling points."[41] Moreover, "the comparison with Selma is apt" wrote one reporter, "because just as southern whites blamed outsiders for Negro militancy" officials in Kenora blamed "outside agitators" from Toronto.[42] These headlines were meant to grab attention, but we cannot ignore the way that such analogies shaped how the issues were understood. They both produced discourse about some experiences with racism and silenced others. The marchers had their experiences translated through analogies that encouraged the identification of racism not as a common experience amongst Indigenous peoples (or other racialized peoples) in Canada but instead as a uniquely local issue that was easily understood as a problem essentially unfamiliar to most of the rest of Canada. Yet Kenora was not Canada's only Alabama or Mississippi, nor was the march the first time that Indigenous rights protest were compared with Black civil rights marches in the United States. As Bryan D. Palmer notes, similar analogies were employed to make sense of the murder of an Indigenous man in North Battleford, Saskatchewan, in May 1965.[43] Rather than universalizing a critique of racism, these global comparisons profoundly localized the experience in a way that sanitized it for the rest of Canada. Instead of becoming an example of how certain types of racial logic shape settler colonialism, and thus the foundations of a nation, Kenora became a problematic place seemingly disconnected from a broader national history.

This is not to say that protestors did not invite such comparisons or derive any benefit from such sensational headlines. If we understand Jim Crow not only as a legal form of segregation but also as a culturally constructed racial order acted out in day-to-day interactions, then comparing Kenora to the Jim Crow South could help speak to the reality of the

daily experiences that the IWC spoke about at the march.[44] When journalist Ian Adams drew attention to the tripartite segregation of laundromats, he was citing an example of how legal categories established by the
Indian Act could become tools for establishing a culture of segregation.
And when the OHRC investigated complaints from Indigenous clientele
in Kenora, they found no shortage of evidence that "Jim Crowism," to
borrow Barrington Walker's phrase, was thriving in the restaurants, hotels, and bars around town, not to mention in the residential schools
which still operated throughout the 1960s and early 1970s in the area.
This Jim Crowism extended from town onto reserves, as the protest delegation illustrated with reference to the types of services available for
"Whites" but not for "Indians."

Not surprisingly, local officials were keen to exonerate Kenora from
the comparisons to the Jim Crow South. While town council endorsed
the marchers' action points, being known as "Canada's Alabama" was
not good for business. Kenora–Rainy River MP John Reid, for example,
used his first opportunity to speak as a newly elected representative in
the federal House of Parliament to reject such unfavourable comparisons. While congratulating the marchers for "an impressive demonstration of solidarity and discipline," he stressed that Kenora was not
another Selma. To do so, ironically, he borrowed a well-worn tactic used
by white Southerners accused of being racist: blame outsiders. The press,
he argued, "came with cameras, with notebooks and with preconceived
ideas. There were those who had covered Civil Rights demonstrations
in the United States and they immediately assumed that this was a similar situation. They compared Kenora with Selma, Alabama. They talked
to townspeople in that peculiar way the press has, and ended up at times
putting words and ideas into the mouths of local residents."[45] Others
commentators blamed different outsiders, primarily Dan Hill, who as a
Black Canadian and director of the Ontario Human Rights Commission, was said to be influencing local Indigenous-white race politics in
an undue fashion.[46]

Rather than distancing Kenora from US race politics, others chose to
make a direct connection between the two. According to this narrative,
racism against Indigenous people was mainly a result of the presence of
white American tourists. As part of their work in the aftermath of the

march, the OHRC conducted interviews with business owners and man-
agers accused of anti-Indigenous racism in the Kenora area. Instead of
denying racist behaviour, they justified it as satisfying the demands of
American tourists. For example, one hotel manager accused of not serving Indigenous clientele told OHRC director Dan Hill that many Americans "have vowed never to come back to Kenora until we get all the drunk
Indians off of the streets."[47] He claimed he was motivated to withhold
service not because he was racist himself, but because the patronage of
white Americans was essential to the survival of his business.

The government of Ontario had launched an advertising campaign
intended to attract visitors from the US Midwest, and close to one million
were travelling newly improved highways each year by the mid 1960s.[48]
The hotel manager's justification was convenient, because American
tourist dollars had become such an important contribution to the regional economy. Such reasoning was also used to explain why Black visitors to the region encountered similar treatment to local Indigenous
clientele. The OHRC document many cases of Black clientele being denied
services at regional motels, restaurants, and tourist camps because business owners said they were satisfying white American desires. One motel
manager claimed that he'd had white Americans check out after seeing
Black people at his establishment. At tourist camps, guests often shared
bathing and washroom facilities; Black presence was framed as bad for
business at these places as well.[49] At a municipal business bureau meeting
in Dryden, a town 150 kilometres east of Kenora, not only were white
Americans blamed for Canadian businesses adopting racist practices,
but white Americans were said to be buying local businesses such as
tourist camps and operating them according to Jim Crow segregation –
antithetical to local values but tolerated because of the financial benefit.
At least one investigator for the OHRC found all such arguments uncon-
vincing. When confronting members of the Northwestern Ontario
Tourist Outfitters Association, R.W. McPhee reported hearing the same
thing he had heard across the region: Black clientele drove away white
business. Yet when he asked for evidence to support this claim, "none
were able to provide specific examples of this happening."[50]

Blaming the white Americans, their prejudice, and their money was
a convenient justification for racism around Northwestern Ontario and

also fit the rhetoric of a period in which the Canadian state was trying to "defend" Canada from the "threat" of American cultural imperialism. As Eva Mackey notes, "The cultural effects of living beside the USA were considered dangerous to a country emerging from colonial status."[51] The disturbing scenes in Kenora and around the Treaty #3 area were presented as if what was happening there was fundamentally unique in Canada. Such discourse ignored, as Robyn Maynard has shown, Canada's own broader history of anti-black segregation that had been common in hotels, hospitals, and other spaces since at least the 1920s.[52]

Comparisons to Alabama or Mississippi also provided a way for commentators to suggest that the experience of Indigenous peoples in Kenora was nowhere nearly as inhospitable as it was for Blacks in the United States. Ellen Simmons, writing for the *Winnipeg Free Press*, said that not only were the intentions of the protestors in Kenora different than those of Black Americans, but more importantly, so were the motivations of Kenora's white residents. She wrote that, unlike places like Selma, Kenora was free of "racial violence" and rarely were there any "overt signs of racial discrimination." According to her, the conflict between Indigenous peoples and whites was not about racism but instead about fundamental cultural differences leading to conflicting attitudes towards employment, capitalism, the modern world, and national citizenship. The townspeople of Kenora were simply frustrated that Indians refused to adapt their behaviour to fit the social expectations of a modern nation like Canada. White employers were not racist, she argued, but were simply tired of seeing Indigenous peoples not show up to work. If "the Indian ... is going to get and hold a job," Simmons advised, "he has to get used to the white man's way of doing things ... perhaps most important and most difficult, he must learn to yield to the white man's preoccupation with the clock." [53] Simmons ended her thoughts on the Kenora march by encouraging business owners to respect "cultural difference" rather than question their own racism.

Simmons's ideas were not unique. As Logan McCallum's research shows, government officials who did job placement work with Indigenous peoples commonly encouraged them to change their behaviour and show themselves to be "Indians" who white employers could trust.[54] "Cultural difference" replaced white racism as the reason for discrimination against Indigenous peoples. This argument was intended to create distance between the situation in Kenora and that in the United States. Organizational problems and cultural difference required technical solutions, not a confrontation with a settler nation's founding ideology. As *Maclean's* magazine insisted: "governments of Canada, unlike those in Alabama and Mississippi, cannot be accused of doing any recent wrong to the native peoples." Though Canada had failed to "bring natives into modern Canadian citizenship" this was not the "same thing as the outright brutality of state troopers in Selma." "We have bigotry…" *Maclean's* admitted, "but no Alabamas."[55]

For those who organized the march, analogies to the Civil Rights Movement proved a double-edged sword. Certainly they helped generate attention for an event that otherwise might not have made waves beyond Kenora. This proved useful when Fred Kelly, one of the main organizers of the march, was fired from his job with the Children's Aid Society in Kenora. Believing the dismissal was connected to government pressure and a local campaign against march leaders, the National Indian Council (NIC) suggested a nationwide campaign to raise money both so Kelly could keep doing his organizing work in Kenora but also, as the NIC's vice-president told reporters, as a way to "draw Indian people together for a common goal."[56] National media ran with the story, calling Kelly "a Canadian Martin Luther King," a comparison the former did not entirely reject. "In a way I was shot down," Kelly remarked.[57] Charles Clark, the president of the Children's Aid Society's board and Kelly's former employer, wanted the comparisons to stop. "We've had enough bad publicity," he exclaimed, "People here are a bit touchy because this situation is being talked about as another Alabama."[58]

On the other hand, while seeing the march in Kenora as a Canadian version of American civil rights protests might have helped publicize it, such analogies also obscured the history of settler-colonialism more than they helped illuminate it. Indigenous organizers in the United States had front-row experience with this. Some voiced concern about having their political aspirations collapsed under the umbrella of "civil rights" because that movement was about assimilation rather than autonomy. "The most common attitude Indians have faced," argued Sioux intellectual Vine Deloria Jr in the late 1960s, "has been the unthoughtful

Johnny-come-lately liberal who equates certain goals with a dark skin. This type of individual generally defines the goals of all groups by the way he understands what he wants for blacks."[59] He thought that this attitude resulted in Indigenous people being understood as a "subcategory of black."[60] If Black Americans had been systematically excluded from American society, Indians, in Deloria's opinion, had been forced into it. Mary Crow Dog, a Sicangu Lakota activist, made similar observations in her memoirs: "like them we were minorities, poor and discriminated against, but there were differences ... The blacks want what the whites have, which is understandable. They want *in*. We Indians want *out*! That is the main difference."[61] In the aftermath of the Kenora march, Indigenous students at the University of Manitoba emphasized the difference between their desires and those of civil rights activists in the United States. "Unlike the Negro of the southern United States," they wrote, "[we] are not demanding equal rights and assimilation."[62] While somewhat flattening the range of political concerns amongst Black American organizers, the refusal to map Indigenous political goals directly onto those of other oppressed peoples was also a refusal to flatten the particularities of Canadian settler-colonial racism, which used legislation such as the Indian Act to homogenize distinct peoples through the disavowal of Indigenous language, culture, and conceptions of nation and belonging.

Fostering political and cultural autonomy while maintaining some relationship with the Canadian state was a hotly contested issue for Indigenous peoples in the postwar period. In 1960, the same year as enacting its Bill of Rights, Canada finally extended the franchise to registered Indians.[63] According to Ellen Fairclough, then minister of citizenship, the vote would "remove in the eyes of the world any suggestion that in Canada race or colour places any citizen in an inferior category to other citizens of the country."[64] Yet "The issue of the franchise," argues Anthony Hall, "was, and still is, at the symbolic core of some of the central strategic questions facing virtually all Indigenous peoples in nation-states not of their own making."[65] It quickly became a point of contention for provincial Indigenous organizations, especially those in Saskatchewan and Alberta, and resulted in protests from Mi'kmaq and Mohawk communities in Eastern Canada.[66] The contentious nature of this type of integration into the settler-state foreshadowed some of the political discourse that became prominent in the late 1960s and early 1970s when young Indigenous activists across Canada, in groups such as the Ojibway Warriors Society, took up the rhetoric of national liberation that had been popularized by the Black Panther Party and the American Indian Movement in the United States and anti-colonial movements across the Southern hemisphere.

Indigenous community organizers in Canada were not alone in grappling with the complexities of drawing on and being compared to Black Americans in their struggle for equality. During the same period, many activists organizing for Quebec liberation from Anglo-Canada also "saw their own experiences reflected in the struggles of African Americans."[67] Some, such as Pierre Vallières, went so far as to call Québécois *Les Nègres blancs d'Amérique.*[68] Austin argues that this rhetoric "can only be achieved by excluding Blacks from the narrative."[69] The Kenora-Selma analogies were not nearly as extreme, but we can read a similar erasure of histories on several fronts. These analogies reinforced the notion that anti-Black racism was absent in Canada and that anti-Indigenous racism was restricted to pockets, like Kenora. In other words, as Barrington Walker notes, they continued the "long tradition of unfamiliarity with the experiences of Blacks in colonial and post-Confederation Canada."[70] While many commentators remarked upon the similarities between anti-Indigenous racism in Kenora and anti-Black racism in the American south, very few tried to connect the experience of Indigenous people in Kenora to Blacks *in* Canada. One exception was Patricia Clarke, writing for the United Church, who included Africville in her invective against "pretty girls" heading south, and Daniel Hill, the OHRC director, who suggested the creation of a mayor's committee in Kenora based on a model used in Amherstview, Ontario, a town remarkable in the mid 1960s for its anti-Black racism. When Black American identities were harnessed to explain the racial dynamic at play in Kenora, at a minimum this disregarded the experience of Blacks in Canada and at worst normalized their perceived absence from the national body.

Race, as David Theo Goldberg puts it, is "heavy." Its "heaviness" is created as "layered, volume piled upon mass, the layers or strata composed of varying substances and differentially born."[71] Differentially born, differentially coded, and differentially enacted through power. In Canada, "the discourse of race has shaped and moulded Canadian history and politics" since European contact with Indigenous peoples and today "underlies public debate" on crime and immigration. Yet in official Canadian discourse, Austin argues, "racial categories, and by extension racism, are present in absentia."[72] David Sealy makes the case for understanding notions of "Blackness" in Canada as directly connected to centrality of imagining Canada as an "un-American" space. One ingredient in this "un-Americanness," he argues, is the assumed absence of "politicized Blackness" in Canada.[73] Anti-racist political activity is then interpreted not as an authentic interpretation of local tensions but instead as the Americanization of Canadian politics.

I agree with Sealy but also want to extend his analysis by drawing on my reading of the history of the "Indian Rights march" in Kenora. I argue that the popular comparison to places such as Selma portrayed white racism in Kenora as specific to locality rather than representative of a broader history of settler-colonialism in Canada. Suggesting that Kenora was "Canada's Alabama" implied that such places stood unique amongst an otherwise tolerant and progressive nation. Discrimination faced by Indigenous people in Kenora could be identified as a cancer needing treatment before this "American" sickness could spread to the rest of Canada. The place of the United States in this history is complex, extending beyond headline-grabbing analogies to "the South." For example, I have already noted the way that local businesses deflected charges of racism by blaming the behaviour of white American tourists for discrimination against Indigenous and Black clientele. Here racism was excused as crucial for economic survival where American tourist dollars were important to the local economy. This is a strange twist on Russel Lawrence Barsh's observation that Canadians have tended to define their "integrity and self-respect" by claiming that, unlike Americans, we have "abstained from the evils of slavery, imperialism, racism and ethnic bigotry."[74] Even when racism was evident, and in some cases not even denied, the symbolic and real presence of Americans allowed its perpetrators to lay the blame elsewhere.

These omnipresent comparisons between Indigenous protest in Northwestern Ontario and Black protest in the American South meant that those marching down Main Street in Kenora were not being understood completely on their own terms. In the 1960s, the possibility of a "politicized Indian" seemed as unthinkable to white Canada as Sealy says the "politicized black" has been. An event such as the Indian Rights March helps demonstrate how 1960s structural racism, and the racial codes and discourses that supported it, are best understood through the interplay of transnational, national, regional, and local differences that helped name a social phenomenon in some places while also reproducing an absence. White residents also resisted such identification by arguing that cultural difference, ignorance, Indigenous incompetence, or American financial power motivated their actions. Racism thereby became an American problem, imported into Canada through the financial power of tourists. These symbols allowed white Canadians in Northern Ontario to sanitize their self-perception, at times even describing themselves as the true victims of the moment. Their denial of racism did not require them to confront naturalized assumptions about colonial hierarchy. As journalist Ian Adams wrote upon visiting Kenora in the summer of 1965, "[m]ost white adults, would refuse to admit there was a colour bar. 'There's no discrimination because of colour but because they are Indians,' was the way it was explained to me."[75]

In 1966, a "Mayor's Committee" was established at the insistence of the marchers. The committee consisted of local professionals such as social workers and doctors, staff from the Ontario Human Rights Commission, and march participants, including Peter Seymour and Fred Kelly, the latter continuing to report from the Indian-White Committee. As had been noted in the declaration read to town council, officials had already set up such a body in Amherstburg, Ontario, to deal with racism against Blacks. At the first meeting of the Mayor's Committee in Kenora, OHRC director Dan Hill promoted the Amherstburg model. There, Hill argued, the formation of a mayor's committee came out of "inter-racial friction and tension, along with unemployment, poverty and poor living conditions among the Negro minority, climaxed with the burning of a Ku Klux Klan cross and the desecration of a Negro church."[76] The Kenora committee began 1966 with a full agenda of issues: employment, housing, dialogue between whites and Natives, and improving the "image of the Indian."[77] The committee cast a wide net, yet there were people who continued to doubt that Indigenous peoples faced problems in the Kenora area. That summer, the newly elected mayor admitted having given little thought to the direction of the committee. According to OHRC staff, the mayor had not noticed any "aggrieved Indians coming to see him" and "[h]e said he certainly wasn't going after them." When presented with the idea that perhaps the he could do more to encourage dialogue, Mayor Carter reportedly replied that they "didn't have to be encouraged to pick up their welfare cheques."[78] By July, only six months after the committee came into existence, Mayor Carter complained that people were blaming him for the committee's ineffectiveness instead of Indian Affairs. Defensive about himself and about Kenora, Carter used the July meeting to suggest a new direction for the committee. His main goal now was to "protect Kenora from ... unfavourable publicity."[79] Ironically, in trying to "protect" Kenora from unsavoury comparisons to Selma, town officials were using the same type of rhetoric common in the American south. Defensive white citizens in the southern United States blamed outsiders, especially communists, for stirring up hatred amongst local Black folks. This, as historian Jason Sokol argues, "enabled whites to deplore civil rights protests without revising their paternalistic views of blacks."[80] Within Indigenous-settler conflicts, the attempt to deny the legitimacy of Indigenous claims by blaming outside interference has remained a popular tactic well into the twenty-first century.[81] In an article on the Civil Rights Movement in the United States, Steve Spence suggests that in the 1950s and 1960s "[p]eople throughout Africa and Asia knew exactly where Alabama was, and what it stood for."[82] It was a symbolic reference point that also significantly shaped the meaning attached to anti-Indigenous racism and protest in mid-Sixties Canada.

The march in Kenora opened up new understandings about race, racism, and inequality within Canada. It did not immediately alter the daily experiences of Indigenous peoples in the region, nor across Canada. It did, however, inspire young Indigenous men and women to further challenge the logic that dictated daily life. In doing so they produced knowledge critical to how we now interpret the relationship between empire and land and that between settler-colonialism and Indigenous dispossession. In reminiscing about the significance of the march on its fiftieth anniversary, Fred Kelly told reporters that "this was the beginning of a new assertiveness. These people were reclaiming some of their own dignity by being who they are. I saw my people walk down the street with a new gait, a bounce in their step, and I noticed it immediately."[83]

CHAPTER 2

"Resolving Conflicts"
Culture, Development, and the Problem of Settlement

The march in Kenora sparked discussion about the role of culture in addressing inequities in "modern Canada." The IWC used tactics such as the march to challenge the popular notion that Indigenous culture was the root cause of socio-economic disparities. These tactics were also challenging dominant settler-colonial notions of what counted as a productive life. It was a theme Fred Kelly would return to in February 1966, when he took to the stage at Lakehead University in Thunder Bay, Ontario. Kelly started by telling the audience that because of protests such as the march in Kenora three months before, "the non-Indian is beginning to listen to the Indian talk."[1] Then he touched upon an idea that the IWC had spent much of the previous two years challenging: that Canada has an "Indian problem." He remarked that "the gap between the Indian and white socio-economic standards is not the Indian's problem. To insist that it is so is to put the onus of fitting into the main-stream of society upon the Indian alone."[2] Decades later, Mark Rifkin would write that the notion of an "Indian problem" is a "set of epistemological and discursive strategies" that puts Indigenous peoples into "a state of exception, as a 'special' or 'peculiar' aberration ... The problem of settlement appears instead as the characteristics of Indianness, a localizable phenomenon that can be delimited, contained, regulated, and acknowledged in its alterity."[3] This observation, while couched in different language, is essentially what Kelly shared with his Thunder Bay audience.

Kelly also said that what many described as a "clash" between Indians and whites was a tension between different ways of understanding the world, with that of European settlers having become predominant. He denied being an authority on the topic of "Indian culture" because he didn't want to generalize the experience of Indigenous peoples in Kenora to other Indigenous communities across North America, many with languages and customs different than his own.[4] He suggested, though, that settler discrimination was born out several key differences from Indigenous peoples, including placing self above community (or the individual above the collective), being beholden to a rigid sense of time, being overly concerned with material gain, and celebrating the ownership of private property. This last point was a key point for Kelly in the "breakdown" of settler-Indigenous relations in the Kenora area. According to him, "Indians" were traditionally communally oriented people focused on "being" rather than "becoming," and therefore valued work not only for material gain but also for the satisfaction of completing a task.[5] In other words, the time it took to complete a task was inconsequential and the drive towards a goal beyond its completion was unnecessary. As unlikely as it might have seemed in 1966, just months after the march, Kelly suggested that these differences were not unresolvable. He ended this talk the way he had others throughout 1965: recommending dialogue. "Remember," he said, "human history is determined not by what happens in the skies, but by what takes place in the heart of man. And let us not forget that love and tolerance are the most beautiful trees in the forest of happiness."[6]

Kelly's challenge to the common understanding of the "Indian problem" had started with the IWC demand that Indigenous and settler life be seen as mutually constitutive. In doing so, he and others were framing "the Indian problem" not as one born out of indigeneity but instead as a problem of European settlement. Kelly was also essentially flipping the anthropological gaze, pointing it back towards settlers. These types of conversations resumed in a series of seminars titled "Resolving Conflicts" which took place throughout the spring of 1967 at Beaver Brae High School in Kenora's north end. The Indian White Committee received funding from the University of Manitoba, the Ontario Human Rights Commission, and the Ontario government to run the program. Over a three-month period, a range of speakers, including well-known scholars such as D'Arcy McNickle and Ruth Landes, spoke "about Indians and cross-cultural tensions." Each lecture was followed by a question and answer period with the audience.[7] The topics covered were fairly wide-ranging, but their primary purpose was to familiarize listeners (presumably white Kenora residents) about Anishinaabe culture specifically and Indigenous customs generally. Such an approach presumed that the discriminatory attitudes of whites could be changed by framing Indigenous culture within a global understanding of Western and non-Western knowledge.

Historian Mary Jane Logan McCallum suggests that there were "three oft-repeated, circular, and interconnected narratives about Indigenous modernity" in mid-twentieth-century Canada. The first was that traditional Indigenous economic practices were failing within the modern capitalist economy; the second, that equality in Canadian society could only become a reality with full-time employment, and the third that it was the job of the state to help transition Indigenous peoples into such jobs through training and education.[8] In ways that I discuss below, the seminar series complicated such narratives, but did not completely break free from the logic of cultural integration. What was made clear during the seminars though, as from the talks Kelly gave earlier, was that Indigenous participants were not keen on neatly fitting into a liberal capitalist framework if it meant total assimilation. A close reading of these lectures illustrates how discrimination came to be understood as the result of three interrelated processes: the outright repression of Indigenous customs by the West, the imposition of Western notions of progress upon Indigenous peoples, and the fact that Indigenous cultures had some characteristics that could be adapted to fit settler-colonial modernity. Thus the focus of many of the talks became explaining Indigenous culture, particularly habits and customs, to its presumably white audience. The talks challenged dominant thinking about the relationship of Indigenous peoples to modernity by reframing the Indian problem as a problem of settlement. Yet the problem of settlement was also somewhat narrowly conceived as a problem of cultural recognition which created barriers to full participation of Indigenous peoples in the town's economic life. Little to nothing was said about the problem of settlement related to land, dispossession, and broken treaty promises.

The seminar series and Kelly's talk also fit within a global context in which popular notions of progress and development were being reshaped to account for cultural integration. This context allows us to better understand why and how the speakers, most of whom were non-Indigenous and not local, so often relied on a dichotomous understanding of Indigenous culture vs Western culture. Early postwar discourses of global development were deeply influenced by the belief that "traditional" culture was a barrier to progress into modern capitalism. This was certainly a common view in the aftermath of the Indian Rights march, when mainstream media suggested that because Indigenous peoples had failed to embrace modern capitalism, they deserved some of the blame for the way they were treated, especially by business owners. These contested understandings were not unique to Kenora, nor to Canada. As part of the West, Canada often saw tradition as a barrier to "progress" (in other words, capitalist consumer society) in the Third World in the same way they saw the relationship between Indigenous peoples and progress in their own country. By looking at the global context in which the seminars took place we can see, in the words of historian David Meren, evidence of "intersecting notions of 'modernization,' liberal-capitalist preoccupations, and racialized understandings of development."[9]

At the onset of World War II, nearly a billion people lived under European colonial rule established over the previous four centuries. By comparison, the transition from colonization to decolonization took place quite rapidly. In 1945, for example, the United Nations was made up of fifty-one member states; by 1965 that number had grown to 117, thanks to independence movements across Africa and Asia.[10] This period of rapid decolonization also saw the popularization of a Three World theory by which to understand geopolitics. "Third World," a term often credited to French demographer Alfred Sauvy, referred to people living in formerly (or in some cases still) colonized places, primarily in Africa, Asia, the Caribbean, and Latin America. It announced itself, according to Vijay Prashad, as a *political project* rather than a *geographical project*, at gatherings such as the Afro-Asian Conference in Bandung, Indonesia in 1955 and the Afro-Asian Women's Conference in Cairo, Egypt in 1961.[11] What this meant is that the Third World saw itself as a non-aligned movement of countries seeking alternative political paths outside of the struggle between Western capitalist countries and the Soviet-led "Second

World." Remaining non-aligned proved difficult because, after centuries of imperial plunder, many Third World countries still struggled economically after they became independent. In the context of the Cold War, the Soviet Union and the Western countries looked to bring these non-aligned countries into their respective orbits. Both camps identified economic development and foreign aid as key tools in securing former colonial subjects as new allies. Speaking to the United Nations general assembly on 25 September 1961, President John F. Kennedy proclaimed that the 1960s were to be a "Decade of Development." Kennedy added that the United States would set an example of how wealthy nations could "freely" share capital and technology "to help others help themselves."[12] The job was to not only to bring technical assistance to the Third World, but also to instill the attitudes that would open people up ideologically to the benefits of capitalist consumer society.[13]

In the Western context, this zeal for assistance and development was shaped by the core tenets of modernization theory. It had many proponents, most famously Walt Whitman Rostow in his book, *The Stages of Growth: A Non-Communist Manifesto*. A key advisor to Kennedy in the early 1960s, Rostow suggested that societies progressed through stages of development in linear fashion, the way children attained adulthood. They began in traditional societies, then moved through three stages before arriving at high-mass consumption. For Rostow and other modernization proponents, this was a process that the United States and other "highly-developed" Western nations had already completed, so now it was their job to shepherd other nations through these stages.[14] Canada too saw itself as a guiding big brother, especially with countries such as India who were also former colonies of the British Empire.[15] As David Webster argues, "[t]he Canadian model of decolonization proposed in effect that other countries follow" what Canada believed was its "path 'from colony to nation'": orderly, evolutionary, and achieved in a way that "did not cast off the colonizer's legacy but built upon it."[16]

It might be useful to pause and reflect here about how like the "Third World," the "West" is also an idea and, in the words of Stuart Hall, a "*historical*, not a geographical construct." Hall argues that "the West" has functioned as concept in four ways, including to "classify societies into different categories." It has also functioned to create a "system of representation" by which to generalize what "cultures, peoples and places are like." A series of binaries are established whereby the "West" comes to be associated with urban/developed, and the "rest," to use Hall's term, as non-industrial, rural, and thus underdeveloped. This also gets mapped on to certain moral categories where the "West" is associated with progress and therefore seen as functioning well, while the non-West is associated with tradition and backwardness and is therefore in need of fixing. This creates a hierarchy whereby the West is seen as the standard that all non-Western nations are imagined as having to catch up to.[17]

These attitudes helped shape the Western notion that the Third World was in third place: defined by what it lacked, always trying to catch up to the other two worlds, especially the "First." This notion was reinforced by the terminology that sorted nations into two distinct categories: "developed" or "underdeveloped." Initiatives such as the "decade of development" helped create an industry of experts to spread knowledge globally, transforming the underdeveloped masses of the world into modern citizens. While the primary target of their alleged expertise was Third World countries, similar logic and analogous language was applied to communities, especially racialized ones, within Canada and the United States. In the United States, for example, a major initiative of the Kennedy administration was the creation of the American Peace Corps in 1961. To prepare for their missions to Africa, Asia, and Latin America, volunteers were sent to communities across the United States whose poverty and culture were thought to resemble that of "underdeveloped" countries. As Alyosha Goldstein notes, "[a]gency planners supposed an intrinsic parallel between culturally unfamiliar poor communities in the United States and impoverished countries abroad."[18] Hawaii was selected for imagined similarities to Southeast Asia, while American Indian reservations in New Mexico served as training grounds for those going to Indigenous communities in Latin America. Yet as Goldstein suggests, local organizations could also try to take advantage of such comparisons by looking to "draw on the confluences of US policy constructions of the foreign and underdevelopment."[19] For example, D'Arcy McNickle and the National Congress of American Indians used the perceived "foreignness" of American Indians to insist that they receive technical aid earmarked for Third World countries.[20] It was one of several ways that Indigenous and other racialized communities would come to identify and be identified with the Third World and notions of being internalized colonies within Western nations.[21]

Indigenous peoples in Canada during this period were also being interpreted through the language of international development. In part this was because, as J.R. Miller, writes "[t]he postwar decolonization movement throughout the world raised questions among thoughtful Canadians about how long Canada could go on treating native communities as internal colonies."[22] Like they had with the scenes from the Kenora March, commentators made sense of Indigenous inequalities through Third World comparisons. An anthropologist named Antony John Lloyd, for example, noted that pressures of modern economic life were parallel conditions shared by both the "underdeveloped nations" of the Third World and by "the native peoples of Canada."[23] Similar rhetoric was employed by the Ontario Human Rights Commission in their claim that "in many parts of Canada, Indians are penned up in slums reminiscent of the most backwards parts of the world."[24]

That such parallels influenced how Canada viewed development in both the Third World and Indigenous communities here is a point reinforced by the work of David Meren, Erika Dyck, Maureen Lux, and Will Langford, among others. For example, Meren shows that when Canada began development aid contributions it took advantage of former missionary networks and adhered to modernization theory's key tenets, including the established dichotomy which positioned Third World peoples as underdeveloped and backwards.[25] The Colombo Plan in 1950 became Canada's first major effort at foreign aid and technical assistance. It focused primarily on poverty in India, Pakistan, and Ceylon, offering capital investment and technical assistance through a series of bilateral agreements between donor and recipient countries. It merged Canada's interest in poverty alleviation through capitalist economic development with Cold War geopolitical concerns about poverty being a key factor which might push Third World countries towards the Soviet model.[26] Will Langford makes the important observation that much like the community development programs in India and Pakistan in the 1950s, those directed at Indigenous people in Canada were meant to

encourage "changes in the behaviour of the poor."[27] Erika Dyck and
Maureen Lux show how debates about population control in the Global
South also shaped the Canadian government's interventions in Indigenous women's reproductive rights across northern Canada.[28] They draw
out the transnational connections between how the perception that poor
people's inability to take "care of their reproductive bodies" "threatened
to destabilize the global economy" and shaped how "Canada's North became a proving ground for testing competing interpretations of population control."[29] These imagined parallels influenced Canadian desire
to treat Indigenous peoples as "underdeveloped" communities within
Canada, and continued to shape development imaginations throughout
the late twentieth and early twenty first centuries. One study from the
1990s, for example, compared the international development experience
of Basarwa communities in Botswana with Indigenous communities in
Australia and Canada to make the argument that the latter can be understood as "the 'third world in the first.'"[30]

In the early 1970s, Palmer Patterson published a wide-ranging mono-
graph suggesting that the histories of the formerly colonized peoples of
the Third World would provide Canadian readers a framework by which
to see "Indians more clearly as colonial people" and not as "ethnic" minorities in Canada. Patterson argued that Indigenous peoples in Canada
and those in the Third World shared histories such as being victimized
by the "divide and conquer" tactics of colonizers, the devastating impact
of foreign disease, the negative impact of Christian missionaries, new
political systems (band councils in Canada) imposed by foreign powers,
the expropriation of land, and the imposition of capitalist ideologies
upon traditionally non-capitalist societies.[31] The discourses of development are somewhat complicated to unpack because their use is not con-
sistent in meaning. But as we will see most clearly in subsequent chapters,
before the advent of terms such as the "Fourth World," Indigenous writers and activists also used "Third World" much as Black Power groups
in the United States did: to announce that they were internally colonized
peoples who drew inspiration from formerly colonized peoples globally.

Development as a framework was predicated on what Westerners believed the Third World lacked. Indigenous communities in Canada were

understood in much the same way, by their reported inability to adapt
to modern society. Sally Weaver argues that the turn towards a community development approach in Canada came from "the emerging nationalism of decolonizing third-world countries."[32] Ultimately, it was an
idea about how the state could better integrate Indigenous peoples into
Canada's economy and into liberal democracy by addressing poverty
and inequality locally. "Community Development" programs were supposed to spur Indigenous communities into the "liberal ideal of self-
reliance," Will Langford argues, by using an "applied social science
whose pedagogy presumed that once people learned about their common problems and identified their 'felt needs,' they could use small-scale
community organization and the decision-making mechanism of de-
liberative, consensus-based democracy to undertake planned, rational,
and cooperative solutions."[33]

In writing about this period of Canadian Indian welfare and social
policy, Hugh Shewell has said that

> Whereas Indian policy in the period since Confederation had rep-
> resented, in most respects, a continuation of imperial subjugation
> rooted in paternalistic assumptions about the Indians' natural in-
> feriority and backwardness, the post-World War II period marked
> a decided shift towards policy based in the production of knowledge
> and universal truths. While social science sought to compare, un-
> derstand, and explain similarities and differences among social
> groups and societies, it also sought to level difference and to find
> attributes that would provide a core of universal knowledge through
> which all humanity could be seen as one, as essentially the same. As
> an idea it was perhaps noble, but profoundly Eurocentric in its as-
> sumptions about the measurements that would determine what all
> humans ought to be.[34]

Much like Third World peoples, Indigenous peoples were understood
through categories popularized by a modernization lens and understood
as "fixable" through social scientific processes. By the 1960s, the phrase
"the Indian problem" signalled a range of meanings in Canada. On the
one hand, it suggested that Indigenous peoples were unable to assimilate

into mainstream Canadian culture and thus presented a problem for modern Canada. In a slightly different way, the phrase might signal how Indigenous life was imagined as being always in crisis and thus a problem for the government to fix. Mortality rates, for example, were double what they were for non-"Indians"; while welfare rates were nearly ten times higher for "Indians" than for non-"Indians." What Shewell argues is that for the government, "'The Indian problem,' which had up to this time been essentially defined as a moral and political question of how best to manage status-Indian and to induce their assimilation as Canadians, was now perceived in more secular terms as an objective problem that could be subjected to the scrutiny of science and the application of scientific knowledge to the policies of the state."[35] These ideas took shape through government-funded studies such as that undertaken by anthropologist Harry B. Hawthorn. Completed in 1966, the Hawthorn Report suggested that "Indians" in Canada were "citizens minus." To become "citizens plus" required that Indigenous peoples be offered opportunity and cultural respect by ending all assimilative programs, including residential schools.[36]

The new role afforded to social-scientific thinking coincided with shifting interpretations of the roles played by culture and tradition as tools of integration and progress. The early post-war years in Canada saw the state enlist anthropologists in the attempt to build comprehensive knowledge about Indian bands. Until then, the prevailing wisdom portrayed Indigenous culture as "static" and thus an impediment to economic and political progress. In adopting Community Development as a strategy for Indian Policy, the Indian Affairs Branch (IAB) believed that combining funding for cultural programs, recreation, non-profit projects, and physical infrastructure with leadership training would create self-sufficiency.[37] Langford makes a critical intervention when he points out that this change in approach might best be understood as a move from assimilation to integration. People were no longer expected to completely forgo their cultural traditions and practices as long as there were ways to use them to integrate into Canadian society. If early colonial strategy was to "kill the Indian to save the man" – to replace Indigenous identity with Anglo-Euro settler cultural values – by the early 1960s this was partially shifting to the idea that "Indians" were another ethnicity who could become fully Canadian by blending in. In other words, it was through the tolerance of cultural difference and the promotion of community development that dominant society would best help the "Indian" integrate.[38]

The Indian rights march and Fred Kelly's talk at Lakehead can both be read alongside the growth of community development notions of self-sufficiency, and that cultural sensitivity by white Canadians would lead to less discriminatory behaviour. Of course, this was not a universal idea among either Indigenous or non-Indigenous actors. As the testimonials and documents after the march demonstrate, people still held strongly onto the idea that the way to "get rid" of the Indian problem was for "Indians" to stop being "Indian." In trying to break down this logic, protestors in Kenora insisted on shared responsibility and mutual respect. Yet while much of what had been said until that point might fit the logic of integration forwarded by community development discourse, tension remained about the role of Indigenous tradition and culture in this process. Was it to be abandoned, in the name of liberal democratic progress, was it to be made expedient for the facilitation of integration into liberal capitalist economies, or was it to be preserved, rediscovered, and protected for the development of a sense of Indigenous autonomy in economic, social, and political life? These are some of the questions that emerged, and remained largely unresolved, in the seminar series in Kenora in 1967.

The series began with the Métis writer and historian D'Arcy McNickle (at the time a professor at the University of Saskatchewan) as the first speaker. An anthropologist with a reputation as one of mid-twentieth-century North America's most recognized scholars of Indigenous history and culture, McNickle was also known in the 1950s and 1960s for drawing attention to the perceived parallels between "underdevelopment" in the Global South and poverty on Indian reservations in the United States. As the chairperson of the Indian Tribal Relations Committee of the National Congress of American Indians (NCAI) he proposed a ten-point poverty reduction program, modelling it after President Harry Truman's technical assistance program.[39] Though mostly ignored by the American government, the NCAI resurrected the plan in 1953 and submitted it to US Congress. Alyosha Goldstein argues that "the terms outlined by the proposal replicated the language supporting technical assistance to impoverished nations abroad, where U.S. policymakers' focus on technical support and the expansion of industry and market relations was combined with an emphasis on national self-determination in order to attract that participation of newly decolonized states."[40]

McNickle's talk in Kenora did not focus on underdevelopment and national self-determination in the United States. Instead, he made the case that Indigenous cultures challenged ideas and practices that were common in international development circles. Here he employed an inside/outside or local/global binary as a way to situate what he believed were key cultural differences between being Indigenous and being non-Indigenous. He argued that the "habits and customs" of Indigenous peoples made profit-driven economic development on reserves difficult to develop. As he had done previously in his references to Third World "underdevelopment," McNickle situated these cultural differences as something that Indigenous peoples shared globally. "One could go anywhere in the world where there are native people living" he told the audience, "and find ways that seem strange" to outsiders. This included how they defer to elders even when they think they are wrong, abide by superstition, and are not interested in private property and profit.[41] The point he was trying to make is that such differences should not be seen as evidence that they were lacking something essential. Not being inclined to the "habits of capitalism," McNickle insisted, was not a defect; instead of imagining that Indigenous peoples were indifferent to "progress," McNickle encouraged respect for a different definition of living a meaningful life. To not respect Indigenous cultures, McNickle argued, was to encourage further conflict with settler society. McNickle suggested that since Indigenous communities had been forced to adapt their behaviours to fit mainstream capitalist society, it was time for white "Europeans" to respond in kind. McNickle insisted that the idea of human perfectibility was a particularity of Western culture, not a universal fact, nor was there just one definition of what counted as the "the good life." In the end, Western development schemes would only work if, in turning towards some of the practices of modern life, Indigenous peoples could also remain true to their cultural values.[42]

The general message of the seminars was clear from the outset: the dominant society had to begin recognizing the value of Indigenous culture if they expected Indigenous peoples to integrate into the mainstream. These were themes that the second speaker, James Howard, repeated. Director of the University of South Dakota museum and an anthropologist by training, Howard said that Kenora had neither "an Indian problem" nor a "white problem" but instead a "community problem."[43] "Today, in 1967," he explained, "there is still a basic lack of understanding of the Indian on the part of the White man."[44] Yet he also suggested that this lack of understanding was, in part, because Canadians were more moved by poverty elsewhere than in their own country.

Like concern with Black civil rights struggles in the United States, foreign aid could be seen as symbolic of the way Canadians were more interested in distant inequities than local ones. The attention that Canada paid to Third World development with the Colombo plan in the early 1950s had grown by the mid 1960s. At the time of Howard's talk in Kenora, for example, aid to Anglo-Commonwealth countries in Africa had gone from $135,000 in 1958 to $35 million in 1966.[45] This newfound preoccupation with the Third World, according to Lackenbrauer and Cooper, offered a potent symbol with which to "to embarrass the government for the plight of Aboriginal peoples at home."[46] The issue was regularly commented on in mainstream Canadian publications. One person wrote to *Maclean's*, for example, to chide Canadians for supporting "far-away causes," while turning a "blind eye to the extermination of our own Eskimos."[47] Following the Kenora march in November 1965, a letter to the *Toronto Telegram* scolded Canadians for their concern for "overseas causes" and their ignorance of "the poverty of Canada's Indians."[48] A community development worker in Kenora shared similar thoughts: "We continually hear of young Canadians going abroad to help underdeveloped nations. This in itself is a worthwhile cause," but so too would be going to Northern Ontario.[49] Another person believed that Canada's mission to create "civilized" Africans was failing, so foreign aid should be directed instead towards creating "civilized" Indians in the Kenora area.[50] The same letter suggested that even if aid to Africa (Tanzania specifically) was successful, "the next generation" of Africans is going to call us "exploiters and imperialists."[51] He sensed no risk of such backlash from Indigenous peoples here.

In Kenora, James Howard did not go as far as these letter-writers and suggest that Canada redirect all of its foreign aid spending but, as Mc-Nickle did before him, he argued that Canadians needed to be more open to seeing Indigenous cultural values as complementary to "modern" social life. He also said that teaching white people how to stop being conquerors would further the "development" of Indigenous life without compromising identity.[52] For him, "nation," "science," and "progress" were European cultural values that had been used to suppress Indigenous peoples. Lack of awareness by settler society about Indigenous culture plays "a great part in preventing Indian development, which holds back the Indian and keeps him from taking his rightful place in Canadian and American society."[53]

An even more pointed critique emerged the following week from John Steinbring, a sociologist from Wisconsin who taught at United College in Winnipeg. Like the first two speakers, Steinbring leaned towards explanations of culture that emphasized fundamental differences. But rather than promote culture as a tool of integration, he focused on how Indigenous cultures had been fundamentally altered by settler arrival. He had made a similar point, even more forcefully, in a lecture given in Winnipeg just days before. There he said that the main thing that mainstream white society could do to address the "Indian problem" was to "leave the reserve Indians alone. Don't break their culture." And this meant stop trying to change Indigenous peoples by changing their behavior. In Kenora, he reminded the audience that cultures were prone to disfigurement from external factors. In this case, external factors such as industrialization and European migration had forced what he said was a cultural practice of mobility into a pattern of permanent settlement. For Steinbring, permanent settlement along with "a money-centred system of economic exchange" had wounded "Ojibwa" cultures.[54]

Steinbring, like Howard, was critical of Western values, especially as they pertained to science and education. He suggested these were assimilationist tools that had led to Indigenous "cultural extermination."[55] Exterminating culture was akin, for him, to the extermination of a people. And he believed Canadians needed to take more care in the words they chose. Unlike most other speakers, Steinbring refused to use the term

"Indian," instead employing the term "Native." He reasoned that "it confuses the native people of Canada with recent immigrants from Central Asia" and that this confusion resulted in "native peoples" further losing claim to distinctiveness.[56] He made several pointed critiques meant to shake up white settlers, especially those who hoped to bring "progress" to reserves through education. First he criticized residential schools, then those individuals who moved to reserves to teach, saying they repeated "modern" society's "faith" in science, and were uninterested in "Ojibwa" knowledge systems. "It is a faith," Steinbring told listeners, "which has brought us a feeling of power over everything. And, it has not stopped when it comes to people, or to the doors of another cultural world (in which this faith is not proclaimed)."[57] To impose Western science on people who had "distinctly different cultural configurations" was nothing less than "inhumane."

As the evening wound down, Steinbring said that "resistance" in Kenora was a sign of health because it symbolized a life force. He finished with a call for more culturally sensitive interactions between the "external culture's" bureaucracy and "Ojibwa" cultures, for more intercultural training amongst professionals such as teachers, extensive modifications to Indigenous education (including closing any residential schools still operating in the area) and, finally, the abandonment of scientifically driven assimilation theories that had "deculturized" people in an effort to turn them "White."[58]

While having slightly different focuses, McNickle, Howard, and Steinbring all agreed that settler society needed to respect cultural differences before Indigenous peoples would be able to enter mainstream Canadian society. Discrimination against Indigenous peoples could only be rectified through acceptance of the differing cultural values. McNickle's problematization of the "Indian problem" through a respect for cultural difference set the tone for the lectures that followed. Many of the speakers shared the idea that Anishinaabe culture was antithetical to capitalist values. And in this context, such difference was viewed positively, because it would help the rebirth of both cultural traditions and community values. Over the course of four months, most of the speakers conveyed a similar message, albeit with slightly different perspectives. Most subscribed to the idea of culture being a way of life that had its own internal logic that was, for the most part, essentialist but at the same time could provide tools for integration.

As with the first three speakers, Joan F. de Pena used her 3 April talk to criticize the way Western culture had impacted non-Western cultures. De Pena, a graduate of the US Peace Corps training program with anthropological fieldwork in Puerto Rico, was a professor at the University of Manitoba. She set out detailed definitions of core concepts such as "human behaviour," which she argued was a common denominator for all societal problems. She then defined "culture" as "the sum total of learned human behaviour." Her ultimate message – a point common to many of the previous sessions – became clear near the end of her talk: Westerners should stop trying to alter Indigenous peoples culturally. De Pena explained this by introducing the topic of "ethnocentrism": the attitudes and behaviours that define a particular group of people. When cultures come into contact, those who hold power tend to change the others and this, de Pena suggested, was a problem that every dominant society needed to address, in Kenora and elsewhere. "As a people of a western culture," she said, "we are steeped in long-range plans for desired goals and tend to assume that other cultures understand and want these same goals and methods of planning ... We, of the western cultures, are often so blind that we tend to impose our assessments of what is needed without even asking members of non-western cultures to express their own assessments of their needs."[59] As an example, she pointed out fundamental differences in how cultures organize time. Non-Western culture – a code which in this context meant local Indians – "have no background planning for activating, or completing long range goals." This claim was contrasted to a cultural behaviour she believed Westerners should appreciate: "They can, on the other hand, deal successfully with goals whose completion will provide them with a better life in the foreseeable future."[60]

The subsequent question and answer period that evening highlighted a problem that appeared in many of the first papers. That is, while advocating recognition of the inherent value of Indigenous culture generally and "Ojibwa" culture specifically, those categories started to narrowly define what it meant to be "Indian" into essentialized categories. This is clear in de Pena's response to an audience member who asked if it was really all that "necessary for contacting cultures to have knowledge of each other." Yes, de Pena said, "knowledge of *expected* (emphasis mine) behavioural reactions" was key to overcoming conflict encountered through contact. Gender roles were one site of presumed predictability numerous commentators drew on, though they disagreed on the specific roles of men and women. E.S. Rogers, the curator of ethnology from the Royal Ontario Museum, suggested that the nuclear family was the prime economic unit for local Anishinaabe communities and was generally inhospitable to modern capitalist development. Men and women, he said, shared equally the economic duties of production and consumption. This assertion would be contradicted the week after by Steinbring, who argued that "Ojibwa" culture is "male oriented" and that "primary economic roles are filled by men."[61] While de Pena and others were trying to disrupt the kind of moral judgements that white society made about Indigenous behaviours, their attempts at understanding the other presumed a fixed and predictable way that Indigenous people would act. This predictability was presumed to be key to addressing the types of structural inequalities and racist attitudes Indigenous peoples encountered daily in Kenora. But what would happen if Indigenous peoples didn't act in the fixed ways that these theories suggested? A question that was not addressed, unfortunately.

The theme of Western time as a cultural construct that de Pena discussed was also picked up by Nancy Oestreich-Lurie from the University of Wisconsin in her talk entitled "The Indian Moves to an Urban Setting." Like others, she rejected the idea of an "Indian problem," asserting that "When you define people as a problem, you do not really want to get rid of the problem; you really want to get rid of the people so you do not have to notice them."[62] Oestreich-Lurie suggested that Indigenous people had yet to assimilate into mainstream urban life because of a fundamental difference in how they understood the relationship between time and space. She offered a different way to think of the migration from reserve to city. Instead of thinking about Indigenous peoples as permanently moving from one place to the other, she suggested considering this more akin to commuting to work.

Perhaps the most radical statement of the series was her reminder that Indigenous peoples were the territory's original residents. In other words, they had made meaning of that place before European settlers had arrived. "For Indian people," she said, "the 'New World' is the same as their old world."[63] This meant that their communities were adapting to urban industrial development, but attempting to do so without abandoning traditional conceptualizations of time and space. In an era seemingly obsessed with bringing colonial subjects into a modern world, this night the audience were challenged to imagine that there existed more than one way to be "modern."

Oestreich-Lurie did this by encouraging the audience to reconsider the concept of time. She spoke about the idea of "Indian time," a popular, but at the time a distinctly pejorative term from the perspective of settlers. In "Decolonizing Time Regimes," Kathleen Pickering writes that moving from task-orientated production to what she calls "governance by the clock" is not only a technique to regulate the capitalist workday, but an ideological issue with deep moralistic overtones.[64] As she argues, a key function of settler-colonialism has been to use capitalism "to bring civilization, progress, and individual identity to those labouring under 'inferior' time systems."[65] What her research into work on the Pine Ridge reservation in South Dakota showed is that "Indian time" is really just a task-oriented approach to work rather than a clock-oriented one. In his talk in Thunder Bay, referenced at the beginning of this chapter, Fred Kelly had made a similar observation. Pickering advises readers not to interpret "Indian time" or her specific examples of Lakota task-orientated practices as indicating a "resistance" to working in the labour market. A task-orientated approach not only helped maintain cultural practices that colonialism had not been able to regulate, it is also a strategy to get by, to survive periods where well-paying work is hard to find.[66] But in the postwar era of decolonization and international development, this material and moral disconnect from capitalism was seen as part of the "problem" that needed fixing. What Oestreich-Lurie tried to do in her Kenora talk was to suggest that "Indian time" was not undesirable but potentially a better way of orienting the workday. "We have always thought of 'Indian Time' as a bad thing, but forward-looking industrial planners are beginning to wonder about the excessive rigidity of schedules," she explained, in a nod towards a post-Fordist workday.

The irony here is that at the same moment that people in a Kenora high-school gymnasium were being told that "Indian" time might be an innovative approach for capitalist workdays, hippies and counterculture figures across North America were appropriating a version of Indigenous culture in an effort to escape from modern society. As Philip Deloria notes, countercultural movements borrowed such symbols of Indianness, including "Indian time," as a way to resist a society that robbed them of their individuality through micromanagement. Thus, in the late 1960s, Indigenous cultures helped imagine many new ways of organizing the world. As Deloria remarks, "whenever white Americans have confronted crises of identity, some of them have inevitably turned to Indians."[67]

Abandoning the physical and psychological markings of being colonized and inferior was the message of two of the final speakers. A.D. Asimi, a former community organizer in Karachi, Pakistan, argued that the way to "the good life" for Indigenous peoples was to accept capitalist values and to abandon past markers of colonial life. "The pursuit of progress," according to him, necessitated moving from reserves into the city. For Asimi, "taking progress to the reserves" was useless because "the reserve will never be for the Indian anything but a reminder of his primitiveness ... His confinement to the reserve represents the confinement of his people from their liberty, independence and ancestral heritage." He insisted that progress was "not the one defined by [Indian] culture but that of the non-Indian."[68] Decolonization for Asimi was not about resisting modernity but instead about being allowed to become modern, about escaping the enclosures imposed by colonization. Such messaging said nothing about treaties or land questions. It would become a message made popular nationally with Trudeau's proposed "White Paper" on Indian policy in 1969.

The four-month-long series ended much like it began, with a notable academic attempting to offer a broader perspective that challenged notions of an "Indian problem" in Kenora. Anthropologist Ruth Landes concluded the cross-cultural seminars with a topic that was probably on the minds of many, given the times: protest. This was not accidental, as according to Landes's biographer Sally Cole, after taking a position at McMaster University in Hamilton Landes began "to appreciate the intense and growing political issues of aboriginal self-determination and land claims in Canada."[69] Landes was neither a stranger to Treaty #3 territory nor to Indigenous peoples of the region. In the 1930s, she did her PhD fieldwork in Manitou Falls, a community along the Rainy River between the towns of Fort Frances and Kenora. This research, primarily based on stories provided by a couple of Indigenous informants, provided the foundation for several studies on "Ojibwa" culture. To this day her studies remain controversial, both because of her practice of paying informants for stories and for her argument that Ojibwa culture was highly individualistic rather than communitarian.[70] The period saw the republishing of her work from thirty years before.[71]

Landes began her talk in Kenora by shifting discussion away from the local concerns towards global issues. Situating the local within the global had been a focus of other speakers: J. Howard, for one, connected local Indigenous cultures to Indigenous cultures across the Americas. Landes drew attention to "the conquered" peoples of the world which, alongside Indigenous peoples in Kenora, included Black Africans in Rhodesia and South Africa and the "American negro." Indians, Landes told listeners, were only a "problem" because the "conquerors" defined them as such. In "frontier" towns, such as Kenora, being "conquered" included white attitudes and practices that drew authority from biological notions of Indigenous inferiority. For Landes, such ideologies restricted the possibilities of life for local Indigenous communities.[72]

Landes distinguished herself from the other speakers who promoted a shared "Indian-white" response by arguing that it fell solely upon Indigenous peoples to decolonize. This was not a question of integration, but instead liberation. Direct reference to anti-colonial liberation had only been mentioned once previously during the series. When Steinbring talked about national liberation, he had noted that "what very few people in the dominant external culture realized" was "that resistance (and the organization of defenses) is an absolute sign of health and life. We should welcome resistance because it immediately shows us that the Ojibwa people think they have something worth defending."[73] Whereas Steinbring spoke somewhat generally, Landes drew upon specific examples from the

United States. Black Power groups, most notably Black Muslims, she noted, were beginning to refuse their identity as "conquered," and therefore could be a model for Indigenous peoples in Northwestern Ontario.

If Landes had ended her talk then, it would have made for a surprisingly radical end to the speakers' series. But what first appeared to be a radical analysis of colonialism as a global system ignored the local protest that had ignited the speakers' series itself when she concluded by criticizing Indians in Kenora for their "self-pity." She bizarrely upheld the legitimacy of the so-called "Indian problem" and returned to her controversial idea that Ojibwe culture is characterized by individualism. The "Indian problem" she concluded, "in part then, can be accepted as *the failure of Indians in this particular area to contribute effectively to an examination and programming of significant changes* (my emphasis). There are reasons for these other than conquest. One reason is the Ojibwe tradition which is highly individualistic. But civilizations and groups of men do not survive without adaptations. Nobody ever gives freedom, opportunity, riches as a gift."[74] The return to cultural essentialisms, which had been a driving message for integration and acceptance of Indigenous difference throughout the series, was flipped on its head. Here Landes was essentially blaming Ojibwe culture for settler-colonial dispossession and impoverishment. It was a confusing way to end the series.

When the speakers' series wrapped up in May 1967, comparing the situation of Indigenous peoples in Kenora to other communities globally had become more commonplace. Beginning with McNickle's reference to American Indians and ending with Landes's invocation of Black Muslims, global comparisons were invoked as a way to understand local issues. The seminars demonstrate that scholarly opinion about Indigenous peoples, colonialism, and racism were not necessarily unified. Numerous speakers invoked Indigenous cultures and Western culture as two different ways of life, Western structures as barriers to Indigenous integration, and Indigenous culture as having characteristics that were adaptable to Western modernity without losing oneself. Yet while both Indigenous and non-Indigenous speakers encouraged a critique of Western and Eurocentric thinking on progress and modernity, no one addressed the question of land and settler-colonial dispossession. While these discussions were taking place, there was another set of ideas taking shape. Indigenous writers and activist-intellectuals were advocating more radical approaches to reimagining the world in the image of the colonized beyond cultural recognition and integration. Here important philosophical and political connections were being forged with the de-colonizing Third World, especially with Caribbean activists and with Black liberation thinkers in the United States. A new set of ideas was developing that fused culture with more radical demands for redressing hereditary and historical connections to land. These ideas would inspire the emergence of what came to be called "Red Power."

CHAPTER 3

"The quest for self-determination"
The Third World, Anti-colonialism, and "Red Power"

On 17 October 1967, Robert Thompson, a Social Credit MP from Red Deer, Alberta, made headlines when he said he had received information from short-wave radio operators in British Columbia, Alberta, and Northern Saskatchewan that Radio Havana was broadcasting a daily half-hour program giving instructions about "subversive activity and guerilla warfare" to people in Quebec and the "Indians and Métis" in Western Canada. Thompson said that the host of the program was a "former Indian resident" from Western Canada who was "interspersing his English talks with phrases in the Cree language" while reading excerpts from Che Guevara's *On Guerilla Warfare*. A source had told Thompson that the broadcast "concerned discrimination against Canadian Indians" and "advocated Red power."[1]

External Affairs Minister Paul Martin said he would investigate by conferring with Cuban Ambassador Americo Cruz. This reassurance did not dampen rumours about Cuba's intent to foster an Indigenous revolt in Canada. Soon after his initial charge, Thompson made an even more dramatic accusation: that Cuban-inspired Indigenous militants had stolen weapons from an armory in Winnipeg.[2] "It is well known," he insisted, "that Cuba follows a policy of subversion in Latin America and South America and there is no reason why this same policy would not be directed against Canada."[3] An unrelated report from Havana seemed to confirm that Cubans *were* interested in what was happening far north of them.[4] While covering the visit of famed Black Power theorist Stokely Carmichael to Havana in 1967, reporter Wayne Edmonstone told the *Toronto Star*'s readers that Cubans had been asking him about the situation of Indigenous peoples and Québécois in Canada. Speaking directly to Thompson's claim, Edmonstone argued that if Cubans "read the story a few days ago of the little Indian girl who dies of malnutrition on a reservation in one of the richest countries in the world ... they'll feel themselves justified" in trying to provoke a revolt in Canada.[5]

While journalists such as Edmonstone enhanced the plausibility of Thompson's allegations, most journalists dismissed the prospects of Cuban involvement in Indigenous rebellions in Canada. "Bizarre," said the *Toronto Star*.[6] The *Montreal Star* poked fun at Thompson by publishing a cartoon depicting Fidel Castro at a podium, cigar in mouth, fist in the air, inciting the crowd with chants of "Vive Red Deer, Alberta, libre!"[7] Perhaps the most caustic was *Toronto Star* columnist Gary Lautens, who wrote that he had intercepted messages from Cuba. "It was pure luck," claimed Lautens: "[y]esterday, while looking out my window, I noticed white puffs in the sky ... of course – smoke signals!" Then he listed the ways that the "Indians" were told to attack the "White man's city," only to dismiss these by saying: "[t]ake it from me ... the White Man doesn't have anything to worry about."[8] The *Winnipeg Free Press* suggested that Cuban distaste for Canadian winters was the real reason to disregard the rumours: "There is no Che in Canada: there is just an alleged Indian in Havana. The Indian is probably grateful for a season out of the coming cold ... If Cuban based insurrection comes it will play for only a summer season: the Cubans will prefer the heat and the sultry eyes of the Latin quarter to the cold reality of our northern winter."[9] Such casual dismissals overlooked an important fact: The Cuban state and Indigenous groups, primarily those in the United States, had been making overtures to each other since the Cuban revolution in 1959. Soon after Fidel Castro and his revolutionary forces had deposed Fulgencio Batista and taken power, American Indians from several nations found themselves in Havana for the "26 July Movement" celebrations. A delegation of eleven Miccosukee Indians led by tribal spokesperson Buffalo Tiger had been invited to Havana after they sent a letter of congratulations to Castro.[10] A Cuban official replied saying the Cuban state would "formally recognize" the Miccosukee as a sovereign nation, and invited the delegation to Cuba for the July celebrations.[11] This exchange did not go unnoticed by the American government, which was "not pleased at the prospect of an American ethnic minority having to turn to a Communist nation for support in achieving its political rights."[12]

Wallace "Mad Bear" Anderson was also at the same celebration. A member of the Tuscarora nation located close to Niagara Falls, Anderson was a longtime activist who had been involved in Indigenous sovereignty struggles both in the state of New York and in Southwestern Ontario. Cuba was one of the first countries to recognize Six Nations of the Iroquois passports and gave an official state welcome to Anderson. Castro, Anderson said, "rolled out the red carpet for us, including police escort in Cadillacs, bands, and machete-waving Campesinos."[13] Roxanne Dunbar-Ortiz, a long time Indigenous activist, recalls that when she met Anderson in 1970, noticing a poster of Che Guevara on her wall, he "reached in his back pocket and took out this picture and there he was arm in arm with Fidel Castro and Che Guevara."[14]

Cubans may have recognized Indigenous national sovereignty, but they wouldn't admit to using Radio Havana to incite rebellion in Canada. Armando Lopez, Radio Havana's news director, said that the French-language short-wave programs were mainly music, news, and features that were "transmitted to improve our already good relations with Canada."[15] Robert Galvez, Cuban first secretary in Canada, acknowledged that Radio Havana broadcast programs into the country, but claimed that these were English- and French-language news programming – not *On Guerilla Warfare* being recited in Cree.[16] Cuban ambassador America Cruz also denied Thompson's accusations of subversion.[17] Paul Martin, while not making his official report public, said that Ambassador Cruz's denial satisfied his concern.[18]

Thompson's charges against Radio Havana came in the fall of 1967, just after millions of people from around the world had visited Montreal for Expo 67. During Expo, rumours had circulated about guards at the Cuban Pavilion training Quebec separatists in the Laurentians.[19] At the same time, significant attention had been drawn to the Indian Pavilion at Expo. As Sean Mills writes, "the Indian Pavilion ... portrayed the impact of colonialism on Native populations, provoking a public unused to seeing history through the eyes of the marginalized."[20] The pavilion, Jane Griffith argues, was an act of public pedagogy that critiqued "historical and present-day settler colonialism nested within the Centennial's unabashed patriotism."[21] Griffith suggests that this was a clear indication of Indigenous resistance. It was a moment where Indigenous control of Indigenous education became actualized.

Of course, Che did not lead a rebellion in Western Canada (in fact Guevara's death in Bolivia was made public around that time), nor did the Canadian government discover any reason to believe Thompson's charges, but it is clear that by 1967 the possibility was growing that this could happen – that Indigenous activists in Canada might see their experiences on reserves and in towns like Kenora as connecting them to other racially oppressed and formerly colonized peoples. In this chapter, I discuss how Indigenous activists and writers encountered ideas about global decolonization and engaged in a process of depicting Canada as a colonizing state, a historical narrative that had not been popularly accepted at that point. What was later named "Red Power" was a framework that interrogated the specificity of settler-colonialism locality and Canadian government policy using globally circulating ideas about decolonization and anti-racism. As noted in this book's introduction, scholars have pointed to the White Paper (The Statement of the Government of Canada on Indian Policy) as a watershed moment in Indigenous activism. Erika Dyck and Maureen Lux, for example, call it "a touchstone in national Indigenous political resurgence."[22] We can see the 1969 White Paper within the broader context of the government's use of policy to shape "a liberal course for Canada." The White Paper, Dyck and Lux argue, "maintained that Indians' disadvantaged social, economic, and political position in Canada stemmed not from unfulfilled treaty promises or systematic discrimination but, rather, from their different legal status."[23] To address this problem, Canada made three related proposals: to nullify treaties, to end use of the Indian Act, and to get rid of the Department of Indian Affairs. The response from most Indigenous organizations in Canada condemned these proposals, especially the failure to adequately consult on the ramifications of such actions as nullifying treaties. Harold Cardinal, a Cree lawyer from Sucker Creek First Nation, called it "cultural genocide" in his widely read and influential text *The Unjust Society*, published in response to the White Paper, which was repealed in 1971. The "defense of treaty rights and Aboriginal rights and demands for greater economic and educational development" remained key points of contention for Indigenous activists.[24]

I do not contest that responding to the White Paper was a formative moment in Indigenous activism in Canada, but I also would argue that we can expand the vision that Indigenous activist-intellectuals shared in rethinking Canadian history in the period by considering other events. If we attend to other experiences that were shaping radical Indigenous imaginations throughout the period, we can see responses to the White Paper as part of a continuum of debates in places such as Kenora as well as in the global sphere. In this chapter, I want to engage with the turn towards the Third World, to other Indigenous peoples globally, and to Black Power politics as a way to read discussions around land, education, culture, and economic rights. The type of knowledge Indigenous activists, writers, and filmmakers in Canada is crucial to understanding how the language of decolonization would come to shape "Red Power." Decolonization in the Third World "offered indigenous peoples a new way to see the world, one that combined grievance and resistance with solidarity."[25] Such challenges began to help reconfigure white global political dominance.[26] Indigenous actors began to reimagine the British empire's former colonies such as Canada as states practicing colonialism at the same moment that old empires crumbled. Scholars, activists, musicians, and filmmakers built an intellectual framework for decolonial thought that still reverberates today.

In this chapter, I follow some of the ways that Indigenous anti-colonialism in the mid-1960s and early 1970s was envisioned in three distinct mediums. The first is grassroots organizing and the circulation of ideas through conferences and community newspapers. The second is the interactions between Indigenous thinkers and organizers in Canada and those elsewhere, such as the Black Panther Party in the United States and Black Power figures from the Caribbean. Indigenous anti-colonial thinking in Canada, as demonstrated through figures such as Howard Adams (Métis), Lee Maracle (Stó:lō), and George Manuel (Secwépemc), combined personal experience with transnational examples of anti-colonial liberation; travel outside of Canada, in their case to China, Tanzania, and California was key to this circulation of ideas. Finally, cultural production

was an essential tool Indigenous activists used to articulate decolonization in this period, and it helped construct critical knowledge and language about Canada as a settler-colonial state.

One important site of intervention that Indigenous intellectuals, activists and writers made in this era was in retelling Canadian history from
the point of view of the colonized. In 1967, the National Film Board created the "Challenge for Change" series to produce films that, as Maria de
Rosa recalls, could become a "catalyst for social change and political empowerment"[27] and a way for some of "the most disadvantaged" populations to speak directly back to Canadians. While the possibility for radical
social change might have been limited by their reliance on government
funding for these projects,[28] groups such as the Indian Film Crew made
films that fundamentally reshaped how one saw the relationship between
Indigenous peoples and the state.

One such film was *The Ballad of Crowfoot* by Mi'kmaq and Scottish/
Irish singer and songwriter Willie Dunn. Released in 1968 by the National
Film Board, Dunn's film tells a history of colonization through the figure
of Crowfoot (Isapo-muxika), a chief of the Siksika and a founder of the
Blackfoot Confederacy of the Western prairies. Set to music and lyrics
written and performed by Dunn, Crowfoot is shown leading a resistance
against settlers and the Canadian government in the West in the late nineteenth century. He is simultaneously in conflict with others who are involved in the lucrative whiskey trade. Ultimately, he and other Plains
Indigenous nations signs agreements with Canada at the same time as
the North-west Rebellions. Dunn's message seems to be that disease,
famine, and death made signing treaties a last-ditch effort at survival.
The promise of food, protection, and land, however, is almost immediately broken, and Dunn's Crowfoot is left to wonder if his decision made
the Louis Riel–led Métis resistance vulnerable to defeat. In the final minutes of the film, as the situation becomes even more dire, the images and
music speed up. The scene builds to a dizzying momentum as pictures
from the nineteenth century morph into newspaper clippings about the
inequitable state of Indigenous life in late 1960s Canada. At the moment
in which Dunn's guitar seems on the verge of disintegrating, the film goes
silent, and all that is left is a still image of Crowfoot as the screen fades
to black.[29]

Dunn's *Ballad of Crowfoot* is an example of how Indigenous artists and filmmaker were crafting a new historical narrative in which Canada develops because of settler-colonial dispossession of Indigenous land and cultural erasure. It tells this story by beginning with a society into which disruptive settlers bring disease and death. The chaotic conclusion brings viewers right up to 1968 – the year when revolution in the First World seemed possible for many. *The Ballad of Crowfoot* was a "staple of 1960s basement coffee houses."[30] It also received significant global attention and was screened at film festivals in Buenos Aires, New York, and Chicago.

Philip Deloria has written extensively on the role of the symbolic Indian in American counter-cultural movements. Deloria argues that hippy movements and the New Left more generally imagined American Indians such as Sitting Bull, Geronimo, and Red Cloud as symbols they could employ to frame their opposition to the US war in Vietnam. As Deloria writes, "countercultural rebels became Indian to move their identities *away* from Americanness altogether, to leap outside national boundaries, gesture at repudiating the nation, and offer what seemed a clear-eyed political critique ... [t]o play Indian was to become vicariously a victim of United States imperialism."[31] Moreover, he explains, radicals could imagine parallels between "red" Indians and the "ideologically 'red' Vietcong."[32] So could government officials. The symbolic contestation over how to reimagine Indigenous figures from Canada's past as a way to speak about the present was a key site of struggle in the late 1960s. The *Ballad of Crowfoot*, for example, was part of larger discussion around Métis history and Louis Riel. In Manitoba and Saskatchewan in 1969, the hundredth anniversary of the Red River resistance sparked debates about Riel's importance to Western Canadian regional identity and history. In Manitoba, a campaign began to have him named the "father of the province," and in Saskatchewan a statue of Riel guarded the legislative grounds.[33] Television documentaries, biographies, an opera, and even a stamp all commemorated Riel, though not all carried the same message. Activists from various political causes adopted him as a symbol. In 1970, for example, the FLQ named a cell of their organization the Louis Riel Wing in recognition of his symbolic status as a French victim of English-Canadian injustice.[34] As historian J.R. Miller explains, "Riel and his 'adjutant' Gabriel Dumont became Canadian versions of anti-imperialist guerilla fighters in the febrile orations of student radicals of the later 1960s and 1970s"[35] or, as Doug Owram suggests, "Riel had become a sort of northern Che Guevara."[36] Others believed Riel was an earlier example of global anti-colonialism. In the foreword to his play *The Crime of Louis Riel*, John Coulter wrote that Riel and the rebellions were "precursors of later and present uprisings all over the world, particularly the so-called Third World."[37]

Government officials were aware that Indigenous intellectuals, film-makers, and grassroots activists were looking to history in order to con-textualize the present. Because of this, such histories became a profound site of contestation in this period. James Prowse – appointed to the Senate by Prime Minister Lester Pearson in 1967, the same year MP Robert Thompson claimed that Radio Havana was inciting Indigenous revolu-tion – said he was alarmed by reports that the Native Alliance for Red Power had posters of Che and of Eldridge Cleaver on their walls and used "black militant" jargon as way to get attention.[38] Prowse wanted to direct the attention of youth away from the likes of Che in favour of Louis Riel. Prowse pushed the government to grant pardons for Louis Riel and other figures from the Northwest resistance such as Poundmaker (Pîtikwa-hanapiwiyin), Big Bear (Mistahimaskwa), Crowfoot (Isapo-muxika), and Gabriel Dumont. He hoped this would encourage kids to see them as both significant Indigenous historical figures and as Canadian patriots who helped build the Western provinces.[39] The Justice Department replied that the government did not grant posthumous pardons, but the senator was not defeated. He went across the country campaigning for the redemption of Riel. In Brandon, Manitoba, he explained to the Women's Canadian Club that Riel was a person on whom the "under-privileged members of society" could pin their "hopes and pride."[40] In-stead of an "anarchist and a murder," as one person in opposition to the pardon called him, Prowse described Riel as a figure committed to non-violence. He had prevented guerilla warfare and bloodshed by bringing a cross, not a gun, into battle.[41] To Prowse, Riel stood as the opposite of Third World radicals.

Weeks after the Cuban broadcast affair disappeared from the public eye, Howard Adams, a Métis activist-intellectual and teacher from

Saskatchewan, explained that while Indigenous people were indeed talking of rebellion, they were not waiting for instructions from Radio Havana,[42] or others. Rather, Indigenous activists were finding examples of resistance around the world not only as a way to make sense of what was going on in Canada, but also to align themselves with others who had or were still trying to decolonize. In doing so, they were creating an anticolonial framework which extended beyond Canada's borders and local histories of colonial encounter as a part of a broader Third World struggle. One such person was George Manuel, a Secwépemc writer who would in the 1970s theorize the concept of a "Fourth World." He travelled extensively as the National Indian Brotherhood's president in the late 1960s and early 1970s, and his trips sometimes sparked controversy for the way he interacted with others who had experienced colonization. For example, on a trip to New Zealand that he made with Canadian government officials, including then minister of Indian affairs Jean Chrétien, Manuel connected with Maori Council and other Maori members of parliament. Manuel disagreed with the Canadian government's attempt to portray the Maori as Indigenous people who had integrated into mainstream New Zealand society. He argued that the Maoris had been confronted by a value system not of their own making, an experience he shared in Canada. His particular focus was the school curriculum, which he called "destructive to a very great degree" because of its endless promotion of material accumulation. He finished by telling the *Indian News* that this "will destroy mankind, unless native people, Indians and Maori get together to do something about it."[43]

Manuel's trip to Tanzania for its tenth anniversary celebration in 1971 also worried Canadian officials. Because he was a last-minute invitee as part of the official government delegation, Canadian diplomats only became aware of Manuel's presence after headlines in a Dar es Salaam newspaper quoted him saying that he came to help Indigenous peoples in Canada "seek solidarity with other members of the Third Humanity."[44] As his biographer Peter McFarlane explains, Manuel "was quoted as describing the Europeans in North America as colonialists and said that the objectives of the Indian movement were akin to those of socialist Tanzania."[45] For Canadian diplomats, another concern was the rumour that Manuel had reacted positively to the suggestion that armed struggle might be a useful strategy for Indigenous peoples in Canada. The Tanzanian press picked up on the tension-filled meeting, responding with articles that focused on anti-Native discrimination, including statistics on mortality rates, education, and employment. Throughout the trip, Manuel drew attention to Canada's role as a colonizer at home and abroad. A meeting he arranged with workers from the Canadian International Development Agency reportedly turned "heated" when he characterized white Canadians working in development as "colonizers," a description the workers themselves disagreed with. McFarlane notes that by the time Manuel's trip had come to an end, Canadian diplomats believed that he had single-handedly ruined Canada's good reputation in Tanzania.[46]

Third World socialist states such as Tanzania not only inspired Indigenous thinkers like Manuel, they were seen as potential allies because they were understood as having been colonized. China stands out, because, as historian Robin D.G. Kelley has written in reference to Black radicals in the United States, it offered them "a 'colored' or Third World Marxist model that enabled them to challenge a white and Western vision of class struggle – a model they shaped and reshaped to suite their own cultural and political realities."[47] This model viewed peasants rather than the urban proletariat as the agents of revolutionary change, embracing "socialism from below." And, perhaps as importantly, the Chinese model elevated the importance of "cultural revolution" as a key component of any liberation struggle.

The appeal of Maoism and the Chinese experience more broadly was not lost on Indigenous activists in Canada, a topic I return to in chapter six. In 1975, for example, a group called the Native People's Friendship Delegation sent twelve people for a tour of China. One delegate, Clem Chartier, said that their purpose was to "learn from China" and to "express solidarity and friendship to the Chinese people."[48] The group believed it was travelling to a once semi-colonized place that had achieved independence through a socialist revolution. Ray Bobb, another delegate, explained that China was important both because of the revolution and because it provided an opportunity to talk with Mongolian "national minorities." Bobb was impressed with the way China treated Mongolians and also with the way China had used "revolutionary theory" to "liberate their country from foreign and domestic oppression."[49] Upon returning to Canada, people were interested in hearing about the experiences of the delegation, so another type of travel became important. An American Indian Movement chapter in California brought Lee Maracle – at that point of one of Canada's most important and recognized Red Power activists – to San Francisco to talk about the trip. The group that brought her, including Roxanne Dunbar-Ortiz, was interested to "apply Marxian analysis and national liberation theory to the history of colonization of Native Americans in North America, and to figure out a strategy for decolonization." She writes that she and a "half-dozen other Native Marxists in the Bay Area," met once or twice a week "studying Mao and the Chinese revolution. We regularly exchanged reports between our group and the Vancouver one."[50]

The circulation of knowledge about colonized peoples outside of Canada took a number of different forms. It could involve trips such as those discussed above, but for many more people the most accessible information was found in community newspapers. In the late 1960s and early 1970s, *Akwesasne Notes* was perhaps the community paper most dedicated to fostering a global Third World that included Indigenous peoples and other racialized minorities in Canada and the United States. Its scope widened year after year. *Notes* helped create an analysis of colonialism that was pan-Indigenous, focusing especially on Latin America, with extensive investigative reporting into issues like the violence in Guatemala that saw tens of thousands of Mayans displaced and murdered throughout the 1970s. The "Letters" section was a dynamic political space that often covered two or three full pages and was read by people across the world. Maori readers were frequent contributors. One reader from the Maori Culture Club wrote, "it seems that the problems faced by your native people, are almost identical to the problems of our Maori people."[51] Another reader from New Zealand, after noting that "our country was colonized in a similar fashion," suggested a book for *Notes* readers: *Wretched of the Earth* by Frantz Fanon.[52] The physical space where *Notes* was published became a critical site for fostering transnational Indigenous identity. One activist remembers that at the offices of *Notes*, "one could at any time meet Aborigines of Australia, Lakotas from

Pine Ridge, Mapuchis [*sic*] from Chilé, or Mayans from the hills of Guatemala, the grandparents of all Turtle Island."[53]

What *Notes* also provided was a sense that Indigenous peoples and Black Americans were, as one article reprinted from the pan-African press put it, "Natural Allies," who had helped each other from the time when enslaved Africans arrived at what became the Americas.[54] How Black and Indigenous communities might join together in a common struggle became a popular topic in the late 1960s, when radical Black Power groups in the US begin to define themselves as "colonized." One of the most powerful statements of this new identification was *Black Power: The Politics of Liberation in America*, published in 1967. Written by Stokely Carmichael and Charles V. Hamilton, it argued that that structures of white supremacy that oppressed Black people in United States and elsewhere were best understood as colonial. "Black people in the United States have a colonial relationship to the larger society," they write, "a relationship characterized by institutional racism. That colonial status operates in three areas – political, economic, social."[55] In making this claim, Carmichael, Hamilton, and other radical thinkers of the time were reimagining "urban conditions and race relations" within a global context, according to Bridgette Baldwin.[56]

Carmichael compared the contemporary situation of Black Americans to the historical conquest of Indigenous peoples – another example of how Indigenous people were present symbolically but absent physically from many of the counter-cultural and radical political movements of the period. In *Black Power*, Carmichael and Hamilton also used the Indian as a symbolic figure of the past that could teach lessons about the genocidal potential of internal colonialism in the present and helped show how anti-Black racism could be understood through the language of colonization. And at a rally in Oakland, California on 2 February 1968 attended by nearly five thousand people, Carmichael and other Black Power organizers, including H. Rap Brown and Eldridge Cleaver, invoked the figure of the Indian to emphasize the urgent need for Black resistance. Rap Brown told the audience that the anti-colonial movement in the United States was a "revolution of dispossessed people in this country: that's the Mexican American, the Puerto Rican American, the

American Indian, and black people."[57] In a fiery hour-long speech, Carmichael covered significant ground, ranging from the meaning of Third World solidarity to what he believed was the failure of the civil rights movement. The "survival of black people" against genocide was the guiding thought when he said "the honky had to *completely* (emphasis mine) exterminate the red man, and he did it ... [a]nd he did where he does not even feel sorry, but he romanticizes it by putting it on television with cowboys and Indians."[58]

Carmichael shared a similar perspective when he spoke at the Congress of Black Writers in Montreal in 1968. "I don't think that white Canadians would say they stole Canada from the Indians (laughter). They said they took it – and they did (applause and laughter). Well then, it's clear we can't work for these lands, we can't be for 'em, so we must take them. Then it's clear we must take them through revolutionary violence."[59] The Royal Canadian Mounted Police Security Service were paying close attention to this speech, and others.[60] The frequency with which Black Power radicals were crossing the border from the US to Canada concerned both the RCMP and members of the Canadian government, who argued that Stokely Carmichael should not be allowed into Canada.[61]

Another visit that drew attention was that of Fred Hampton, chairperson of the Illinois chapter of the BPP, to Western Canada in 1969. Student activists invited Hampton, along with two other BPP activists, William Colvin and Jeraldine Elridge, to speak in Regina, Edmonton, Calgary, and Lethbridge; their goal was to raise money for Bobby Seale's defence as part of the Chicago Eight conspiracy trials. It was clear from the beginning that along with fundraising, Hampton was interested in investigating how Canada treated Indigenous peoples. In Regina, for example, he refused to speak with the press because, in his words, he did not like what Canadian papers "printed about Indians." He made similar remarks in an interview with a local alternative paper, *Prairie Fire*. Hampton also met with local Indigenous activists which, along with the BPP's liberationist language, not only caused controversy in Regina but also caught the attention of Saskatchewan's Attorney General. By the time the three Panthers arrived in Edmonton, immigration authorities had ordered Colvin and Elridge deported back to the United States on the grounds that they were travelling with false papers. Hampton "voluntarily" followed them back soon after.[62] A week later Hampton was murdered by police in his Chicago apartment.

Carmichael and Hamilton's *Black Power* and both Fanon's *Black Skin, White Masks* and his subsequent *Wretched of the Earth* were important contributions to what scholars such as Emma LaRocque have identified as the "resistance literature" of the era. LaRocque writes that "Certainly, many native works cannot be considered works of resistance in the tradition of liberationist Third World thinkers and writers or the explosive Black writers of the 1960s ... but, as I have argued, a simple assertion of one's (native) humanity is a form of resistance, given the magnitude of dehumanization over a span of 500 years."[63]

In British Columbia, one group paying attention to Black Power politics was the Native Alliance for Red Power (NARP).[64] Lee Maracle, a Stó:lō activist-intellectual, played a key part in NARP, and recalls how decolonial Indigenous politics in Vancouver drew from both Indigenous experiences and the writings of racialized non-Indigenous peoples globally. In her memoir *Bobbi Lee: Indian Rebel*, she writes that members of the Black Panther Party regularly made trips from California to Vancouver and helped to shape NARP's direction. The Panthers provided a model for their political manifesto as well, as it listed ten points like that of the BPP.[65] Maracle even said at one point that they just changed "Black Power into Red Power."[66] They raised money by selling the Panthers' newspaper on university campuses.

Maracle also notes that those, like her, interested in Indigenous decolonization in Canada were drawing from other Third World theorists, most notably Frantz Fanon. Maracle recalled that "like every other Third World person in the world we studied [Fanon's *Wretched of the Earth*] and I remember we formed a study group to study it because we just couldn't understand it."[67] When asked to expand on what Fanon meant for her, she said,

It sort of came about later in my life, but it started in the Sixties, this whole business of supporting other struggles in the hope that we'd be able to collaborate someday. Well the hope shouldn't be what determines whether we support other struggles. It should be our sense of humanity. I think Fanon taught me that, you know,

that little *Wretched of the Earth*, that the struggle is one for humanity
first and foremost, everything else is secondary. I think that's true
for me personally. And it wasn't true for all of us. But it is true for
those people who started the little Red Power group way back in
the Sixties. It is true for us, in our own way, doing what we can based
on our sense of humanity.[68]

Howard Adams was also interested in how theories of decolonization
and anti-imperialism in the Third World and from Black Americans
might help engender not only a wider radical Indigenous politics in
Canada but also a deeper understanding of his own subjectivity as a
Métis person within a settler-colonial state. In numerous publications
and a 1970 interview, Adams spoke about how his experience at Berkeley
in the early 1960s shaped his own liberationist politics. Having seen police
arrest Black protestors and being exposed to the writing of Malcolm X
led Adams to believe had "no choice" but to become involved in the struggle for Indigenous rights and nationhood to "reappropriate his Métis
identity."[69] What Adams saw in Black nationalist politics was a way to
counter the psychological impact of colonization, most notably the
shame of being Indigenous. He also began to recognize that the similarities between Indigenous peoples and Black North Americans could be
explained through a broad colonial framework. "When you come right
down to it," he told reporters, "it's fairly plain to see: we're both conquered
colonial people. We're both exactly the same." These similarities, Adams
believed, meant there was an unspoken solidarity: "I felt very strongly
about [Black] oppression and consequently as a colonized native we understood one another immediately – there was no need to explain causes
to each other."[70] Adams repeats this perception in his 1974 memoir and
manifesto, *Prison of Grass: Canada from a Native Point of View*; similarities between Blacks and Indigenous experience meant they understood
each other "immediately."[71]

Like Maracle, Howard Adams found Frantz Fanon especially important in developing his own sense of radical Indigenous politics. In *Prison
of Grass*, Adams writes about colonization as both an economic and racial
project. He deploys Marxian insights about how "[r]acism ... arose from
economic functions inherent in capitalism"[72] but goes beyond them to

treat ideology and culture, especially education, as equally important aspects in the settler-colonial project. Like Fanon, Adams writes about how colonized Indigenous peoples were psychologically oppressed through the constant shame they were taught to feel, relating this to his own experience as a young adult when he constantly tried to shake-off "the ugliness of Indianness."[73] "Even in solitary silence, I felt the word 'savage' deep in my soul."[74] Adams explained that the colonizer purposefully educated the colonized to feel inferior and that successful internalization of this sense of inferiority through education, including residential schooling, is where the colonial project drew much of its power. Drawing from the work of Paulo Freire, Adams writes that this internalization of inferiority significantly impacted the ability of Indigenous peoples to advocate collectively for their own interests because "[s]everely oppressed people who do not understand oppression prefer domination. They refuse to listen to a call for freedom."[75] For this reason, Adams believed that Indigenous liberation requires both the dismantling of capitalism in favour of a socialist economy and Indigenous control of their own education as a way to reverse the psychological impact of colonization and the shame it instills in the minds of Indigenous peoples in Canada.

The conclusion of *Prison of Grass* provides a framework for Indigenous peoples' liberation, which he called "Red Nationalism" and others called Red Power. He suggests that it would take the form of a nationalism, because nationalism "is neither objective nor tangible: on the contrary, it is subjective, spiritual, ideological, and surrounds people continuously. Nationalism gives spirit and content to a community of people by bringing them together under a common history and state of mind."[76]

Demonstrating what Edward Said says is how theory can travel, *Prison of Grass* shows the way that ideas from elsewhere can land in new places where people can rethink them according to their particular needs.[77] In this case, Adams points readers to the importance of Third World nationalism because he believed it could inspire them. At the same time, he admits that Indigenous peoples in Canada are too few to reclaim all of their disposed land and will likely not have the power to become a new country, like so many across Africa, Asia, and Latin America.[78] Still, "Red nationalism" rejects reform that might lead to assimilation into the ways of colonial capitalist society.[79] According to Adams, this new form of nationalism is about gaining control over Indigenous economic, social, political, and cultural affairs, beginning with "complete local control of Indian reserves, Métis communities, and native urban ghettos."[80] Indigenous intellectuals like Maracle and Adams were rewriting the history of Canada as a settler-colonial state long before it became common scholarly discourse. This emergence of a new Canadian history and a decolonial politics of the present was the endeavour of filmmakers, artists, and musicians, as well as activists in the late 1960s.

Jan Carew was one of the most vocal advocates for the possibility of radical Black and Indigenous solidarity in Canada. Carew was a Guyanese writer who called Canada home in the late 1960s. Having also served as Guyana's director of culture in 1962 and as a special cultural consultant to Kwame Nkrumah's government in Ghana, Carew understood colonialization and decolonization as global processes.[81] Soon after he arrived in Toronto in 1968, he organized the Afro-American Progressive Association (AAPA) with Ted Watkins (a former player in the Canadian Football League) and Jose Garcia (a Dominican-born electrician). The AAPA objectives were clear: become involved in "the worldwide Black Liberation struggle," "inform Black people living in Canada of conditions which exist in Canada and worldwide," and structurally reshape society. They considered educating each other about current events, history, and anti-colonial theory as an important political intervention. In addition to news coverage which focused primarily on national liberation conflicts across Africa, they recommended a reading list that included Frantz Fanon's *Wretched of the Earth*, Nkrumah's *Neo-Colonialism: The Last Stage of Imperialism*, and an audio recording of Malcolm X's "the ballot or the bullet."[82]

The AAPA's Black liberation politics and their critique of European colonialism and industrial capitalism were controversial. Carew especially was understood as blaming "whitey" too loudly. After reading commentary by Carew in the *Toronto Star*, one person wrote to remind the AAPA they were "in a country where 99.6% of the population is white."[83] But if "whitey" wasn't too interested in the AAPA, some Indigenous activists were. Years later, Carew remembered that some of their efforts were to make "very close ties with the militant Indian groups." Of Amerindian ancestry himself, Carew drew both from his personhood as well as his knowledge of history in trying to bring Black and Indigenous activists together. As he wrote in numerous publications and shared with me in conversation, "wherever the insurgencies against slavery were most dangerous to imperialists were where Africans and Indians joined forces. That's why there were ferocious attempts to divide them."[84]

Shared histories of oppression and resistance also drew attention from some of Canada's most important Black newspapers. In the late 1960s *Uhuru* (Montreal) and *Contrast* (Toronto) both published articles calling on Black and Indigenous communities in Canada to recognize their shared dehumanization by white society. As one writer for *Uhuru* noted, as the "wretched of the earth" it was time for both to "cooperate" for "mutual benefit."[85] *Contrast* applauded the attempts by the AAPA to bring "Black Power" and "Red Power" together, but also suggested that structural change was not possible unless white working classes saw racialized peoples as allies instead of enemies.[86] *Contrast* also reprinted a poem titled "I Am an Indian." Written by Gail Bruyere, a grade eleven student from Fort Frances, Ontario, the poem explores her experiences as an "Indian girl" in Northwestern Ontario. The poem ends with Bruyere deflecting attention away from her own hardships: "[M]y trivial hardships here in Fort Frances aren't nearly as bad as the hardships many Negroes must face." "Indians and Negroes," she goes on to write, "are brought into the world by the same process as are all human beings and are made in the same image of their Divine Creator. They should not know hate and defeatism – *but they do*."[87]

The talk of Black Power joining forces with Indigenous activism moved from the page to the stage in 1969. On the evening of 21 February 1969, Toronto's burgeoning Black Power movement marked the fourth anniversary of Malcolm X's assassination by announcing a new alliance with Indigenous peoples. As Fred Kelly explained during the event, both groups were "prey to the policy of divide and rule" and both suffered "the atrocities of a colonial situation."[88] That colonialism marked Black life was a new discovery for Kelly, who admitted that until then, he "was almost brainwashed" into thinking that Black people were inferior to

'Indians.'[89] Three months later, Kelly found himself on stage with some of the period's most recognizable Black Power advocates, including Kathleen Cleaver, Emory Douglas, and Jan Carew, for a rally at the Ontario College of Education in Toronto.[90] Cleaver and Douglas walked the audience through the BPP's approach to revolutionary change and compared the treatment of Blacks in the United States to those in Canada. For Cleaver, the main difference was that it was "highly unlikely" for a Black person to be shot dead by a police officer in Canada.

When Kelly joined the others on stage, attention was focused on the possibility of a wider movement that would not easily separate Black and Indigenous struggles. Kelly told the crowd of nearly six hundred that for Indians to achieve political power, they needed to collaborate with other "persecuted" peoples. This was an idea Cleaver endorsed, citing the historical precedent of how American Indians had helped Black men and women flee slavery in the United States.[91]

After the rally, Kelly reiterated the need for more drastic action and broader thinking by young Indigenous peoples. He called this "Red Power." Red Power was driven by "the quest for self-determination." Red Power would not advocate violence, nor would "it fear it." It had a disregard for the establishment, for "the system," and for the colonialism that continued to subjugate Indigenous peoples. Red Power, he declared, "has a heated impatience for negotiation. Its ideology and terminology is derived from the third-world movement."[92] Howard Adams shared similar thoughts: "Leaders spoke of our struggle in the context of imperialism in the Third World. It helped to feel that we were part of a global revolution against oppression."[93]

Yet making common cause with a global revolution was not a given across any identity spectrum in the 1960s. In June 1969, Black Panther Kathleen Cleaver, sociologist Margaret Norquay, a student activist named Jennifer Penny, urban studies theorist Jane Jacobs, and Abenaki filmmaker Alanis Obomsawin joined host Adrienne Clarkson on CBC television's *Take 30*, a panel discussion forum. For thirty minutes, the five women debated many hot topics of the day, but racism and identity became the central themes. Cleaver and Jacobs, the two Americans on the panel, agreed on most issues; yes, "the system" oppresses everyone, but racism adds a layer that white activists are unable to truly understand.

This includes how mainstream media ignores state violence, and that changing "the system" from within is futile and thus direct action, even violence, is necessary for oppressed minorities to be free.

Obomsawin was quickly becoming known for her critical portrayals of Indigenous life in NFB documentaries. Given Obomsawin's status as an advocate for "Indian" rights, viewers might have expected her to agree with Cleaver and Jacobs. She did at times, but not when the latter two voiced support for armed struggle as a necessary tactic of political and social change. However, rejecting violence earned Obomsawin a scolding not from Cleaver or Jacobs but from Jennifer Penny, a student activist. Penny told Obomsawin that "the system" had taken away not only her dignity but that of all Indians. With a finger pointed at Penny, Obomsawin's mild manner turned to anger: "How do you know? Even if you live next door, you could never tell because you have different eyes than us, you hear different things, you see pain someplace, I see pain in another place. This is where you could never understand us." Penny refused to back down, reiterating her point that Indigenous peoples had been "destroyed" by "the system."

The discussion ended with the Cleaver upholding Alanis Obomsawin's confidence in Indigenous resilience. When the white student insisted that the system will "chop up" Indians, Cleaver objected, on the contrary, that the system cannot "destroy the spirit of the people."[94]

This panel demonstrated that, while the idea of a shared oppression and shared anti-colonial politics took shape in the late 1960s amongst "colonized" peoples, it could not be assumed. There were differences that needed to be teased out, some of which Manuel would do in writing *The Fourth World: An Indian Reality* in 1974. At the time, though, the attempt to develop a broader anti-colonial framework in which to reframe Canada as a colonial state betrayed the simplistic picture painted by politicians such as Robert Thompson according to which Indigenous peoples were pawns being played by Third World Marxists. What this chapter has aimed to demonstrate is how Indigenous activists, writers, academics, and filmmakers were involved in a process of reimagining Canadian history by articulating both how Canada's colonial past continued to inform its present and how this history could be understood on global terms. They were doing this through critiques of Canadian

"Indian Policy," as demonstrated by Cardinal and also by connecting with others who saw themselves as Third World people. "Red Power" situated itself at the intersection of local, national, and global histories. As we will see in the next chapter, this type of framework was beginning to shape how Indigenous activists in places like Kenora began to interpret and challenge the various forms of dehumanization and dispossession that had continued since the 1965 march.

CHAPTER 4

"Nobody seems to listen"
The Violent Death Report and Resistance to Continuing Indifference

Nobody seems to listen. Not in Ottawa. Not in Queen's Park. Not in Kenora.
Concerned Citizens Committee, Confidential First Draft, 1973

Throughout 1973, graduate student Lynn Kauffman was in Kenora con-
ducting anthropology fieldwork on a Doris Duke American Indian Oral
History grant that had as its purpose "collecting testimony from Indian
people."[1] Remembered both for her fortune and her eccentricities, Doris
Duke reportedly initiated the oral history project at the behest of her
friends, including actor Marlon Brando.[2] Kauffman came to Kenora just
as this funding was winding down, which may have been because Duke
was "wary of associating herself with rebellious causes."[3]

Kauffman was not in Kenora to write about "rebellious causes"; she
was there to record and document Ojibway language and customs while
working at the Kenora Museum. Her work put her in contact with the
Anishinaabe artist Norval Morrisseau, who was becoming famous for
his vibrant paintings of Anishinaabe culture and history. The spring of
1973, however, saw Morrisseau incarcerated in the Kenora jail for a six-
month period after being detained for various minor offences. The war-
den gave Morrisseau a second jail cell to use as a studio, which was where
he painted some of his most iconic pieces, including *Fish Cycle*, *Loon
Cycle*, and *Indian Jesus Christ*.[4] Kauffman was one of the many people
who interacted with Morrisseau during his time in Kenora. She writes
that she would take him from jail to the museum on day passes. "Joyce,
Regie, and [m]yself drove to the prison and picked Norval up – They issued

a pass till 5pm," Kauffman writes. "He is an extremely intelligent man and fascinating to be around ... he likes to talk and he is especially interested in having legends, stories, etc. written down and preserved."[5] During this time, two documentaries about Morrisseau, *The Colours of Pride* and *The Paradox of Norval Morrisseau*, were made.

Kauffman's field notes offer unique insights into Morrisseau's creative vision. They are also a window into the discrimination that still shaped everyday life in Kenora, eight years after the Indian Rights march put such issues on the front pages of national newspapers. For example, prior to her first meeting with Morrisseau, a member of her host family told her she was not to be alone with him, saying "Be sure you have a man with you all the time; you never know what he might do."[6] Indeed, discussions about "Indians and problems" are a common theme recorded in Kauffman's notes about her experiences at diners, bingo halls, bars, private residences, parties, on reserves, and at the Indian Friendship Centre in Kenora. Like those Ontario Human Rights Commission workers from the mid-sixties, Kauffman witnessed her share of in-your-face hostility as well as more subtle, unspoken, quieter forms of racism towards Indigenous peoples. At one local restaurant, while she was eating with Indigenous friends, she noticed how "the waitress, a young white woman ... paid more deference to whites."[7] Two stereotypes are frequently addressed throughout Kauffman's notes: "the drunk Indian" and "the lazy, ungrateful Indian." While there was general contempt for the "drunk Indian," Kauffman notices how much white people enjoyed telling stories about them. White men especially seemed compelled to make comments about "drunken squaws," a derogatory phrase used to describe Indigenous women.[8] After attending the trial of two men accused of petty crimes, Kauffman recalls hearing similar comments outside the courthouse. Unsolicited, one man came up and told her that he knew Indigenous women who would "fuck" for booze or the cash to buy a bottle.

Kauffman's notes recount frequent assertions that laziness was at the root of "Indian problems." At lunch one day, a man remarked to her that, in the 1920s, Indians made things but now they were just "lazy and shiftless."[9] To what did people attribute this alleged change in behaviour? For some it was white benevolence, reinforcing long-standing paternalistic attitudes. After church one Sunday she was told "that the Indian problem here is similar to the black problem in the states – Indians are reproducing very fast; everything is given to them; they ask and they get."[10] Such discourse was common. When the possibility emerged in the early 1970s for the Kenora Métis and Non-Status Indian Association to help Indigenous residents procure affordable mortgages through the Federal Government Housing Program, one citizen expressed displeasure by writing to MPP Leo Bernier to complain about "Indians" taking advantage of "government sponsored programs." The resident told Bernier although "the reputation of the Indian definitely precedes him" they were not voicing their objection to having Indigenous peoples build houses near them "on the ground of racial prejudice but rather on the grounds of land value depreciation."[11]

This chapter returns to Kenora a year prior to the six-week armed occupation of Anicinabe Park in the town's south end. It does so to argue that what emerged as Indigenous anti-colonial praxis interrogates the lived history and the specificity of place, while simultaneously naming a global process of settler colonial dispossession that drew power from the types of discursive and material practices discussed above. I use this chapter first to examine how Indigenous peoples in Kenora faced, in the words of Mary Jane Logan McCallum and Adele Perry, a structure of indifference that "shapes and produces life chances."[12] I look at key examples by which to better understand the local context for emerging anti-colonial movements, such as fires on First Nations communities, mercury poisoning, and the Violent Death Report. Sherene Razack observes that these types of narratives "produce the story of the Indian on the brink of death, repeating the narrative of the vanishing Indian that has been dear to white settler societies from the time of their inception." Razack calls this the "oldest settler colonial story."[13] These attitudes extended beyond dinner tables, diners, and street corners to infiltrate the legal system and healthcare. Though at this point the book might be feeling a bit repetitive, having touched on these issues in the first two chapters, it's important to remember that settler colonialism is systemic erasure and dehumanization and not a single event to be washed away easily by singular acts of resistance.[14]

Yet Logan McCallum and Perry also make clear "while recognizing the very real, persistent, and exhausting spectre of Indigenous death in Canadian cities" it's also necessary to challenge the erasure of Indigenous peoples' agency in asserting desire for change from Canadian history.[15] Indigenous organizations and groups around Kenora and the Treaty #3 area initiated a variety of responses to challenge the continued impact of settler society noted above. This included helping create the Concerned Citizens Committee, advocating directly to government, publishing educational material, organizing conferences, and finally, towards the end of 1973, using direct action by occupying the Indian Affairs office in Kenora. All of this took place as rumours swirled of a "Red Power Rebellion" coming to Kenora in the aftermath of the American Indian Movement's armed occupation of Wounded Knee in South Dakota earlier that year.

In early November 1972, local MPP Leo Bernier received the following letter:

Dear Mr. Bernier,

Today we buried a teenaged boy who died by gunshot at his own hand. A week ago another boy killed himself with an overdose of drugs. During the past year and a half, a girl and a boy both died in front of trains. They were all Treaty or Non-Status Indians, and all of them lived within a radius of twenty miles. Two of them had been out of school for a short time, and two were in their last elementary years. They died either by their own hand or by violent means, and it seems that their deaths are connected somehow. As Principals of the local Schools, we knew these students personally, and are deeply concerned. What hope, what future, lies ahead for present Indian pupils if nothing is done?

On 13 November 1972 Bernier replied with three letters. One went to the two school principals who had sent the original letter, to suggest that there were "many contributing factors beyond government control." The Addictions Research Foundation received a letter in which he promises funds to help initiate "remedial measures" to perhaps "save a few young lives." The third letter went to the attorney general of Ontario, high-lighting the dire situation in Bernier's constituency regarding sudden death amongst Indigenous peoples.[16]

A month earlier, in October 1972, a group calling itself "concerned cit-izens" gathered at the Indian Fellowship Centre in Kenora to discuss data relating to "violent death" and to formulate potential responses. The group was made up of both Indigenous and non-Indigenous men and women from various organizations, social services, and government agencies. Many of these groups were part of the Social Planning Council (SPC), an umbrella organization with a wide array of participants from the Addictions Research Foundation, the Native Women's Association, the Cecilia Jeffrey Residential School, and the Ontario Human Rights Commission. Participants who were not part of the SPC included members from the Grand Council of Treaty #3, the Kenora Métis and Non-Status Indians Association, and the Ontario Provincial Police. The Concerned Citizens Committee would meet once a month for close to a year, eventually publishing a report called "They Were Young People," but also popularly referred to as the Violent Death Report.[17]

The committee began by asking the province to gather information on the number of unnatural deaths amongst local Indigenous peoples. Inquests had been held before into such types of death in Kenora. Such was the case when Chanie Wenjack, a twelve-year-old boy, died after running away from Cecilia Jeffrey residential school in Kenora in the fall of 1966, though as Tanya Talaga makes clear, the inquest focused mainly on whether or not the person he last had contact with when he reached the community of Redditt sent him out again without food. In other words, there had been little attempt to ascertain why so many kids were running away from this residential school.[18] The province denied the committee's request, but changes to the provincial Coroners Act in 1966 allowed them to obtain coroners' reports.[19] The committee's first meeting emphasized the gravity of the situation by having a member read a list of Indigenous men, women, and children who were determined to have died "violent" deaths between 1 January 1972 and late October of the same year. In just eleven months, forty-six people, ranging in age from one to sixty-nine years old, were listed as having died because of "over-dose," "exposure to the elements," "suicide," "car accident," "hit by a

train," "drowning," and "beatings." By the time the committee produced
its draft report in June 1973, the list included an additional one hundred
and eighty-nine violent deaths since 1970. The geographical boundaries
of the study appear somewhat arbitrary but covered several of the largest
nations in the Treaty #3 territory as well as Kenora, the area's most populous municipality.

Several interpretations circulated to explain these deaths. One was that
they were the result of destructive behavior resulting from alcoholism.
This interpreted the "violence" as essentially self-inflicted and was a de-
cidedly apolitical understanding of the situation. Another explanation
was that structural inequalities were the root cause of "violent death"
whether they involved alcohol or not. Members of the committee, especially those associated with Indigenous organizations, tried to steer the
discussion away from always blaming alcoholism for the deaths in favour
of considering other potential causes such as relations with local police,
the politics of displacement, and mercury poisoning. This is not to say
that intoxication was ignored but that they insisted that it wasn't the only
factor that ought to be considered.

This was an important argument because, of the forty-six names on
the original list, thirty had the phrase "& alcohol" listed beside the cause
of death. The phrase "& alcohol" influenced discussions not only among
the committee but whenever settler society tried to make sense of Indigenous life and death in Kenora. During their first meeting, the relationship
between violent death and alcohol quickly became a contentious issue.
The group had come together partly because of accusations that law enforcement and the wider justice system were treating Indigenous death
less seriously than deaths among white residents. When questioned about
why he refused to open inquests into any of these deaths, the chief coroner, Dr Burris, stated that "alcohol was almost always a factor" even when
the victims had drowned, been hit by a train, or been stabbed. Other possible causes were ignored, the implication being that this person's death
was unworthy of investigation if intoxicated.[20] Burris told the committee
that unless foul play was suspected or reported, the coroner would not
open an investigation because "if inquests were held for every mysterious
death, there would be one every week." As Sherene Razack argues, like
other healthcare professionals, this assumed that a body was "so deeply

destroyed by alcoholism that nothing else can destroy it, a situation that renders the body one that is not worth caring for and one that can be neglected with impunity."[21] But Doug Skead, of Rat Portage 38A First Nation (Obashkaandagaang Bay), disputed some of the deaths listed as having been caused by "drowning & alcohol," noting that there were rumours in his community that a group of white men were deliberately throwing Indigenous people who were intoxicated into the lake, leaving them to drown. Skead told the committee that police tended not to consider foul play when "an Indian" died because they assumed intoxication was always the real cause of death. Because of this bias, when one man escaped such a drowning attempt, he didn't report it to the police because he was intoxicated at the time and didn't expect to be believed.[22]

When the committee met a second time in 1973, Peter Seymour suggested that alcoholism in the 1970s was unlike that of any previous decade. "Deaths of this nature were unheard of" in 1964, he argued. A government study would later corroborate Seymour's claim. The rate of increase in alcohol consumption in Kenora between 1969 and 1974 was more than double that of the rest of the province. The local hospital also reported that rates of alcoholic diagnosis had "risen rapidly" since the mid 1960s.[23] The difference in explanations offered for this phenomenon is striking. Whereas white residents in Kauffman's notes tended to see Indigenous people as having a predilection to alcoholism, Seymour argues it was a result of the psychological and social impact of the government relocation of numerous reserves in the 1950s. Indeed, research on Grassy Narrows First Nation (Asubpeeschoseewagong) shows that relocation in 1963 significantly increased the rate of "violent death." In the four years before relocation, 91 per cent of all recorded deaths were due to natural causes. Ten years later, this number had dropped to 25 per cent. From 1974 to 1978, 75 per cent of all recorded deaths there were considered "death by violence."[24] As one probation officer concluded, "the problems really started" when the government relocated the community and continued with the impact of mercury poisoning.[25]

The committee's monthly meetings illustrate the different perspectives members had on violent death amongst Indigenous peoples in Kenora in the early 1970s. Discourse attributing "unnatural" deaths to intoxication pathologized Indigenous bodies and treated these deaths as inevitable.

Indigenous representatives challenged this by insisting that the cause was often political and arose from settler attitudes including, but not limited to, the way police treated Indigenous men and women and the material and psychological impacts of displacement. This discussion of policing, alcohol, and death fits into a wider history of governing the consumption choices of Indigenous people. Protestant missionaries, the foot soldiers of assimilation in the nineteenth century, viewed Indigenous alcohol consumption as a significant barrier to their entering the "civilized" world. While there was a "widespread problem of alcohol abuse among settlers and Aboriginal peoples alike," only the latter were banned from purchasing and consuming alcohol. This point of view was closely tied to citizenship. To vote, an "Indian" needed to give up their status and become enfranchised as a "Canadian"; to become enfranchised, one needed to demonstrate "good" moral character, a key marker of which was sobriety.[26] Citizens were the only people who had the right to imbibe.

While *Indian Act* reforms in the early 1950s allowed consumption of alcohol on reserve, the sale of alcohol was regulated by the provinces. Ontario, for example, used an "Interdiction List," which was also popularly referred to as the "Indian List," to prohibit Indigenous peoples from purchasing alcohol up to the 1970s. Interdiction lists allowed the LCBO, under the Liquor Control Act, to ban individuals from purchasing alcohol at its outlets. Individuals on interdiction lists who were caught in possession of alcohol could be detained and jailed. Scott Thompson and Gary Genosko argue that these lists were aimed primarily at Indigenous peoples in Northwestern Ontario. The LCBO was always trying to "curtail Northern drinking," and focused much effort on people coming into town from reserves to buy liquor. When the last interdiction list was used in 1975, Northwestern Ontario represented 89 per cent of the names on the list, while only accounting for 8 per cent of the province's population. The list was almost all made up of Indigenous people from local First Nations communities.[27] These policies tied the politics of colonization to the culture of racism in early 1970s Northwestern Ontario, including Kenora. They reinforced a stereotype which hinged on race. As one Indigenous man stated, "I have been placed in jail here in Kenora when I was sober. And I was jailed for a week. My charge was being drunk on the streets. I hadn't had a drink."[28]

The summer months of 1973 saw Roy McDonald, the band council chief of Whitedog Independent First Nation (Wabaseemoong), worried about another potential form of violent death: house fires. McDonald thought that better policing might help alleviate the situation, and requested that the Canadian government provide two RCMP constables to live on the reserve for a year to train two Indigenous constables appointed by band council.[29] "We have planned and tried other programs," McDonald told member of Parliament John Reid, but, "[t]his one is the need for this community."[30] A little less than a month later, Leo Bernier, the provincial minister for the Ministry of Natural Resources, wrote to Jean Chrétien, then minister for the Department of Indian Affairs and Northern Development (DIAND), expressing his opinion that "favourable consideration of Chief McDonald's proposal might help correct the situation."[31]

McDonald followed up with a second petition asking that the federal government approve special constables from Community Guardians Limited (CGL), a private security outfit in Toronto, in Wabaseemoong.[32] One federal official with DIAND supported this proposal, referencing CGL's work with Ontario Housing Corporation in Toronto and the security services they provided for Rochdale College.[33] Another DIAND employee was not sure if CGL was a social service or a policing service. The question of purpose became inconsequential when a note to Deputy Solicitor General R.M. Warren from Elmer Bell, the chairman of the Ontario Police Commission, cited the "considerable danger" in having private security in the community (though he refused to elaborate on the specifics of this "danger").[34] Warren heard much the same from H.H. Graham, then the Ontario Provincial Police commissioner. In the commissioner's opinion, the fires were not a policing problem but a social problem and, in either case, CGL workers were not trained either to police or to do social work. He emphasized to Warren that policing of reserves "will be met and resolved by us," the OPP.[35]

McDonald received the news that his request for private security guards would not be approved the day after hearing that the federal government had also denied his request for RCMP constables because on reserve policing fell under provincial jurisdiction.[36] He was encouraged to approach the local OPP instead.[37] Aside from the jurisdictional issues which precluded the RCMP's involvement, Leo Bernier suggested that OPP officers were better than the CGL because he thought they commanded the respect of local Indigenous peoples. In his letter to Deputy Solicitor General Warren, Bernier adds a hand-written note: "This appears to be well in hand! L." But just days later, on 29 September 1973, a recreational hall and a house burned down. Focusing on policing and jurisdictional questions may have blinded many officials to an important fact mentioned only once in passing: a memo noting that "there is no firefighting equipment on the reserve."[38]

The two fires do not appear to be simply random acts of destruction. A young woman taken into custody for starting the house fire reportedly told officers why she did it. Police records from the evening note "she stated that her brother [name blacked out] beat up his father and brother and smashed her around. She became very angry and set his house on fire, which was subsequently completely destroyed."[39] In the report the deputy solicitor general received, the girl's actions were not given any special attention. Still, that investigators overlooked the significance of the girl's actions is not surprising, for as Karen Dubinsky reminds us, "[h]istorically, subordinate groups often made sense of their experience in ways we do not immediately recognize as political."[40]

What the report does emphasize is that while charges were laid, "the fires do not have anything to do with the unrest of the inhabitants of the reserve."[41] What he meant by "unrest of the inhabitants of the reserve" was something reported by Frank Wilson in his report to R.M. Warren: that there was "dissatisfaction among young people in the Band, due to the fact that there has been contamination of fishing sites in recent years due to mercury, and they wish to move from this location and establish a Band at another site."[42]

While mercury poisoning would become a more significant issue because of the Anicinabe Park occupation in 1974 and subsequent visits to Grassy Narrows (Asubpeeschoseewagong) by teams of international researchers, it was only in 1973 that Canadians learned something residents of Grassy Narrows and Whitedog had likely already suspected: there was something wrong with the water, and with the fish coming out of it. Since at least 1962, a mill in Dryden had been dumping mercury into the English-Wabigoon river system.

In 1970, when the Ontario government ordered Dryden Chemicals to stop its dumping, the pulp and paper mill had already left at least 20,000 pounds of mercury in the water. Close to ten years of consuming a lethal substance was having noticeable health effects on the residents of both communities. As Anastasia Shkilnyk notes, this was a "devastating blow" to the residents of Asubpeeschoseewagong First Nation. "Having just been wrenched from their moorings on the old reserve, the people were ill prepared to cope with yet another misfortune," she writes.[43] When he first received evidence connecting mercury to negative health effects, Bernier opted not to ban commercial or tourist fishing in the river system. Instead, he told reporters "that this problem of mercury contamination of certain waters is the result of new knowledge that is still imprecise."[44] In the early 1970s, natural causes were reported to account for less than a quarter of all deaths at Grassy Narrows First Nation.[45] Moreover, attempted suicides on reserves were ten times higher there than in Kenora by the middle of the decade.[46]

As Seymour's earlier testimony argued, forced relocation and mercury poisoning received attention from the Concerned Citizens Committee in 1973, but the issue most discussed was Indigenous and police relations. While McDonald advocated for more policing at Whitedog, Indigenous members of the Concerned Citizens Committee worked to problematize the relationship. As had been the case in the first meeting, speakers from the Rat Portage band council and the Grand Council Treaty #3 criticized the police. Peter Kelly, the Grand Chief of Grand Council Treaty #3, told the committee that the "social and economic development of Indians" would not be possible until Indigenous peoples "felt safe."[47] And they would not feel safe until the police treated them better. Kelly wanted the committee to advocate for a six-month project during which the OPP, the RCMP, and the Kenora Police would participate in "awareness sessions" with Treaty #3 and an "equal number of Indians and police would discuss" their differences. Treaty #3 wanted the sessions to be confidential, but hoped that participating officers would influence attitudes among their colleagues after they returned to their detachments.[48] The committee's third meeting saw a proposal from the Kenora Métis and Non-Status Indian Association to set up "Street Rescue programs" that would hire Indigenous officers. Indigenous groups in the committee

stressed that they needed to be consulted when these programs were created. "As an Indian person," Kelly stated, "I want to be consulted. Such
decision should not be made by non-Indians who care about these issues
only from 9 to 5, Mondays to Friday."

The committee's report on violent deaths entitled "They Were Young
People" published its findings in August 1973. The report was written
by Dr J.A. Riffel at the University of Manitoba. It included many of the
statistics noted earlier, breaking down "sudden deaths" into categories
such as the kind of death, season of death, sex and age of the deceased,
location of death, and alcohol involvement. Other than Kenora, which
accounted for the highest number of "sudden" deaths, Grassy Narrows
and Whitedog, two locations with mercury poisoning, were third and
fourth respectively. In summarizing the impact of alcohol, the report
suggested "prejudices" needed to be replaced with "objective understandings," and that no single theory explained all the issues involved.
"Different people drink for different reasons," the report noted, and "a
range of programs must therefore be available." The various reasons for
alcoholism suggested in the report include the loss of traditional life,
anomie, discrimination, inadequate community structures, and inadequate social services. Recommendations ranged from more funding
for social services to better police training, increased Indigenous control
of these services, and more respect for the circumstances people face
on a day to day basis.

Upon returning from a meeting to discuss the preliminary findings
and recommendations of the Violent Death Report, a policy development officer with the provincial government was skeptical of the report.
He wrote to Deputy Solicitor General R.M. Warren explaining that he
did not believe the evidence supported the committee's recommendations. What was clear, though, according to the memo, was "a strong feeling within the Committee and the native population at Kenora that there
has been a much stronger inclination to conduct coroner's investigations
and inquests into the deaths of white people than into the deaths of the
native population."[49] Frank Wilson, Assistant Deputy Minister for Public
Safety, stated that the committee could not produce one example of
racism on the part of the coroner's office.[50] Nevertheless, the government

needed to "consider some extraordinary activities to assuage the concerns of the native people."[51]

F.D. Herman, a civil servant with the province's research and planning branch, was one committee member who continually voiced his skepticism about looking for root causes beyond "& alcohol." Upon reading the committee's first draft report, Herman said the group's analysis was "overly simplistic." Herman continually tried to problematize the use of "violent" as a way to describe these deaths because it was primarily the fault of the individual for becoming intoxicated (obviously this ignored the violent deaths where alcohol was not a contributing factor). Some committee members grew tired of Herman, one saying that arguments about the adjective "violent" distracted people from responding to the recommendations of the report. Herman also worked to undermine the committee's credibility. During a meeting in June 1973 in Toronto with other provincial bodies, Herman claimed that Kenora's mayor, Jim Davidson, was concerned that the report was "biased" and suggested that the Ontario government should conduct their own investigation.

A memo he sent to his superior, W. Welldon, acting director of the Indian Community Branch, outlined Herman's skepticism with the committee's findings, especially around social determinants of alcohol use. In its place, Herman recommended the findings from a different study, called *The Kenora Report* (its original authors were not mentioned):

> They persist in their blindness to white distaste. This fact suggests the most obvious solution to the problem, and perhaps the one most attractive to the residents of Kenora: that is, quarantine. Simply to restrict the Indians to their reserves would wipe out the volume of repugnance in the town, and it might reduce the burden of guilt. There are however, two obvious difficulties with such a policy. In the first place it would have to be totally effective. Kenora is rather easy of access, either by water, road, or rail, and it is questionable whether such a quarantine could be enforced. In the second place, legislators have for too long a time now publicly disavowed the application of systematic coercion to large groups

of Indians not to have convinced themselves privately of the truth of their own homilies.

There exists a second course. The Indian could be erased as he is presently known by a comprehensive and unflagging programme of community development. Chronic drinking is in large part a leisure time activity. The Indian has a great deal of leisure time. Thus, if the Indian could be imbued with a measure of enterprise and capitalist 'frenzy' he would forego the old dissipations voluntarily. Of course, it is necessary to get to them early or else the lesson does not stick. Here again though, the previous objection applies; that coercion is untenable. In any case it would be anachronistic at this time in our history to create zealous Indian entrepreneurs when the nation as a whole is turning toward leisure as a way of life, albeit an affluent form of leisure and not one imposed by poverty.[52]

Herman went on to summarize that he felt the committee had ignored the genetic factors that the *Kenora Report* seemingly adhered to. In responding to the memo, Weldon tried to distance himself from Herman's position. He told D.R. Martyn, the executive director of the Community Services Division, that he takes "exception in the strongest possible terms to a number of points raised" by Herman. A "not helpful" argument which should be "discouraged."[53] This was just one government member on a committee struck to respond to the wide array of ways that Indigenous people, many of them teenagers, were dying. His point of view did not represent the majority of voices on the committee, but as Kauffman's notes from earlier demonstrate, he may not have been alone in suggesting such inhumane "solutions."

Amongst the flurry of memos looking to control the message to the public, Herman's stands out. I also include it to demonstrate that this type of thinking was not monopolized by white folks sitting around diners and bars in Kenora – those most likely to show up in Kauffman's field notes that began the chapter. This attitude also shaped the legal and governance structures which developed policy related to Indigenous peoples. People like Herman demonstrate the severity of the situation and the broader social and political context faced by Indigenous groups advocating for changes that would politicize rather than pathologize violent deaths.

The committee was only one of several groups where Indigenous men and women in the area organized to share knowledge and challenge these forms of settler discourse and dispossession. There were a range of different tactics from publications, to conferences, to an occupation that announced "Red Power's" arrival in Kenora. Treaty #3 publications demonstrate concerns around both culture and education. In 1972, their research found that Indigenous children in the Kenora area were not being given enough opportunity to learn in Ojibwe and to study Anishinaabe traditions. This was partly because their teachers, on reserve, in the public-school system, and in residential schools had very little training in "the history of the Indians of the Lake of the Woods-Rainy River area, or of treaties and Indian rights." Moreover, "no teachers had any training in teaching English as a second language to Indian people." The report supported the idea that "Treaty #3 and the bands [should] take over the educational field."[54] An educational program proposed for Whitedog in the summer of 1972 anticipated having "Indian children more involved in our culture" by being taught by area elders and other "people knowledgeable of history, traditions, art, singing and dancing, and the Ojibway language."

Another concern is evident in the special issue of the *Council Fire*, a Treaty #3 publication, focused on education. Along with a curriculum in languages which better reflected Anishinaabe knowledge, the articles express concern about the "boarding home situation." This issue began to be discussed in the early 1970s, as Kenora's last residentials schools shut down and Indigenous kids began attending high school in Kenora.[55] Those who needed busing in from reserves were either forced to board in town, often with white families, or would stay at Cecilia Jeffrey Residential School (which was in operation as an Indian Residential School until 1976). Kauffman mentions the boarding home situation in notes about discussions she had with a young Indigenous woman. The young woman says that at least if students were boarded at Cecilia Jeffrey, they would be around other Indigenous kids, as opposed to living at a white home where "they are lonely and uncomfortable."[56] These were also some of the concerns expressed by a group called Kenora Students Residence Committee of Treaty #3. Made up of high-school-age students from various Treaty #3 communities, they argued that most students hated the boarding home experience. Few of these places allowed students to have friends over, and they were forced to find alternative accommodation if the boarding home family left for the weekend. The Residence Committee also noted many students had "trouble with drunk landlords." This had profound effects on both their psyches and their scholastic performance because, as one student said, they "didn't feel very secure in a boarding home." The committee connected this insecurity to the high dropout rate amongst Indigenous kids in Kenora. As a way to be "with fellow Indians," the committee advocated using the recently closed St Mary's Residential School as communal residence for students who had to live off reserve to attend school.

The situation faced by these students also concerned Indigenous women's groups. Upon returning from the National Native Women's Conference held in Saskatoon in March 1972, Agnes Mills, an executive secretary with Grand Council Treaty #3, reported that Indigenous women across Canada shared similar concerns: education, culture, health, and native women's rights, especially those pertaining to marriage, which had recently gained national attention because of Jeannette Corbiere-Lavell's efforts to challenge gender discrimination in the Indian Act. Mills's article lists a broad range of issues, including "poor sewage and housing ... and better pay and working conditions," especially with the summer tourist season about to begin. Mills also noted that they were concerned with the quality of education on reserves, the high drop-out rate of high school students, and the situation of boarding homes in the Kenora area. She suggested the importance of a women's meeting to find solutions in Treaty #3. "Well, so much for 'women's lib,'" she writes at the end of her report. "We are not trying to take over the matters on the reserves. We just want to help improve things and work together in doing so."[57] While just a quick reference at the end of a much longer article, the reference to "taking over matters on reserves" indicates some of the hostility Indigenous women faced not only from non-Indigenous Canada but also from Indigenous men in their advocacy efforts. As Erika Dyck and Maureen Lux make clear in their research on Indigenous women's activism around reproductive rights in this period, women's struggles, especially for marriage rights, were "dismissed at the time by the Indian Brotherhood as anti-Indian, unauthentic, and indeed dangerous to Indigenous sovereignty and self-government," because amending the Indian Act threatened the authority of "band governance."[58]

Interest in working together to improve things extended to other issues whose impacts were just beginning to be understood. In 1973, "The Women's Mini-Conference" held at Grassy Narrows saw mercury poisoning as a central concern. As I noted earlier, in 1973 mercury poisoning was beginning to become a topic of conversation in Kenora because it was finally being covered in the media. Over time, Grassy Narrows and Whitedog have become the best known examples of communities in the area devastated by poisoned water-systems. But they were not the only ones. As Brittany Luby notes, waste dumped into Rideout Bay on the mouth of the Winnipeg River from the Ontario-Minnesota Pulp and Paper Mill in Kenora also affected people living upstream at Dalles 38C First Nation (Niisaachewan). By 1975, the federal government determined that the fish near the Dalles was "unfit for export and human consumption."[59] This had tremendous repercussions for Indigenous employment, making it impossible to legally guide or fish commercially. Luby also shows how it impacted women's "ability to care for their children" because "Anishinabek dietary recommendations for lactating mothers … emphasized the importance of whitefish in breast milk production."[60] Given how many communities were noticing both the "physical and social consequences" of mercury poisoning, we should not be surprised that it was on the minds of Indigenous women from various Treaty #3 communities when they got together at Grassy Narrows.

The "mini-conference" of Anishinaabe women was dedicated to raising awareness about the issue, including passing around posters declaring "Breast milk is Poison" because of mercury. Reports from the conference show that participants were concerned that doctors and nurses on reserve were downplaying the issue in order to protect the pulp and paper mill. To counter this, the conference organizers brought in their own medical professionals to spread knowledge about the impact of mothers passing mercury on to their unborn babies and then, through breastmilk, to newborns.[61]

At the same time as Indigenous groups were sharing information on issues affecting communities in the Treaty #3 territory, a matter to the south of Kenora would have significant consequences. On 27 February 1973, two hundred people affiliated with a group called the American Indian Movement (AIM) took over a small hamlet at Wounded Knee on the Pine Ridge reservation in South Dakota. AIM leaders used the occupation to highlight allegations of corruption amongst tribal governments and to demand American Indian sovereignty in the United States. The seventy-one-day armed protest received wide media coverage as images of shootouts between AIM and National Guardsmen was "spectacular symbolic politics."[62] The old "cowboy and Indian" motif was being played all over again. The occupation ended in early May 1973 with many AIM members surrendering and being arrested. A few of the more high-profile activists, such as Dennis Banks, temporarily fled to Canada.

As the Wounded Knee protest was taking place, CBC Radio broadcast an interview suggesting that Kenora, given its similar tensions, might become "Canada's Wounded Knee." What seemed to spark the story was not only the volatile and dehumanizing situation faced by Indigenous peoples in the Treaty #3 territory but also the expressions of support for AIM from Indigenous groups across Canada.[63] *The Winnipeg Free Press* published an article asking "Could it happen here?" after seventy-five people from Saskatchewan, Manitoba, and Northwestern Ontario met at the Winnipeg Native Club to decide how to support AIM at Wounded Knee.[64] The following day, after appealing to Winnipeggers for donations, upwards of fifty people drove in a caravan to bring food and supplies to South Dakota.[65] Journalism students at Wounded Knee suggested that such expressions of transnational support foreshadowed a more radical approach to Indigenous politics in Canada when they reprinted a conversation with an AIM member for *Winnipeg Free Press* readers:

"We're journalism students from Canada."
"We're from Canada too," he said, "Fort Qu'Apelle."
"You think there'll be a Wounded Knee in Canada?"
"It's possible," he said.[66]

Rumours of an AIM-style direct action coming to Kenora began to develop during a series of confrontational moments between Indigenous peoples and the state in Northwestern Ontario at the end of February 1973. Ontario Provincial Police files note that on 18 February (ten days prior to Wounded Knee) "three female and two male Indians" tried to come into Canada from the United States. When told that they would need to be documented by customs to enter the country, they "[r]efused to be documented claiming rights under the Jay Treaty."[67] The group was citing a 1794 Treaty signed between the United States and the British to help harmonize trade along the boundaries established in the Treaty of Paris which ended the American revolutionary war. Formally known as the Treaty of Amity, Commerce, and Navigation, the Jay Treaty established that recognized Indian nations had the right, in the words of Audra Simpson, to "traverse the boundaries of the US-British divide freely and without levy."[68] Simpson also writes that citation of the Jay Treaty at the US-Canada border two centuries later is still an act of refusal: a refusal whereby "Indigenous border crossers enact their understandings of history and law, understandings that are then received in particular ways."[69] The group of five refused to leave the customs office, resulting in the arrival of four Ontario Provincial Police constables and a high ranking immigration official. Robert Andras, the minister of manpower and immigration, advised immigration officials that if the "American Indians refused to be documented they were not to be permitted entry as Canada does not recognize the Jay Treaty."[70]

Although they were refused entry, another attempt at challenging the legitimacy of the Canada and the United States to prevent Indigenous peoples from undocumented crossing would take place on 3 March. That afternoon, a group of fifty activists from AIM and the Union of Ontario Indians travelling from Thunder Bay passed through Canadian customs but stopped when they reached the midpoint of the Pigeon River bridge, between Canadian and US customs. At the blockade, a police officer reported that when he asked one of protestors (reportedly a member of AIM from London, Ontario) what they were trying to prove, the protestor told the officer that "his people deny being citizens of either Canada or the United States, that the government of both countries are trying to enforce citizenship on them. They claim they are citizens of North America."[71] The blockade ended early that evening with most people returning to Thunder Bay.

By the middle of March 1973, Lynn Kauffman's notebook was filling up with people's speculations about the possibility that Kenora might become the stage for a more direct form of action, maybe one involving guns. At breakfast, the day CBC predicted Kenora becoming Canada's Wounded Knee, a friend asked her if she had heard about a possible "Indian uprising"? Kauffman was also hearing rumours that a white vigilante group was being organized, "just in case."[72] At dinner one night, a member of her host family "was particularly upset with the current situation of B.C. Indians who are attempting to take back lands; [he] is worried that Ojibway and other groups will follow suit and stated he would take up his gun and tomahawk and do some scalping all over again to protect his property."[73] Provincial police were also beginning to wonder what might happen. In a letter to the deputy solicitor general, the deputy commissioner of operations for the Ontario Provincial Police wrote that he had heard an interview in which a "native person made comments regarding the Wounded Knee incident." And "[w]hen pressed by the interviewer he singled out the Kenora area as the most likely location for such a disturbance."[74] The concern was relayed to local authorities in a 15 March 1973 memorandum concerning possible "civil unrest" involving Indigenous activists. Kenora's chief of police, the deputy commissioner, and the district judge thought that law enforcement should prepare for violent unrest, though they did not believe it was imminent. "It occurs to us, and was also mentioned by Judge McLennan," the memorandum notes, "that the most likely point of attack would be the Court House in Kenora, and we have plans for the defense of that building."[75]

The social inequalities discussed in this chapter and the global context in which they were being framed meant that any organized gathering of Indigenous peoples could be seen as the moment when Kenora became Canada's Wounded Knee. When a large powwow took place in the early autumn of 1973, rumours of violence again swirled, and a hospital nurse even reported seeing "an Indian man measuring the bridge in order to set dynamite and blow it up."

No bridges were blown up in Kenora in the fall of 1973. But with issues such as mercury poisoning becoming known, and with what appeared as a general lack of public concern regarding the Violent Death Report, the possibility of a more radical form of action had become appealing, and perhaps necessary. In the waning days of November 1973, a group of several dozen young men and women calling itself the Ojibway Warrior Society took over the Department of Indian Affairs office in Kenora. The group staged what they called "a powwow at Indian Affairs" for thirty-six hours. They used the sit-in to demand greater economic autonomy for local First Nations, government action on mercury contamination, and an end to the physical brutality, discrimination, and racism they experienced in Kenora.[76] The occupation ended without any arrests, but the Ontario government was worried that this type of "civil unrest" would spread to other cities in the province. A memo to the deputy solicitor general dated 29 November 1973 recommends that the OPP prepare for similar occupations in Sault Ste Marie, where the "principals involved in the recent incident in Kenora," would again be active.[77] For his part, Louis Cameron, a loquacious young Anishinaabe man from Whitedog First Nation (Wabaseemoong) who would emerge as a key actor in several high-profile protests, vowed that the violent deaths of his "brothers and sisters" would not be so easily forgotten. The armed occupation of Anicinabe Park on Kenora's south end in the summer of 1974 made sure of that.

CHAPTER 5

The Anicinabe Park Occupation
Red Power and the Meaning of Violence in a Settler Society

On 8 August 1974 a journalist with the Better Reads Collective, a small leftist publisher from Toronto, sat down for an extensive interview with Louis Cameron of the Ojibway Warrior Society. They were at Anicinabe Park, a fourteen-acre parcel of land on the southeast edge of Kenora which was popular with summer tourists and locals because of its lakefront location.[1] At the time, the Warriors and their supporters were refusing to leave the town-owned land; armed, they were occupying it until it once again became "liberated Indian territory." This was week three of the standoff between the Warriors on one side and the Ontario Provincial Police, the town, and the province on the other. About halfway through the interview, the reporter asked Cameron if the ows had decided on the armed occupation of Anicinabe Park after the three levels of government failed to meet any of the demands from the sit-in at the Indian Affairs office in Kenora seven months earlier. "Yes," said Cameron.

> It's a direct result of the takeover. We met with the Attorney-General's representatives, we met the Solicitor-General, we met with the Chamber of Commerce trying to get a change for our people – some justice for our people. We talked and met in different places with these officials. We tried to meet Leo Dernier [*sic*], John Reid – the local politicians here – and we asked to meet with Trudeau. The Prime Minister, he don't care what's going on in this part of the country, and he doesn't know what's going on in this part of the country. We've asked for cabinet ministers to come down to this part of the country, we've asked for Senators to come down to this part of the country, and nobody will get involved be-

cause they know that they cannot do anything – it's our people that are being killed and they know it. They don't want to come down because they can't do anything. It's our responsibility and we have to take that responsibility. If anyone is going to do anything for our people we are going to do it – Indian people themselves will do it for Indian people.[2]

The group at Anicinabe Park, numbering somewhere around 150, was armed with an assortment of hunting rifles and homemade explosives, and demanded real action on a host of issues that had not only come up in the Violent Death Report the previous autumn but had been discussed since at least the Indian Rights march nine years earlier in 1965: housing, policing, jobs, water poisoning, violent deaths, and land. The park occupation was one of many actions Indigenous peoples took across Canada throughout the 1960s and 1970s. As sociologist Howard Ramos notes, the years between 1973 and 1976 saw twice as many Indigenous protest actions and legal challenges take place in Canada annually as any year between 1960 and 1969.[3] Ken Coates writes that such militancy was also inspired by global examples of "a dramatic new rhetoric ... immersed in the language of decolonization and antiracism."[4] I would add that the armed occupation of Anicinabe Park in Kenora from late July until the end of August 1974 demonstrates how Red Power in Canada acted in intensely local ways while also situating itself in broader global anti-colonial contexts from the past and present.

In June 1974, the Ojibway Warrior Society and Grand Council Treaty #3 had put together a plan for a conference to "unify our Indian people." Plans were made to accommodate upwards of 5,000 people at Anicinabe Park. As would become evident in the weeks that followed, holding the conference at that particular location was not a haphazard choice. In separate press releases, Grand Council Treaty #3 and the OWS outlined the main purpose of the events. There were subtle but important differences in their tones. The Grand Council press release was eleven points long and emphasized verbs such as "examine," "question," "understand," and "establish." As they had throughout the early 1970s, they emphasized returning to Anishinaabe knowledge practices as an important aspect of rejuvenating "the Ojibway nation." For Treaty #3, this meant inviting "spiritual leaders, chiefs and all people concerned with the rebirth of our nation" under the teachings of the Midewiwin Society.[5] The Ojibway Warrior Society struck a more militant tone in their press release. Rather than "examine," they argued they must "blame" the Canadian government, the churches, the judicial system, the business community, and the provincial government for the "racism, bigotry, and subtle discrimination that is running wild" in Kenora. The ows also suggested that Indian Affairs had used "tribal government" puppets who were complicit in the "conspiracy to destroy the will of the people."[6]

On the heels of the American Indian Movement's protest at Wounded Knee and an increased number of protests around the region, there were rumours that members of AIM, including its leadership, would attend the conference. This led Crown Attorney Ted Burton to say he was concerned that the conference was just a "cloak for subversive activities."[7] Speculation that white vigilantes were planning to attack conference participants made the town wonder if it had sufficient resources to handle the situation. In response to the concerns of Mayor Jim Davidson, Peter Kelly of Grand Council Treaty #3 wrote that the ows would conduct their own security patrol; however, he also said that the town would be wise to "police their own people, particularly their own police," some of whom were known for their "hostile and prejudicial attitudes."[8] In preparation for the first day of the conference, posters put up by the ows warned participants to be on their "best behaviour" and that liquor and drugs were prohibited, a rule that "Indian security" would enforce.[9] They asked the Kenora Hotel Association to cooperate with this dry policy and close their bars for the weekend. By doing so, the ows emphasized their security responsibilities, while claiming they would not "be responsible for the perpetuation of alcohol, which could lead to definite and serious circumstances."[10] The Hotel Association turned down the request.[11]

The five hundred people who showed up was a smaller number than organizers had hoped for, but they spent the weekend participating in a variety of activities, including drumming and dancing. A wide range of issues was discussed relating to government policies, Anishinaabe worldviews, and ways to "find new direction, and new thinking and practice of our people." The agenda emphasized that while pan-Indigenous in spirit, the event was "first ... an Ojibwa Nation Conference."[12] The event ended with what must have felt like a celebrity appearance: Dennis Banks – the National Director of the American Indian Movement and, at that time, on trial with Russell Means for their roles in the Wounded Knee standoff – had been given special permission to come from the US to speak in Kenora. Crown Attorney Ted Burton suggests that Banks was able enter Canada because "the district attorney and the judge [in St Paul, Minnesota] both held Banks in high esteem." [13]

At the conference, Banks explained how the colonial system inflicted shame on Indigenous peoples across North America. While providing some examples, Banks reminded those listening to him that the colonized did not need much evidence of their colonization, so he would rather talk about how Indigenous people could work together for their own protection. "[W]hen society initiates and creates laws detrimental to our members," he explained "then we must disobey those laws. We must disobey the laws of the crooks. We must disobey the laws of people who have forgotten about mother earth and human rights." The time to resist, according to Banks, was now, "[f]or no matter where they have been born, Indian people are standing up in lonely towns and on lonely reservations to be heard. We have been silent about these injustices for too long, and we have been silent as a group."[14] Those who remained after Banks left the stage were treated to a demonstration of Taekwondo, a martial art designed for self-defense. The message seemed clear. They needed to learn how to defend themselves.[15]

By mid-day on Monday, 23 July, a day after the conference ended, news spread that nearly one hundred and fifty people were refusing to leave the park and also refusing to let visitors back in. The Ojibway Warrior Society were armed, and declared that they would not leave the park until it was "liberated Indian territory."[16] When the ows made their demands public, they provided twenty-five points of contention broken into local, provincial, and national topics. At the top of the list was a claim to Anicinabe Park itself. At issue was the legality of the town's purchase of the land from the federal government in 1959, who had held it as "Indian land" since the signing of Treaty #3. The state insisted that the purchase was legal; the ows, with the support of Grand Council

Treaty #3, argued that not only was it illegal for the federal government to have sold the land in 1959, the land was not the federal government's to sell in the first place.[17] Beyond the disputed ownership of Anicinabe Park there were twenty-four additional points, most receiving only scant media attention, many of which Indigenous activists had repeated ad nauseam over the previous ten years. They included better job opportunities, fairer press coverage, and an end to police brutality by means of the creation of a local "Indian patrol" trained by an Indian police college. As they had in 1973, the OWS reiterated the need for an "investigation into the violent deaths of Indian people in the Kenora area" and compensation for the people devastated by mercury pollution, an act that the OWS called "an outright crime against two communities."[18] "Provincial" issues such as mercury poisoning were joined with demands for Indigenous control of social services around alcoholism and the removal of a particular judge known for his extreme anti-Indigenous prejudices. National issues included dental services on reserves and making reserves economically viable for Indigenous peoples. As the OWS stated, "Indians do not want to be on a reserve of unemployed who are kept available only to do dirty temporary low paying jobs." They also wanted reforms to the justice system that would reflect Anishinaabe worldviews and finally, "speedy and just settlement of land claims."[19]

The occupation quickly gained national attention after AIM activist Harvey Major proclaimed that if police entered the park, or if they were cited for breaching fire regulations, the OWS would go to town and "start blowing things up."[20] While the talk of exploding buildings alarmed citizens, historian Sean Atkins argues that because of that summer's intense forest fires, breaches to fire codes also fuelled animosity against the OWS.[21] One reader of the Kenora Daily Miner and News wrote in, sarcastically recommending that government officials "pay those Indians a good buck for doing a rain dance" to put the forest fires out.[22] Word of weapons in the park immediately overshadowed the concerns outlined by the OWS, and it set the imaginations of newspaper copywriters into overdrive; "Kill or Be Killed," read the Winnipeg Free Press's front page.[23] Federal officials tried to downplay the dispute. Jean Chrétien, the minister of Indian affairs, dismissed it as a "local" event that the federal government did not intend on becoming involved in.[24] Mayor Jim Davidson told the public that this was "nothing more than a sit-in."[25] "Let them have the park," exclaimed Davidson – himself a former member of the Indian-White Committee. "After a week or so they will drift away and there will be no problem."[26] He could not have been more wrong.

The end of the first week saw the beginning of negotiations. As the Ontario government refused to negotiate with a non-elected Aboriginal group, members of Grand Council Treaty #3, including Fred Kelly and the Chief of Grand Council Treaty #3, Peter Kelly, represented the park occupiers, though the ows initially disputed not being at the table. Sitting across the table were Mayor Jim Davidson, Peter Hare from the Federal Department of Indian Affairs, and the provincial representative for Kenora, MPP Leo Bernier.[27] In case these officials were unsure about the ows's determination, Fred Kelly told the group that "the Warriors are prepared to die to protect themselves after bringing out the issues – not to attack the town of Kenora."[28] Town Council remained unconvinced that their weapons were for purely defensive purposes. One councillor stated that the town was "under state of siege"; Mayor Davidson simply did not want a mistake to be made that would be "disastrous for future relations." Moreover, he wanted to prove that Kenora was "not a racist town." In response, a member of the negotiating team offered some historical perspective. Doug Skead and Peter Kelly reminded the group that while negotiating with governments, "Indian people had always had the threat of violence hanging over their heads. Chiefs signed Treaty #3 with government troops standing on alert only five miles away."[29]

The sensational imagery of "Indians with guns" dominated how Canadians were first informed about the park occupation. The *Montreal Gazette*'s initial coverage, for example, was simply a photograph of an unidentified Indigenous man brandishing a rifle with the caption "armed Pow-wow."[30] Members of the ows were almost always pictured holding guns, and often casually. A widely circulated photo depicted two men holding their guns while lying on the hood of a car. These images made the occupation seem like a spur-of-the-moment decision, one without the weight of decades of frustration over inattention to basic human rights behind it. One cartoon depicted the situation as a relic from the past: a Hollywood-style moment when sneaky Indians jumped out of bushes and attacked whites with arrows and tomahawks.[31] Such crude stereotypes were also employed by reporters relating first-hand accounts of their time in the park. Some told stories about the "haunting sounds of tom-toms" and the spookiness of seeing Indians armed with rifles amongst the trees, almost as though they were part of the natural scenery in Kenora.[32] Recalling his night in the park, reporter Derik Hodgson characterized the militants as "thugs," "madmen," and "crazies" who "talked tough" and laughed while pointing guns at people's faces. He described a park inhabited by giggling revolutionaries who spent the night "serenading policemen" with beating drums and talking revolution, employing language they had learned from Algerians and Angolans. Hodgson afforded virtually no space to the occupiers' grievances, not even to their land claim.[33] Mark Anderson and Carmen Robertson also note that in Kenora's newspaper, Indigenous people were regularly described as having a predilection to violence and a lack of self-control, a fact that the occupation, when robbed of any other context, seemed to confirm.[34] If they weren't biologically programmed into these actions, they were simply naïve actors, as one Thunder Bay–based editorial suggested in arguing that the occupation was unnecessary."[35] Their analysis of media coverage during the occupation leads Anderson and Robertson to conclude that the ows's list of demands took "a distant back seat" to sensationalistic images and stereotypical portrayals of Indigenous people.[36]

As had been the case during the aftermath of the 1965 march, commentators worked to distinguish Kenora from the rest of Canada. The only way to truly understand what was happening in this small Alabamalike town was to situate it internationally. One cartoon did this well by depicting a white couple looking at posters for Kenora, Turkey, Cyprus, and Greece, the man asking the travel agent, "Isn't there anywhere the natives are NOT restless?"[37] It was also common to portray the ows as not representative of most Indigenous people in Canada or the Kenora area. The American Indian Movement was the most convenient villain for commentators wanting to blame what would become a six-week occupation on some outside influence. The majority of letters published in local papers expressed anger at the situation.[38] The Kenora *Daily Miner and News* claimed that their survey showed that "as a whole ... members of the Ojibwa people in the Kenora area do not approve of the actions taken by the Warrior Society."[39] And some government-funded Indigenous organizations, as well as eminent figures such as Harold Cardinal, said they supported the purpose but not the tactics of the ows.[40]

AIM's presence at Anicinabe Park is undeniable. The geographical proximity of Northwestern Ontario to Minnesota allowed for easy travel. Moreover, Dennis Banks and the veteran AIM member Harvey Major were significant presences throughout the occupation. AIM's influence may even have been the reason for cheers coming from the park the day Richard Nixon resigned. The loudest show of support in the early stages of the occupation came from AIM when Vernon Bellecourt, then AIM "International Field Director," spoke to an audience of close to one hundred people at the provincial legislature in Toronto. Bellecourt's talk focused on the ows's concerns: unemployment, the need for better social services, mercury poisoning, "white backlash," the land claim, and double standards when it came to experiences with the justice system. These conditions, he concluded, forced Indigenous peoples to take drastic actions such as the occupation.[41]

In blaming outsiders for the tactics used in Anicinabe Park, mainstream media and local commentators were attempting to delegitimize the ows. This fits with what both Ward Churchill and Daniel Francis demonstrate is a long-established narrative of "bad Indians" coming into towns to destroy the harmonious relations between "good Indians" and their white neighbours.[42] During the era of Red Power, the "good/bad" dichotomy travelled with reference to AIM-inspired protests. AIM were the "bad Indians," corrupting otherwise docile Indigenous peoples by promoting the American tactic of armed rebellion rather than the Canadian tactic of peaceful negotiation, a trap that the ows reportedly fell for.[43]

While not as prominent, there were also somewhat positive portrayals of the ows tactics suggesting that they were correcting longstanding historical wrongs. Les Whittington, for example, explained that the ows was "rebelling" against historical injustices and echoing "the posture of their ancestors who fought the white man." The return of militant armed struggle was "nothing less than the renewal of the wars of the last century"[44] (though his references to AIM and Dee Brown's *Bury My Heart at Wounded Knee* might imply that Whittington was picturing the nineteenth-century Indian Wars in the United States rather than what took place in Western Canada in the 1870s and 1880s). A smattering of leftist publications voiced support for the occupation and its political goals. In a multi-article feature that appeared after the occupation, *Canadian Dimension* explained that it grew out of problems "inherited" from nineteenth-century colonial policies. Moreover, the OWS were "good leaders" who "seized the initiative in Kenora, took risks they felt necessary and demonstrated themselves to be skilled tacticians during the negotiations."[45] For one journalist, what was happening in the park was that the OWS were "fed up enough to trade in their copies of Robert's *Rules of Order* for a volume of Frantz Fanon."[46] In other words, they had turned away from using institutions such as the Canadian courts to achieve justice in favour of direct confrontation with the colonial state.

Producing the meaning of the occupation was not limited to media commentators. The OWS also had their own sense of history and were not acting only because of contemporary social and political inequality but were also actively situating themselves within a broader history of colonization. Like other contemporary Red Power activists, they were rewriting Canadian history from the ground up. The OWS acknowledged their intellectual and political debts to AIM as well as to other decolonization struggles, including those in Algeria and Angola. But they were mostly concerned with situating themselves, and the reemergence of the Ojibwa nation, within a longer history of Indigenous resistance in Canada.

The contested ownership of the fourteen-acre park was clear before the conference began. As Cameron explained to Mayor Jim Davidson, the site was chosen specifically because it used to be "reserved for Indian people. Many of our lands have been illegally sold, surrendered or leased for minimal amounts; the Ojibway Warrior Society is now looking into how white people gained control of Anicinabe Park."[47] The emergence of disputed land as a focus of Indigenous protest in the early 1970s is a key reason for describing the occupation of Anicinabe Park as a decolonial intervention in a way that the Indian Rights march in 1965 was not. As Coulthard makes clear, Indigenous anti-colonial theory and practice is "oriented around the question of land."[48] The early 1970s was a period when attaining Aboriginal "title" to land was becoming a possibility. In

1973, a decision the Supreme Court of Canada called the Calder case opened up the possibility that Aboriginal land rights had not been "extinguished through colonial legislation."[49] According to Coulthard, the Calder case forced the state to "recognize Indigenous claims to land where the question of existing title remained open."[50] While the ows did not reference the Calder case directly and the land question at Anicinabe Park was only one of numerous issues the group wanted addressed, Indigenous claims to land they believed had been stolen shaped the imagination of Red Power activists during the early 1970s. The Vancouver-based Native Study Group, for example, argued that, "only national independence and the meeting of land requirements of statehood will end the dependence our people suffer from."[51]

The land question was not influenced only by recent legal developments but also by the ows reading of history. Cameron argued that Indigenous peoples in the region had experienced two phases of European incursion. The first were trappers with the Hudson's Bay Company, voyageurs, and some British immigrants. Indigenous peoples in the area helped settle these visitors and benefitted from the houses and machinery that came with their new neighbours. "Our people were free," Cameron claimed, because Anishinaabe folks were still able to fish, hunt, trap, and generally do their own thing.[52] The second phase, he said, was devastating. It brought "an invasion" beginning in the 1870s. It was during this time of mass migration that the machinery of colonization and dispossession impacted every facet of Indigenous life. Railroads were built, British soldiers put down Louis Riel, Crowfoot, and Chief Redsky, Indian Affairs was established, the RCMP was created, and the Indian Act was written and then enforced by missionaries and the military. In this second phase of colonization they "started taking the land away from people," Cameron observed. Treaties were signed under "force of starvation" and a system of segregating Indigenous people from each other was achieved through the reserve system. Once segregation and restriction of movement was achieved, business took over. We now "have nothing," Cameron argued. There was no economic base for Indigenous communities; "we need something to thrive on – something we can depend on and our kids can grow."[53]

As the main public voice of the ows throughout 1973 and 1974, Cameron was interviewed many times. Throughout these interviews, especially in the twenty-four-page fully transcribed copy with Better Reads, and in the ows literature, it is clear that one of the things that bothered him most was the way that Canadian institutions had separated Indigenous peoples from each other and from the land. It is a theme that he remarks upon many times.

Organizing under the name "Ojibway Warrior Society" also reclaimed the past to imagine a new future. ows literature, along with articles published by the Toronto Warrior Society, suggested that the Warrior Society was a response "to the specific conditions and needs of the people," that sought "justice and the return of the rights of our people." The Toronto Warrior Society created a sense of global anti-colonial consciousness by including a wide variety of international stories in their newspaper, *Native Peoples Struggle*. These included documenting a trip to China by a group of Indigenous men and women, "a message from an Amazon Indian to his North American relatives," and a study comparing the health of Indigenous children in Canada with children in Vietnam. The newspaper also published the stirring "Apolitical Intellectuals," a poem by Guatemalan poet Otto Rene Castillo, "one of the leading poets of Guatemala. In the year 1967, in a show of guerilla strength, he died fighting for his people."[54] In pamphlets and interviews, the ows portrayed itself as a contemporary manifestation of a longer history of anti-colonial struggle. As a result, besides being in solidarity with contemporary global anti-colonial struggles, the "Warriors" who fought in Kenora were the heirs of "Warriors" who "fought the invaders, the British troops, the French troops and the Spanish troops throughout North America."[55] Such a narrative located the Anicinabe Park occupation within a longer history of global anti-colonialism and it explicitly depicts the summer of 1974 as just one moment in a centuries-long local resistance.

For Cameron, the park occupation was also linked in spirit to similar protests by peoples throughout the world. At a Montreal talk, he explained that Anishinaabe people were part of a human revolution that saw Indigenous peoples, Chicanos, and Blacks involved in bringing down "this imperialist monster."[56] He reiterated this point in a conversation with a Winnipeg reporter, telling him that "Indian and non-Indian people everywhere are fighting back. Across Canada, in the United States, in Angola, South America and Africa, people are getting it on."[57]

If the ows spoke of locating the Warrior Society within a broader anti-colonial framework, the resurgence of the Warrior Society was also profoundly local. "It began by itself; a lot of women and a lot of men started expressing: 'Where else can we go?' It serves the people, it puts the aims and aspirations of our people together, especially the feeling of being Indian people. It started from this."[58] As the conference press release emphasized, it embodied a resurgence of Anishinaabe traditions – specifically Midewiwin – in the long history of anti-colonial struggle. The federal government had prohibited the practice for much of the twentieth century until the reform of the Indian Act. Some see Midewiwin as the institutional setting for the teaching of an Anishinaabe worldview; Cameron said it reflected "a full and material understanding of the ways of the Anicinabe people."[59] A ceremony in which healing, drumming, and knowledge of the natural world occupied central roles, Midewiwin's central concept is that not only are human beings, animals, and plants alive, "but so were *some* natural and created objects such as specific stones, locations, dolls, etc. All such beings or creatures, not just humans, were considered to have what in English is termed a soul, and thus to be alive, and have power."[60]

According to Michael Angel, in the eighteenth and nineteenth centuries, Ojibway communities used Midewiwin as a way to slow down the impact of Christian missionaries across central Canada.[61] Some choose to incorporate aspects of Christianity into the practice, while others used it to protect themselves from the new religion. In 1974, with the conference and subsequent park occupation, Midewiwin once again became part of opposition to colonialism. "The Indian movement, spiritually and in every way is part of human revolution," said Cameron. Midewiwin was "not something you pray for, you just do it. It's a search for justice; and practice, not talk about God, is the key."[62] It meant "going through the deep ceremonies, learning about your families and the traditions or history, for the purpose of going forward – not going backward but forward."[63]

At the same time as the ows was trying to revive a traditional worldview, they also cultivated an identity which connected their ideas of radical social change to their willingness to confront structures of colonial power. When asked about the decision to arm themselves, Cameron said it was because other avenues of change, such as pursuing civil rights through the courts, had not worked for "us" like it had not worked for Black people in the United States. Nor would it work, he said, to bring white men to justice for sexually assaulting Indigenous women or to address mercury poisoning at Grassy Narrows and Whitedog. Again he drew on history to contextualize the group's actions, saying that the ows was "standing on the same ground as the leaders of the past," like Riel.[64] Daniel Francis writes that when he closed his eyes to think about the park occupation "the first image that occurred" to him was "a photograph of a young Ojibway man ... sitting on the hood of a car cradling a rifle."[65] The rhetoric of revolutionary violence and its corresponding imagery, brought to life in Canada in moments such as Anicinabe Park, generally "catered to the press's stereotypical image of the Plains Indian Warrior."[66] But it was not an image that these groups necessarily repudiated. As Cameron explained in an interview "the Anicinabe people ... right from the word go, they've been fighting with the gun."[67]

Nor was the choice to adopt the threat of armed revolt unique to the American Indian Movement or the Ojibway Warrior Society. This was a moment when, as Robert J.C. Young explains, "guerilla warfare embodied a seductive and powerful image of a successful mode of political struggle, waged against heroic odds by subaltern peoples of the Third World against the forces of imperialism."[68] Most obvious is that weapons (or even rumours of weapons) helped enhance the dramatic effects of political action.[69] Moreover, as Vijay Prashad argues, these actions made the "identity of the Third World comprehensible and visible."[70]

In Canada during the "Global Sixties," the best known moment of leftist political violence was the Front de libération du Québec. Throughout the 1960s, the FLQ committed numerous acts of violence, including bombings, as it advocated the need for a radical transformation of Quebec society.[71] As Sean Mills recalls, their tactics escalated in 1970 when they kidnapped British diplomat James Richard Cross, an act that set into motion a series of events that came to be known as the "October Crisis." The FLQ's demands were read over Montreal airwaves in a manifesto denouncing capitalism and colonialism. At the same time, Mills notes, this wide-ranging statement was couched in a heavily masculine language addressing itself directly to male workers" which amongst other things "also denounced Pierre Trudeau for alleged homosexuality."[72]

The relationship between anti-colonial politics, revolutionary violence, and masculinity in this era is complicated. Kristin Ross argues that Fanon's analysis "of the colonial situation depends heavily on a Freudian model of castration whereby the (male) castrated colonized subject attains full manhood or 'wholeness' through revolutionary solidarity and the violent overcoming and expulsion of the colonizer."[73] Men picked up guns not only to change material circumstances but "also to create an embodied sense of empowerment."[74] The recovery of a manhood taken away by the colonial state was a recurring theme amongst the most vocal members of AIM and the OWS. At the Wounded Knee trials in 1974, Russell Means told jurors that there were only five ways for Indigenous men to express manhood. These were to be an athlete, or a soldier, to get drunk and beat women, to become a white, or to be an activist. Means choose the final option. AIM, Means explained, provided Indian men a rebirth through radical politics.[75] Similar themes emerged in the narrative surrounding the Anicinabe Park occupation. Cameron often called OWS a "human movement," where "Indian people" could put "their dreams, their hopes, [and] their frustrations together."[76] But he also suggested that by picking up guns, men were reclaiming their identity as protectors of women and children. "When we went into the park to liberate our land we took guns not to attack the community but to protect our women and children from outside belligerence."[77] Lyle Ironstand recalled that he was motivated to pick up a gun and participate in the occupation after his wife challenged him to be like the men who took over Wounded Knee.[78]

This masculinist discourse and self-fashioning bumped up against the image of Indigenous women being as willing to pick up guns as their male counterparts. This seemed deeply concerning to the press; in the early days of the occupation, reports circulated that the OWS had a training school for young women on how to use high-powered weapons. Moreover, when the OWS agreed to end the standoff, the weapons were handed over in a ceremony conducted by its female members. These were images that became especially popular in leftist publications, like that of the female North Vietnamese fighter. Yet scholars and activists argue that

these images of revolutionary egalitarianism were often betrayed by nor-
mative gender roles within the movement. Norma Stoltz Chinchilla says
that women in Central American liberation movements, who were often
celebrated for being militants, still found it difficult to convince male activists to do any form of child-care.[79] Lee Maracle recalls that patriarchal
expectations were "inherent in the character of the American Indian
Movement."[80] "Culturally, the worst most dominant white male traits
were emphasized. Machismo and the boss mentality were the basis for
choosing leaders."[81] While militant women made good press, inside the
movements cooking and cleaning were still women's duties.[82] During the
Native People's Caravan in September 1974, Vern Harper was candid
about this division of labour. "Some of the younger brothers didn't want
to do kitchen detail, and they tried to use tradition – so called tradition
– to get out of it. When they were asked to pick up the mop they would
say 'oh no, warriors don't do that.'"[83] A female board member of the Indian Friendship Centre experienced this first-hand while attending an
AIM-led meeting in Sault Ste Marie in the spring of 1973. She noted that
"this almighty guy" just threw questions at her. "I've been dominated
by someone else for too long," she told a group of other women in
Kenora.[84] Still, despite this experience, she told her group that if AIM
came to Kenora she would still attend their meetings, to keep informed.[85]
Yet as Devon Abbott Mihesuah explains, in AIM, "not all of the women
expressed sentiments that their roles were less important than the men's.
They justified their 'invisible' work by stating that men and women have
specific tasks to perform and all duties are essential to tribal survival."[86]

In thinking about the multiple meanings of violence which circulated
during the occupation, another which stands out is Cameron's. In his
most wide-ranging and complete interview, it is clear that the park occupation, and the takeover of the Indian Affairs building in 1973, were
not only inspired by an analysis of the colonial system but even more by
a sense of loss and desperation amongst those he grew up with. When
asked why Indigenous people lived with high rates of suicide, mental ill-
ness, and alcoholism, Cameron was emphatic:

> Well, a lot of violence is a result of the oppression from the Depart-
> ment of Indian Affairs, methods of division and control over Indian

people. And the businessmen's co-operation with the town police and the federal police is deep down really isolating Indian people. And what I mean by businessmen is the people who plan the business and really profit from the economy of the area. All these things – with education system, the churches – are pushing our people. You know, everybody knows, that people have to be free to express human freedom. They have to laugh, they have to yell and they have to be free to move around. But when you push people into a group like that a lot of that expression turns inside. It's what you call internal aggression … And as a result of that Indians live a dangerous style of life. They fight each other, they drink a lot. And the tendency of suicide is higher.

This is the crime, the injustice that is being committed by the government and by the businesses around the country. They are taking one segment of society and pushing it violently inwards. Now we have to live that style of life which is detrimental to human beings. So we, the Ojibway Warrior Society, believe the only way is to bring that internal aggression outwards. It must go out, we must break out through the same way we got in. We got in by violence, we must go out by confrontation.

As a result of the force of that whole oppression pushing that expression inwards on the Indian people. As a direct result of that they drown, die of fire – little kids and whole families die of fire, and they freeze, or sometimes they shoot each other – or *we* shoot each other, I should say. And when you have nothing on a reserve the houses they live in are being given by Indian Affairs as a token. These houses are death traps, they burn people.

Sometimes they go home along the railroad tracks because they have no car and no money to buy a train ticket. They're drunk and they've got to walk a long way along the railroad tracks. Sometimes they freeze and sometimes they get run over by a train.

We are fighting for the brothers and sisters we have lost, for land we have lost.[87]

By the end of the second week of the occupation, negotiations appeared to have led to a tentative deal according to Kenora's mayor, Jim

Davidson.[88] Such reports, however, were premature.[89] The ows were also growing frustrated that the state would not recognize them as a legitimate negotiating party and that they had to be represented by a group from Grand Council Treaty #3. When they were eventually allowed to represent themselves during negotiations, they believed that their main concerns were being bypassed or not taking seriously. This frustration resulted, in part, because the Department of Indian Affairs sent a representative who had little power to make decisions for the federal government.[90] "We came honestly to talk," Cameron exclaimed, "but we have to return to the park and tell our people there is no hope in these talks."[91] Officials from Treaty #3 denied that the ows had lost the support of Indigenous people in the Kenora area and issued a press release stating that they "wish to reiterate their solidarity with the desire for immediate changes as expressed by the Ojibway Warrior Society now occupying Anicinabe Park. The fact that some Indian people are turning away from peaceful approaches to change is a direct result of years of exploitation and per-secution of Indian people by those with power."[92] Internal disagreements clearly existed between the ows and the representatives from Treaty #3, but the message to the public remained clear: the "divide and conquer" tactics of colonialism were not going to work this time.[93]

With the ows representing themselves, the talks focused primarily on land title and getting the ows to relinquish their weapons. Since their brief takeover of the Indian Affairs building in 1973, the ows had learned that you do not leave the bargaining table until you gain concessions. "We'll live here," Cameron declared. "We may even get married here."[94] The ows presented a complex analysis of economic and social power. Even though the threat of white vigilante action was constant, the ows emphasized that white residents of Kenora were not the focus of their occupation. In fact, for Cameron, what Indigenous peoples and white residents in Kenora had in common was the fact that they were on the periphery of economic power in Canada. "[A]ll their economy is con-trolled from the outside," Cameron explained: "they are controlled either from Toronto or the United States."[95] Yet his recognition of this shared powerlessness was not meant to let white residents off the hook for what was happening to Indigenous communities. When asked to explain what effect the ows wanted to have on the white community, Cameron said that he wanted them to realize that all the stories they'd heard about Indians, whether in school or from local "businessmen," were wrong. He wanted the ows to provide a different perspective. "I think that they have to start looking at things from our side or forever be our enemies ... We've given the white community of Kenora a choice on where they want to stand."[96]

Early into the occupation, police arrested several white men who approached the park with loaded weapons.[97] Individual expressions of hostility became more organized as the occupation went into a third week with no agreement in sight. A group of white citizens began to advocate a more aggressive strategy to end the stand-off and bring "law and order" back to Kenora.[98] One "concerned citizen" rhetorically asked, "[i]n this country, in this province, in this town, is there no one with authority who has guts enough to say, 'The Law is the Law, it will be upheld?'"[99] The first meeting of the Committee of Concerned Citizens (not to be confused with the Concerned Citizens Committee which organized around violent deaths in 1973), organized by alderman (and future mayor) Bill Tomashowski reportedly drew seven hundred residents and resulted in the formation of a twelve-person committee.[100] Particularly vocal was Eleanor Jacobson, a nurse who worked in Whitedog (Wabaseemoong) and would publish a post-occupation diatribe called *Bended Elbow*. She questioned the will of the town to enforce law and order and claimed "there is no racism in Kenora."[101] At the same time that the group denied it advocated violence, one of its strategies for ending the occupation was reportedly to storm the park to "evict" the ows.[102] During the occupation's second week, Cameron reported that shots had been fired in the direction of the park from the outside. He thought it was either white vigilantes or uniformed officers.

The rise of white vigilantism during Indigenous protests in the 1970s was not unique to Kenora. In response to the Menominee Warriors Society's takeover of a building in Wisconsin and the belief that government officials were unwilling to end the standoff, local residents became the "Concerned Citizens of Shawano."[103] Libby Tronnes notes that as the Menominee occupation continued, "the rumors of a large 'citizen army' preparing" to move in "grew more frequent."[104] In Kenora, a person concerned that outsiders would perceive the Committee of Concerned Citizens as a white vigilante group told reporters that "[t]hey don't want to act like a bunch of red necks or the Ku Klux Klan, *but it will be necessary* (emphasis mine) if something doesn't happen soon."[105] Indeed, this was the ows's perception too. A reporter for the *Toronto Star* commented that during one interview, Cameron was continually doodling the letters C.C.C., which "he then changed to K.K.K. (Kenora Klux Klan)."[106]

Amid rumours that police were anxious to end the occupation, and in the face of growing militancy from white townspeople, negotiations took on a more desperate tone. The citizens' meeting spurred action from the town, as officials began to block vehicles from bringing food and other supplies sent by several Winnipeg organizations into the park.[107] Then, on 13 August, the Town of Kenora cut the park's electricity and also revoked a temporary amnesty and arrested four ows activists on charges of "conspiracy" and "unlawful assembly" as they exited the park.[108] At the same time, anxiety over a potential showdown also produced expressions of support from various groups like the Revolutionary Marxist Group, which published letters expressing their support of the Ojibway Warrior Society. To be in solidarity with "those who are struggling," explained the RMG, meant "material aid" as well as verbal support.[109] One particularly respected activist also lent her moral support. At a talk in Winnipeg, Angela Davis expressed solidarity with the park occupiers and told the audience that "by standing up for native rights and combating racism, you're helping yourselves."[110] The Canadian Friends Service Committee, who had organized an ad hoc group "of concern for Ojibway Indians," sent volunteers to act as a buffer between police and rogue citizens and those in the park. They set up tents on a strip of land that the ows gave them, then proceeded to try to "reach the less-sympathetic white population, including the self-styled vigilantes." [111]

Attempts at having human rights committees and government arbitrators oversee the talks could not break the impasse so an unlikely arbitrator returned to Kenora. After much consternation from elected officials, all sides agreed to let Dennis Banks take on the role of mediator.[112] He arrived on 16 August, and three days later the ows agreed to lay down their weapons as an act of "good faith" – not as an act of surrender, as Cameron made clear. "The Ojibwa Warrior Society has spoken," Cameron announced, "we will now see if the government listened."[113] Ten days later, on 29 August 1974, the ows, in conjunction with Dennis Banks and representatives from Grand Council Treaty #3, agreed to a tentative deal with the town, the provincial government, and the federal government, with further promises to study and implement several of the ows recommendations. Grand Council Treaty #3 would file a land claim on behalf of the ows for Anicinabe Park, which, in the meantime, would remain a free camping and recreation space for all visitors. Town council noted that if the land claim had not been settled by 1 May 1975, "the matter of charges for use of Park facilities will be reviewed."[114] As well it was agreed that, for the most part, the park occupiers would be granted amnesty, the conspiracy charges against the four ows members would be dropped, and the charges of unlawful assembly not tried until the land claim concerning Anicinabe Park was resolved.[115]

The threat of punishment for unlawful assembly hung over the heads of a couple of dozen ows activists for nearly two years. In late April 1976, with Treaty #3's request for the return of Anicinabe Park tied up in the federal land claims commission, the charges were dropped.[116] As with the land question, numerous other key issues were left unaddressed, most notably the mercury poisoning which was then (as still now) devastating people living at Wabaseemoong (Whitedog) and Asubpeeschoseewagong (Grassy Narrows) despite now decades-long activism by people in those communities – including some, like Tom Keesick, who were part of the ows. As journalist Heather Robertson said in a *Maclean's* article published months after the occupation, the ows understood "the truth about Indians' situation; they suffer not from neglect but from persecution."[117] As with the Indian Rights march nine years early, and the gestures towards other racially oppressed people, the six-week occupation of Anicinabe Park was fundamentally altering the terms by which Canadian history was to be understood. Indigenous protesters had centered the discussion of colonization so that going forward it could not be ignored. As September 1974 arrived, two new tactics emerged: one a group made up of politicized Indigenous peoples and allies who would travel across Canada to raise public awareness of these issues, and the other an attempt to form a multi-racial coalition of Indigenous, white, and Black activists.

CHAPTER 6

The Native People's Caravan

Surveillance, Agents Provocateurs, *and Multi-racial Coalitions*

The RCMP had the guns, clubs and the tear gas. We had a drum and a sheet
of paper with our demands.

Louis Cameron, November 1974[1]

After the Anicinabe Park occupation ended, Louis Cameron joined the
Native People's Caravan to help gather Indigenous activists from across
Canada to arrive in Ottawa for the opening of Parliament at the end
of September 1974. One of their goals was to demonstrate solidarity
amongst Red Power groups, including the Cache Creek Warriors, which
had endured an armed standoff with the RCMP at a highway near their
community in British Columbia at the same time as the Anicinabe Park
occupation. The Cache Creek Warriors distributed leaflets to motorists
informing them about poor housing on reserves and their rights to
the land under the highway.[2] The blockade only ended after the RCMP
promised to relay their concerns to the BC government.[3] The caravan to
Ottawa also included the Calgary Urban Treaty Alliance. The Calgary
group had already occupied an Indian Affairs office demanding better
social services and had campaigned for more realistic representations of
Indigenous peoples beyond the "cowboys and Indians" stereotype seen
at the Calgary Stampede.[4] As one participant from the Canadian Association in Support of Native Peoples (CASNP) noted, "We were told that
while more 'militant' Natives People were the instigators of the Caravan,
other elements are giving it total support."[5] It ultimately included members from other AIM inspired groups, those from Warrior Societies, peo-

ple from CASNP, Quakers, and, most controversially, the Communist Party of Canada (Marxist-Leninist) (CPC-ML).[6]

Vern Harper, a Cree activist from Toronto who was a member of the Toronto Warrior Society and ran in the federal election as a CPC-ML candidate in the Rosedale neighbourhood of Toronto, participated in the caravan. In his memoirs, Harper writes that the caravan brought together many different political interests, including "native spiritualism," "red nationalism," socialism, Maoism, and national liberation. Harper's desire for a Marxist-oriented movement came from what he said such ideologies "had done for other oppressed nations of the Third World."[7] Yet others in the caravan saw Marxism, even in its Third World iterations, as a Eurocentric ideology that drew energy away from a movement to revive Indigenous knowledges in North America.[8]

The Native People's Caravan is an example of the difficulties Indigenous activists encountered in creating a unified Red Power movement in 1970s Canada. Some of this difficulty was due to ideological differences or differing purposes, as well as tension between Indigenous activists and non-Indigenous leftist groups. Yet this was also generally a tense time for Indigenous activists, militant or not, for other reasons. Threats of violence from non-Indigenous peoples were clearly on the minds of caravanners as they requested RCMP protection at various times in advance of their arrival in a town or city.[9] I pay attention to those tensions in this chapter by describing one of the controversies, the role of Maoists, that followed the caravan on its journey from Vancouver to Ottawa. I also suggest that state security was actively trying to disrupt both Indigenous solidarity and the attempt to generate support from non-Indigenous activists. In 1974, the RCMP described Red Power as the greatest threat to Canadian national security.[10] As such, state security worked to actively manufacture dissent and tension within the movement. Here it is important to discuss the significance of Douglas Durham, an FBI informant and *agent provocateur* within the American Indian Movement. His role in spying on Red Power movements in Canada has been overlooked. The same can be said for Warren Hart, an important figure in the history of transnational surveillance in Canada. Hart first grew to fame as an FBI informant who infiltrated the Baltimore chapter of the Black Panther Party before coming to Canada and being used by the RCMP to spy on

Black Power movements. The evidence discussed in this chapter suggests that the state was increasingly concerned about the potential of non-Indigenous activists becoming allies of Red Power movements and Indigenous activists forming multi-racial coalitions, especially with Black activists. State security used surveillance and *agents provocateurs* as ways to disrupt such efforts.

The Native People's Caravan left Vancouver on 15 September 1974 after a rally attended by several hundred supporters. It made stops in communities across Western Canada on its way to Ottawa. In Calgary, at the Native Friendship Centre, Ken Basil from the Cache Creek Warriors told reporters that while his group and the ows "did not represent all the Indian people of Canada," they were "grassroots people" who were dealing with "real issues."[11] In Edmonton, the Alberta Committee of Native Rights for Native Women reportedly expressed their support, sharing with the caravaners their own struggles to regain status lost through the Indian Act.[12] From its earliest days, the presence of people believed to be communists shaped the narrative of the Native People's Caravan. The CPC-ML helped organize and fund the caravan, and their presence proved controversial. At the caravan's stop in Winnipeg, word came that members of the American Indian Movement, for example, were threatening to withdraw support from the caravan when it reached Kenora because they said that the CPC-ML had taken over and were driving the agenda.[13] Members of CASNP in the caravan noted that whenever a new person joined them, they were listed as either "caravanists" or "Leninists."[14]

The topic of violence, and specifically Louis Cameron's role within the group, received significant media attention as the caravan of activists drew closer to Ottawa. John Price writes that in the media, "[r]umours circulated ... that some young Warriors were prepared to die for their cause and planned to storm into Parliament as human bombs with explosives strapped to their bodies."[15] Anicinabe Park had turned the young man from the Whitedog First Nation (Wabaseemoong) into a celebrity amongst Canadian leftists and one of the most recognized spokespersons for Red Power in Canada. During the park occupation, Cameron provided nuanced analyses of social, cultural, and political contexts in the Kenora area and how they connected to broader colonial histories. Yet, whether it was mainstream media's desire for more sensational rhetoric

or a change in Cameron's own outlook, his public appearances during
the caravan's trip increasingly emphasized the potential for violent confrontation with the Canadian government. The same day as Hamilton's
district labour council and union endorsed the caravan, reporters quoted
Cameron saying that when he arrived in Ottawa, he wanted to blow up
parliament.[16] Vern Harper points out that mainstream media attention
focused primarily on the potential for violence rather than the caravan's
political purpose.[17] Internal memos from CASNP suggested that media
focus on Cameron was unfair because when he spoke, he was only doing
so with permission from the caravan's other leaders.[18] Cameron also denied making such inflammatory statements, reiterating that the press
was trying to discourage Indigenous youth from coming together to join
in struggle.[19]

The caravan with approximately one-hundred fifty participants arrived in Ottawa at the end of the month in time for the opening session
of Parliament. George Manuel, then the president of the National Indian
Brotherhood, said that the caravan chose Ottawa as their destination because "peoples of the Third World" would recognize the capital's importance as a symbol of colonization.[20] While the RCMP band serenaded
Chief Justice Bora Laskin with "God Save the Queen" to mark the occa-
sion, the caravaners and their allies countered with drumming and the
AIM anthem.[21] They also arrived with demands outlined in a ten-point
manifesto. It demanded increased accountability from Indian Affairs,
that funds budgeted for Indian Affairs go directly to Indigenous communities, recognition of treaty rights for both status *and* non-status Indians, and better funding for Indigenous-controlled education. It also
demanded better health care provision, shaming the government by saying that if so-called "underdeveloped" countries such as Cuba and China
kept their citizens healthy, an industrialized First World country like
Canada should be able do the same for *all* of its people.

The wide-ranging ten-point manifesto, however, was almost entirely
overshadowed by events referred to in the press as the "The Riot on Parliament Hill." Cameron and Harper offer slightly different accounts of
what happened that afternoon. Cameron says that despite the large police
presence in front of them, protestors pushed through barricades to find
an "open area" to continue singing and drumming before being crushed.

It was the "national guard," as he called the police force armed with bay-
onet-adorned rifles, who made the first move on the protestors, not the
other way around as the press reported. Asked why the police would provoke such a confrontation, Cameron said that they were retaliating "on
the native people for their armed insurrection at Anicinabe Park."[22]

Harper's account differs slightly from Cameron's. He suggests that
moving past the barricades was deliberate provocation, and thus a be-
trayal of the caravan's vow that there "would be no violence."[23] During
the confrontation with police, Harper's sixteen-year-old child was in-
jured. Still, Harper believes that the police came prepared to intimidate
Indigenous peoples across Canada. "I feel the riot squad was used on us
to accomplish a number of things," Harper writes. "One was to show Native people across the country that if they supported us or got involved
in the Native liberation movement, this is what they would get."[24]

Non-Indigenous Canadian leftists were also convinced that whether
or not they provoked the confrontation, the state ultimately benefitted
from it, because Canadian television sets broadcasted images that portrayed Red Power in Canada as a violent threat to national security.[25] In
The Young Worker, for example, writers blamed the government's "total
unwillingness to even meet with the leaders of the caravan" for the confrontation. The police actions, they suggest, were "just one more episode
in the continuing 400 year old campaign to keep the Native peoples from
regaining their rights and from establishing control over their own future."[26] In fact, this was the first time that the RCMP had used a riot squad
against protestors on Parliament Hill.[27]

Just as the RCMP's role in the clash drew criticism, so did the alleged
role of the CPC-ML. By the mid 1970s, there was a growing presence
of Maoist organizations in the United States and Canada, including
the CPC-ML, Canada's largest group.[28] Maoism as a political theory had
gained popularity amongst North American militants, especially with
certain Black Power factions in the United States and activists organizing
under the banner of Quebec liberation. Sean Mills writes that in Montreal, Maoist groups "flourished, often attracting hundreds of members,
publishing weekly newspapers, and playing an influential if controversial
role in union and community organizing."[29] As we saw in chapter three,
Maoism also appealed to Red Power activists, especially those on the

West Coast like Lee Maracle, Clem Chartier, and Ray Bobb, who visited China in 1975. For Chartier, the trip was an opportunity to "learn from China" and "express solidarity and friendship to the Chinese people."[30] The Native People's Friendship Delegation wanted to connect Indigenous peoples in Canada to other people who defined their experience with the West through the lens of colonization and imperialism. The delegation also wanted to connect with those who had liberated themselves through a Third World socialist revolution.[31]

The presence of Maoists and their Marxist-Leninist ideas within the caravan was controversial because some feared they were becoming the dominant voices of Indigenous organizing. Other leftists, such as those who wrote for the Trotskyist paper *The Young Worker,* argued that Maoists acted as though they were the leaders of the Parliament Hill protests. Some Trotskyists believed that the CPC-ML had turned Indigenous activists off communist theory altogether. Furthermore, *The Young Worker* blamed the CPC-ML for allowing the state to portray Red Power not as a mass movement of Indigenous peoples but as a group directed by a small number of non-Indigenous activists.[32] Other caravaners writing in *Canadian Dimension* and the Vancouver-based Trotskyist paper *Western Voice* were also critical of the CPC-ML role in the caravan. Dave Ticoll and Stan Persky suggested that Maoist involvement had dominated the caravan from beginning to end. But they also reminded readers that not all the Maoists were white; some were members of Vancouver's South Asian community who "itself is increasingly victim to racist attacks."[33] They credited the CPC-ML for providing the caravan financial and logistical assistance while also acknowledging that their involvement was a major source of conflict amongst Indigenous activists. Indigenous publications were also critical of the Maoist role in the Parliament Hill confrontation. *Indian Record,* for example, reprinted a *Toronto Sun* article criticizing the role of non-Indigenous Maoists, while *The Native Voice* followed suit with an *Edmonton Sun* article claiming that AIM would withdraw all support if "leftists continued to get involved."[34] *Native Voice* also claimed their sources told them that AIM split from the caravan in Kenora because it had "been infiltrated and is now directed by radical leftists." The same source blamed Maoists for "the complete disintegration of what was ... a Canadian Indian Movement."[35] Moreover, as John

Price argues, their presence contributed to the ability of Indian Affairs to deflect "blame from both the police and Indians by emphasizing that White Communist agitators were involved in the demonstrations."[36]

In the aftermath of the protest on Parliament Hill, a small group of caravaners took over a vacant mill on Victoria Island in Ottawa, calling it "the Native People's Embassy." *Akwesasne Notes* remarked that the embassy "reflected in miniature the entirety of the three centuries of how Europeans have related to native peoples."[37] The group published its own newsletter in which it established that they, like other Red Power activists, were part of long history of Indigenous leaders, "Riel, Dumont, Big Bear and Poundmaker" who were attacked by the RCMP when they choose to "struggle against the federal government's policies of violating our land and hereditary rights."[38] Early enthusiasm for the embassy dissipated as conditions deteriorated and conflicts in the group re-emerged. Another source of tension was the constant surveillance by the RCMP. One CASNP memo simply said: "This telex is bugged as are our phones." In an attempt to boost morale, AIM sent Douglas Durham to the embassy. Durham had only been part of AIM for a year, but he had already become the group's director of security and Dennis Banks's confidant. In Ottawa, he gave press conferences and talked with those who were still occupying the "embassy." He "fit in well," said Harper.

But the person AIM sent to boost morale, Banks's closest ally, was an FBI informant and *agent provocateur* who was gathering intelligence on Indigenous activists. Durham first became known to AIM when activist Ron Petite introduced him to Banks after Wounded Knee in 1973.[39] With help from the FBI, Durham had entered Pine Ridge during Wounded Knee as a photographer with press credentials for *Pax Today* – a leftist newspaper located in Des Moines, Iowa. Durham made an immediate impression on the group, telling everyone that he was a former police officer. This made some AIM members uncomfortable, though Petite supposedly convinced Banks that AIM could benefit from Durham's skills as a photographer and pilot. Former AIM activist Aaron Two Elk remembers that Banks thought Durham's alleged law enforcement experience could give AIM "special insight about the way the police worked."[40] When Dennis Banks fled the United States for the Northwest Territories,

Durham accompanied him. He quickly gained trust within AIM and was soon Banks's full-time bodyguard. Yet AIM activists such as Vern Belle-court and Anna Mae Aquash were both sure that Durham was an FBI agent, but Banks did not believe them.[41] By the time Durham was exposed as an FBI operative in 1975, Banks and Russell Means had given him control AIM's finances and security arrangements.[42]

Durham's biography is the stuff of Hollywood thrillers: he said that he had received CIA training at a secret camp in Guatemala and was part of the US Bay of Pigs invasion in 1961. Separating fact from fiction is difficult, however, because, as journalist Steve Hendricks writes, "[t]he CIA will say nothing of Durham's claims and is shielded by law from having to."[43] Durham would turn accusations about his true identity back upon those who suspected him, a technique called "badjacketing." Informants use this technique in order to deflect suspicion onto others, not only to protect their identities but also to create mistrust and division within an organization. Durham used this strategy to turn AIM against Anna Mae Aquash, which ultimately led to her murder. It was also rumoured that he played a role in the deaths of two other Indigenous activists: Harvey Major in 1974 and Juanita Eagle Deer in 1975. Durham is also thought to have been involved in the extradition of Leonard Peltier in 1976. When "Durham's undercover status was exposed," writes Sandra Baringer, "reactions among AIM leadership ranged from shock to denial and redirection of suspicion against each other. He had penetrated to the heart of the troops and when the dust had settled, some of the things that remained visible were the bodies of dead women."[44]

Durham's brief period in Canada is an example of how informants were used to disrupt movements by Indigenous people and people of colour in 1970s North America.[45] When Durham's true identity was revealed, Vern Harper claimed that he had not shared any information with Durham that he had not also shared with others, but he still thought that his conversations had given the FBI and RCMP "a lot of information."[46] Louis Cameron thought that Durham was not around only to collect information but also acted as an *agent provocateur*, attempting to get Indigenous activists to ramp up violent confrontations with the state. Cameron told a reporter that during the park occupation, Durham "tried to get our people to make explosives and bombs ... to break up into small terrorist groups like the FLQ." Cameron also revealed that Harvey Major, a Des Moines, Iowa–based AIM activist who was in Kenora during the park occupation, didn't trust Durham. "He told me to be careful," Cameron remembered, "and to watch him." The OWS evidently agreed, unanimously voting against Durham's suggestion to break into small terrorist cells.[47]

Durham came to Kenora at least two times during in the summer of 1974. Once was in late June as part of the Ojibway Nation conference before the occupation; the next time was in August, when Banks was mediating an agreement between the OWS, the police, and various levels of government. According to crown attorney Ted Burton, he and Durham grew close during those summer months. "I had many phone conversations with Durham in succeeding months," wrote Burton. "He continued to give me good advice on how to wind down the volatile situation in Kenora." Durham also put Burton in contact with the governor of Wisconsin, who Burton claims was trying to find "a reasonable way to deal with the seizure by local Indians of a monastery in Grisham" Wisconsin that summer.[48] Here Burton is referring to the Menominee Warriors Society takeover of a building on disputed land. As in Kenora, Durham participated in those negotiations as an AIM representative.[49]

Burton says that he was so close to Durham during the park occupation that he later helped facilitate Durham's participation in the caravan. If this is true, it was done behind the back of Warren Allmand, Canada's solicitor general in 1974. While the RCMP had given Durham clearance numerous times to act as an FBI agent in Canada, Allmand told journalist Barbara Frum that he had nothing to do with Durham's participation in the Native People's Caravan. And upon questioning by Perrin Beatty, a Progressive Conservative MP, Allmand reiterated that the RCMP had not sanctioned Durham's participation.[50]

One of the most thorough accounts of Durham's time in Canada comes from Durham himself. As an FBI agent who had infiltrated one of the United States' most high-profile activist organizations in the "Global Sixties," he was asked to testify at the Eastland Committee on Revolutionary Activities of the American Indian Movement. Durham's testimony fell back upon a common trope employed by state security in Canada and the US, situating Indigenous protest not on its own terms but instead as part of a worldwide communist conspiracy. In turn, Durham portrayed himself as a defender of freedom.[51] Citing Kenora specifically, he reiterated Burton's claim that he was the mediator between the police and the Ojibway Warrior Society. But more importantly, he was there to observe the "communists" who he claims were not only present at the park but were also the main inspiration for the caravan.[52]

When asked about the park occupation, Durham again emphasized the role of the CPC-ML in helping to finance it. Moreover, he claimed that he and Banks had tricked the police, town officials, the government, and the public into believing that the OWS and AIM had destroyed their weapons as part of the mid-August agreement:

Mr. Durham: The agreement was reached that the arms would be turned over to responsible government authorities and that a negotiation period would come for the transfer of title. Actually, in Dennis Banks' own handwriting, he handed me that note saying that the arms will be hidden and kept inside the park. They were buried, along with the Molotov cocktails. Approximately four old, rusty rifles and shotguns, were turned over in front of the press, and I received the honor of destroying approximately three or four of the at least 30 Molotov cocktails that had been assembled in the park.

Two days previously the press had pictured Indians assembling a large number of Molotov cocktails, and yet were willing to accept the fact that there were only three of them when I destroyed them for the press. The weapons, rusty and inoperable, were placed in a blanket and surrendered ceremoniously, while the others were buried in the park. Negotiations began, until the press left; then the principals in the occupation decided to depart for western Canada, began building a caravan to travel to Ottawa, the seat of the capital of Canada, to demonstrate violently. They did in fact do that, and in a press release to the Toronto Globe and Mail, Reporter Rudy Platiel portrayed the caravan as being Communist inspired, I will submit that article to the subcommittee.

Mr. Durham: Also, again, during this occupation. George Roberts
of Los Angeles became involved and sent a telegram to the Canadian government, threatening a precipitation of an international
incident of unknown proportions if the Government of Canada
attempted to dispossess the Indians of Kenora land.[53]

It is difficult to believe that Durham's testimony was entirely truthful.
He was a performer, a chameleon who could change his narrative when
it suited his needs. He also clearly understood his audience, knowing
that his portrayal of Red Power movements as communist-driven con-
spiracies would justify his being hired to speak to them. This was clear
when the John Birch Society organized a tour about AIM with him as a
speaker. As Berringer notes, Durham needed an income and, to achieve
it, his narrative about AIM underwent revision.[54] Although Durham
had originally stated sympathy for the cause if not the tactics of AIM, by
the time of the Birch tour he was portraying AIM as a new front in the
war against communism. Yet AIM was keen to disrupt this sort of narrative, showing up to confront Durham and to challenge his depiction
of their movement.[55]

Like the FBI, the RCMP's extensive surveillance of Indigenous activists
was also influenced by imagined links to communism, resulting in Indigenous activism as another kind of "red scare." As David Austin shows
in his work on RCMP surveillance of Black Power activism in Canada,
accusations of "communism" had become a way to imply, without saying
explicitly, that the people in question were not able to organize themselves and that their grievances were being manipulated by outside
forces.[56] In the early 1970s, "communism" crossed paths with a second
elusive category: "terrorism." Reg Whitaker suggests that concerns about
communism and terrorism dominated RCMP surveillance at the time.
They believed the first movement was directed from Moscow and Beijing
while the second was controlled from "indigenous non-Communist
bases" such as Palestine and Northern Ireland.[57] The "terrorist" category,
for example, was used to direct intelligence-gathering about the FLQ. Rumours persisted throughout the period of associations between AIM and

the Palestinian Liberation Organization, while Canadian reporters sometimes offhandedly compared Red Power to the Irish Republican Army.

What seemed also to concern the RCMP were the overtures between
Black liberation activists in Canada and Indigenous groups, as well as
the inroads that Indigenous liberation was making amongst sympathetic
white allies.[58] As Austin writes, "the RCMP understood what others who
have written about the sixties and the new left have often failed to acknowledge. Despite their small numbers ... Blacks in Canada were playing a significant role in shaping attitudes and politics." The RCMP feared
that Black radicalism "would spread and 'contaminate' Whites."[59] We can
observe similar concerns in RCMP surveillance conducted in the 1970s
around Indigenous activism. A report from the RCMP's Saskatoon office,
for example, suggested the need to fire certain Métis teachers who intelligence officers deemed were political subversives. Of utmost concern in
the report was "the gravitation of Caucasian persons who are militant/
dissidents in their own right, to the various native organizations."[60]

The RCMP were also concerned with how fertile university campuses
and adjacent communities were for Indigenous activism.[61] It is there, according to Steve Hewitt, that the RCMP "launched its most determined
effort to destroy its opponents," especially those they deemed as "violent
revolutionary threats."[62] As the home of Canada's first Native Studies
program, Laurentian University in Sudbury was a key site for RCMP
surveillance. Even the most banal action, such as enrolling in Native
Studies, might be interpreted as support for AIM. Terry Pender writes
that at Laurentian, the RCMP justified its surveillance of the Native Studies Program "by saying it was vulnerable to infiltration by the Marxist
Study Group, a handful of students who met once a month, for a few
months."[63] Pender notes that surveillance on campus bled into the community, with Sudbury becoming known to the RCMP as a "breeding
ground for AIM radicals."[64] "Barbra," an organizer of the Trent Homo-
phile Association in Peterborough and a student in the Native Studies
program there, suggests that activists in gay rights groups were also at-
tracted to Indigenous protest movements in the early 1970s.[65] The active
presence of numerous gay and lesbian activists in the caravan forced

some reflection amongst caravan leaders. "We had a couple of gay sisters on the Caravan," Vern Harper writes, "I think a lot of us were opening our eyes for the first time."[66] Again, what might have proven most dangerous from the state's perspective was the possibility of broad based multi-issue movements amongst the oppressed.

According to historians Gary Kinsman and Patrizia Gentile, leftist social movements that were active in the early 1970s were almost always seen by the RCMP as being associated "with Marxism, even if in an unaligned way."[67] The RCMP was not always incorrect in this assumption. Certainly the CPC-ML did play a role in both the Anicinabe Park occupation and the Native People's Caravan. Other Marxist groups also expressed their support for Red Power.[68] One was the Revolutionary Marxist Group (RMG).[69] During the third week of the park occupation, the RMG's Winnipeg chapter sent out a press release expressing "solidarity with the Ojibwa struggle."[70] They argued that capitalism was the root of racism, that Indigenous struggles for land were just (unless profit was the root motivation), and that Indigenous resistance in North America started with "the European invasion of the Americas in the sixteenth century."[71] They also argued that what was happening in Kenora was connected to struggles against the Mackenzie Valley Pipeline in the Northwest Territories and against the James Bay Hydroelectric project in Northern Quebec. Such "solidarity," however, was not without criticism of the Warriors. They disagreed with the OWS demand for Indigenous representation in the police force and demands for Indigenous business opportunities. "Red capitalism," they said, "will follow more or less, the same rules as white capitalism." Still, despite these concerns, the RMG advocated for Indigenous movements, hoping that the support voiced by some Ontario trade unions during the caravan would spread. The "Revolutionary Marxist Group unconditionally supports the struggle of the Ojibwa People," their press release ends. "Solidarity means more than verbal support, however, it means material aid to those who are struggling." Certainly the RMG's "Red Forum" in January 1975 stoked the RCMP's fears that white allies were developing close ties to Indigenous causes. At this meeting in Regina, RMG members concluded that the collapse of class-based exploitation was a key to success for Red Power and that it

was "abundantly clear to us that all socialists must give complete and un-
conditional support to the right of native people to determine their future
as a nation or as several nations."[72] Yet potential obstacles still existed to
achieving true solidarity. One was the RMG's belief that Indigenous activists were "politically far less developed" than other groups on the left.[73]

The RMG was part of an attempt to create a broader anti-racist coalition with Black Power groups such as the Black Workers Alliance and
various Warrior Societies. The western Canadian chapters of the RMG
caused the RCMP concern. By the end of 1975, the RMG was claiming that
through "long and patient work" they had made excellent connections
with the Ojibway Warrior Society, that in Regina "important links" had
been made with the Métis Society and other Indigenous militant protestors, and that in Vancouver they had "established a good relationship
both with the left of AIM and with some militants from Mount Curry."[74]
The RMG believed these successful ties were forged primarily because the
group understood "how to do support work" – meaning they tried not
to impede Indigenous independence with their own political convic-
tions. Yet they also admitted constraints in organizing, such as feeling as
though if they pointed out links between Indigenous struggles and working-class struggles they were interfering with the former's autonomy.[75]

In addition to their attempts to connect to Indigenous politics, the
RMG was trying to make ties with Black Canadian activists, especially
around the question of immigration policies. They also were trying to
emphasize to the "white-left" the "links between Canadian imperialism
and the Caribbean revolution."[76] For the RMG, the time seemed ripe for
such alliances because they believed that Black radicals had moved away
from nationalism in favor of a "left-marxist current." Yet there were difficulties in establishing alliance-based work across racial identities. These
included the problems of sectarianism, which the RMG blamed on the
CPC-ML and the Black Workers Alliance.[77] The RMG also argued that this
was a "nationalistic" phase of political awakening that will take work from
"politicized black and native militants ... to overcome." Yet they argued
that "with respect to the politicization of vanguard elements who are
white, the question of racism is critical, for a number of reasons." This
included the large number of Third World immigrants who now made

up a significant part of the working class, the "genocide of the Native people," and the role of Canadian imperialism in the Caribbean.[78]

From 1965 until he was deported in 1976, Roosevelt "Rosie" Douglas played an important role in raising awareness about the status of immigrants in Canada, and Canada's imperialist role in the Caribbean. He was also a key figure in Canadian and Caribbean Black Power movements, especially in Toronto and Montreal, during the period. Douglas was a central figure behind numerous conferences in the late 1960s which, according to David Austin, "ignited the Montreal black community" and helped mobilize "African-descended peoples ... throughout Canada against racial oppression."[79] Douglas had been arrested for his participation in the 1969 "Sir George Williams affair."[80] The arrest made organizing difficult for Douglas and eventually led to his being declared a national security risk and deported to Dominica in 1976.[81]

Before his deportation, Douglas embarked on a tour across Canada. It served two purposes: one was to bring attention to his own case in hopes of preventing the deportation, while the other was connecting with other groups that he believed were marginalized because of race or citizenship status. The "Rosie Douglas Tour" hit some hotspots of Indigenous activism in Canada, including Thunder Bay and Grassy Narrows (Aubpeeschoseewagong) just north of Kenora. Across Western Canada, Douglas included visits to Winnipeg, Regina, and Vancouver. While he toured Canada, Douglas had a close companion, his bodyguard and driver, Warren Hart.[82]

Douglas gave two very well attended talks in Winnipeg, where he was joined by Louis Cameron. The RMG remarked later that the Winnipeg stops were two of the most successful of the tour, as more than five hundred people heard Douglas use a relatively new concept to describe Canada: "settler-colonial." Canada is not a "conquered colony," he said, it is "a settler-colony" and "founded upon the premise of racism." He also concentrated on immigration issues, outlining how throughout its history, the state had used border control as a way to keep "black people out of Canada." Dismissing rumours that he would go work for Solicitor General Warren Allmand in exchange for his deportation being halted, Douglas stated that "If you're committed to something you're going to fight to the end. That's the only kind of fight I understand ...

There is no signing of any peace treaty in between. The last time people signed peace treaties in this country you can see what happened to the native people."[83]

Douglas ended with an appeal for local committees to raise awareness about another deportation case: that of the 1,500 Haitians who were about to be forced from Canada back to Haiti, where, Douglas argued, they would face persecution by the Duvalier government.[84] While Montreal was the centre of Haitian anti-deportation activism, Douglas took his message across Canada. It gained traction in unexpected places. In December 1974, for example, the anti-deportation campaign received a cheque from a person living in Attawapiskat. Attached to the cheque was a letter reading: "From a remote Indian reservation in Ontario, I wanted to tell you now I found the Haitian affair shattering." The Winnipeg meeting also spurred action on behalf of the Haitians from a newly formed anti-racism committee that elected September Williams, an organizer for the Black Action Movement, as committee co-chair and Leslie Currie "of the Ojibway people" as secretary.[85] The group planned a teach-in and demonstration, both in support of Haitian deportees' issues and to raise funds for Lyle Ironstand's defence against charges stemming from the Anicinabe Park occupation. According to the group's literature, "if we know these things and do not act, then we become the torturers, executioners and prison bars."[86]

In Regina, he joined Rod Bishop of the Métis Society of Saskatchewan. According to an RCMP surveillance report, Bishop gave what was "a long dissertation on the native children who were sent from Northern Saskatchewan to the United States." For his part, Douglas gave a speech that RCMP surveillance characterized as "the usual rhetoric concerning racism and imperialistic repression." He also reportedly "denounced" the CPC-ML in what the informant believed was an attempt to resurrect Vern Harper's credibility (Harper had just left the CPC-ML).[87]

RCMP files redact the names of their informants. It's plausible, however, that this information came from Warren Hart. In 1975, Hart was publicly identified primarily as Douglas's bodyguard and driver. By the end of 1979, however, he had gained a different type of fame. The RCMP hired Hart in 1971 as part of their effort to infiltrate Black Power groups in Canada. Hart was a known figure in counter-intelligence communi-

ties, as he had performed similar tasks for the FBI, infiltrating the Black
Panther Party (BPP) in Baltimore, Maryland. Hart spent four years
alongside Douglas, driving him around in a Lincoln Continental. The
RCMP worked hard to keep Hart's identity a secret. After Douglas was
jailed in 1973, the RCMP arranged for Hart to be deported to make it
look like he too had been arrested. Upon returning to Canada after Douglas's release, Hart told Douglas that he'd snuck across the border to re-
join him.[88] When told about Hart's true identity, Douglas responded in
much the same way as Louis Cameron did when confronted with the
truth about Durham. Denial. First, he denied that Hart had gained any
significant knowledge of the movement. Then he claimed that he'd
never trusted Hart because his driver was never bothered by the police
even though the car was loaded with guns, but he kept him around
anyway to help pay for the trip across Canada.[89] Douglas's insistence
that Hart had gained little knowledge was met by the latter's claim
that he "knew everything [Douglas] was involved in – even the colour
of his underwear."[90]

Hart did more than gather intelligence. He was also an *agent provocateur* whose activities sometimes resulted in tragedy. In his memoirs,
former Black Panther activist Marshall Eddie Conway remembers Hart
as one of the founders of the Baltimore chapter of the BPP. Conway
writes that they "would eventually discover that our Defense Captain,
who was the highest-ranking Panther in the state of Maryland, was a
paid agent of the National Security Agency."[91] According to Dylan Ro-
driguez, when Conway discovered Hart's true identity, Hart had Conway
targeted by the FBI's Counter Intelligence Program. Conway was arrested
and charged with the murder of one police officer and the attempted
murder of two others. David Austin suggests also that Hart was "implicated in the assassination of Chicago Black Panther Fred Hampton." Internationally, Hart reportedly failed in an assassination attempt on Tim
Hector, a journalist who had revealed "an international plot by the Cana-
dian-American multinational Space Research Corporation, which Hart
worked for at the time, to illegally ship" weapons from New Brunswick,
through Antigua, to South Africa.[92]

Despite his being implicated or suspected to have had a role in the
deaths and unjust arrests of BPP activists, the RCMP used Hart not only

to gather intelligence but also to persuade movements in Canada to take violent tactics further than they had originally intended. We know this, in part, because of Hart's testimony at the McDonald Commission. Formed in 1977, the commission was tasked with investigating the actions of the RCMP security services after an earlier commission had uncovered evidence of illegal activities against radical political organizations in Quebec. During his McDonald Commission testimony, Hart provided significant details about the license the RCMP gave him. From originally spying on Black Power movements in Canada, his role was expanded to include intelligence-gathering on "black, Canadian Indian, immigrant and labour groups in Montreal, Toronto, Kenora, Lethbridge, and Vancouver."[93] According to Hart, the infiltration of Indigenous groups was one of his most important tasks.[94] Much like Durham, Hart used the media and the commission to create a narrative about himself, one in which he saved Canadians from the violent designs of Indigenous activists. He explained to reporters that on several occasions, Indigenous groups asked for his help in blowing up buildings, because it was common knowledge that Hart was a demolitions expert. He said that this included requests by the Ojibway Warrior Society to help blow up a bridge and by a group in Alberta to destroy a pipeline.[95]

His McDonald Commission testimony reveals that Hart had plenty of opportunity to influence groups while accompanying Rosie Douglas across Canada. This included an alleged trip to Anicinabe Park during the occupation. He also described meetings in 1975 with Ojibway Warriors Society lawyer Donald Colborne in Thunder Bay, with various Indigenous groups in Winnipeg, and a visit to the Mount Currie reserve in British Columbia. Hart's testimony to the McDonald Commission is reminiscent of Durham's to the Eastland Committee. Both men were keen to describe Indigenous protests as "communist plots." Both tried to portray themselves as patriotic citizens protecting the country from attack. There is a counter-narrative to Hart's testimony, however, as he was only one of many people to testify at the McDonald Commission. Witnesses challenged his self-portrayal as simply an informant, arguing that he had encouraged Indigenous protestors to adopt increasingly violent tactics. According to lawyer Clayton Ruby, Rosie Douglas was never asked to testify in front of the commission.[96] But others were. In a summary of

Hart's testimony, Don Colborne's deposition is quoted extensively. Colborne testified that when he met Hart in Thunder Bay in June 1975, Hart "several times stated that he intended to steal weapons from persons in Thunder Bay" and to find ways to attain military-grade weapons.[97] Though Hart denied these allegations, other witnesses offered similar testimony. For example, one individual claimed Hart offered unlimited supplies of weapons to AIM during his trip to Mount Currie in BC, and volunteered to train them "in the use of dynamite and other types of explosives."[98] Hart again denied the accusation.

Because of these allegations, Noel Starblanket, then the president of the National Indian Brotherhood, demanded a criminal investigation into Hart.[99] Starblanket believed he should have had the opportunity to examine Hart himself because of his admission that he was asked by officials to train activists in guerilla warfare (during Douglas's 1975 tour) only to then have the RCMP swoop in and raid the camps. The intent was to create the perception that the RCMP was successful in rooting out internal threats to national security.[100] Hart was not a rogue agent, however, but part of a larger effort to disrupt Indigenous political movements and their sense of common cause with other anti-racist activists. Depositions taken by the National Indian Brotherhood show that RCMP agents often used dirty tricks to gather intelligence. A woman serving time in a Kenora jail in 1976 testified that two members of the Winnipeg RCMP offered her money in exchange for information on the Winnipeg AIM chapter, on activists involved in Leonard Peltier's campaign, and on people working with Treaty #9 who had "leftist" leanings. [101]

Almost a decade after Hart testified, a federally commissioned report concluded that in deporting Hart, the RCMP had acted "disgracefully" out of "fear of public disclosure" of Hart's true identity.[102] Consequently, Solicitor General James Kelleher awarded Hart $56,000 in compensation.[103] After their moments in the spotlight, both Warren Hart and Douglas Durham escaped into lives of obscurity. Both are now dead, like others who came into contact with them while they worked for the FBI and RCMP in the 1960s and 1970s. The histories of Hart and Durham read like spy films, but their activities had real-life consequences. While they presented themselves as heroes, their activities were costly both to the movements they infiltrated and to later public perceptions of Indigenous protest. Social movements in North America, including Red Power groups, sometimes resorted to armed insurrection as a tactic of political change. Yet within most of these groups, there was a range of opinion as to what was appropriate action. Agents such as Hart amplified the possibility of revolutionary violence. By doing so, they gave states the license to repress movements advocating multiracial and transnational oppositional politics.

More than three decades after Warren Hart, Douglas Durham, the FBI, and the RCMP collapsed complex movements for social justice into categories such as "communist" and "terrorist," Indigenous activists are still imagined as threats to national security. In early 2007, a leaked draft of a Canadian army counter-insurgency manual listed Hezbollah, the Tamil Tigers, and specific Indigenous groups in Canada as insurgents against whom tactics such as "ambushes, deception and killing" would be legitimate tools. As the Grand Chief of the Union of British Columbia Indian Chiefs explained, this was evidence of the "deliberate criminalization of the efforts of Aboriginal people to march, demonstrate and rally to draw public attention to the crushing poverty that is the reality within our communities."[104]

This chapter has demonstrated that the possibility of a broader movement of racialized and working-class people centering Indigenous rights provoked concern amongst state actors. When state actors and popular commentators saw connections between global forms of anti-colonialism and anti-racism, they concluded that a "foreign influence" had corrupted local Indigenous peoples. In the case of Kenora, it did not matter if that foreigner was from Toronto or Tanzania: there was a deep-seated belief that Indigenous peoples only voiced a desire for systematic change because an outsider had told them to do so. On the contrary, what this book has worked to show is that Indigenous activists, across a range of contexts and for a range of purposes, saw the transnational in a much more complicated fashion and interpreted comparative examples of racism, colonization, and dispossession not as guides on how to challenge settler-colonialism but as ideas they could adapt to their own local context when they saw fit. In reflecting upon the role of the RCMP and Canadian state in attempting to disrupt Indigenous political protest in the period, members of the Native People's Caravan had this to say:

They are racist because they say Native People are not capable of organizing themselves, that they need some outside force to push them into waging struggle, that Native People are not capable of directing their struggle, that they need to be "manipulated." Their racism extended to the fact that Native People were "used as pawns" for someone else. And further we weren't responsible for our actions. In fact, the opposite was true ... We bear full responsibility for our actions and made a deliberate conscious decision to build fraternal ties with those who concretely supported our struggle to regain our land and hereditary rights. The federal government has always promoted their racist line that Native People are capable of nothing, in order to justify their interference in our internal affairs ... History shows Native People never stopped fighting, were courageous and fought tenaciously to defend their land and hereditary rights against the colonialist aggressors and now against their capitalist successors.[105]

Dear Louis Cameron

Dear Louis Cameron,

This is not the first time I've written you a letter like this; but I still never get it quite right. I first wrote it in 2010 when I found your name in the obituary section of the Kenora newspaper. I check that section every few days, as one does when one lives far away from where they grew up and needs to know if it's time to write a condolence card. Seeing that obituary took my breath away because I hoped we would still have time to meet. I was wrong.

A picture of you during the occupation of Anicinabe Park is framed on my wall. Years have passed since I first learned about you and engaged with the ideas that the OWS put forward in 1974. Those ideas are still so prescient because Canada continues to benefit from settler-colonial dispossession. Late last summer, I reread the long winding interview you gave in the midst of the park occupation. Your words were not for me but reading them fundamentally changed the way I understand the world and settler complicity. They changed the way I understand the history of the place where we both lived, where we probably crossed paths, and which produced such different lived experiences and expectations. In your few surviving interviews, you were so generous in situating white working-class alienation alongside the much more precarious and unjust circumstances you found yourself and other Indigenous folks living through in Kenora and in Treaty #3 nations. Others have built newer or more detailed critiques, but you exposed me to the colonial foundations of Canada unlike anyone I had ever read.

The person who wrote your obituary said many beautiful things about you. They shared how you lived according to the principles of Mide-wiwin, which you were orienting towards when the Ojibway Warrior Society was just forming. The obituary says you were still playing in drum circles. Alongside other activists, you first appeared in the public spotlight in 1973 during the Indian Affairs office occupation as a voice articulating demands for justice, not only for the return of land but on a host of social issues, many of which had most recently been recounted in the Violent Death Report. Two short but dramatic years later, you left the national spotlight. Some old sixties activists capitalized on their public image in their later careers, writing books, becoming professors or even film stars. This was not your experience, was it? You paid for trying to stand up for what you believed in. I've read and heard stories about things that hap-pened to you around Kenora after Red Power faded from fashion. I don't need to repeat those stories here but I wonder, if you had not stood up for what you believed in, would you have lived an easier life in later years?

Also, I suspect that in 1973 and 1974, that type of future didn't seem possible. Too many people you knew, your age and younger, were dying. You said as much. The houses you lived in were "built to burn down," you said in that interview I reread a few months ago. Your words sounded matter-of-fact. You were tired of the disregard for Indigenous life by white people in town, in government, as employers, as newspaper re-porters and as police officers. You were also tired of the way colonization had turned Indigenous peoples against each other. In fact, that seemed to bother you as much as anything. In 1974, you explained that this con-flict was the result of both the material and the psychological effects of colonialism. I learned so much from that insight. Reading that *led me* to Franz Fanon – another theorist who thought that way.

What does it mean when the past is continually reliving itself in the present? From what I know, you were a close reader of history. You sit-uated everything you did within a much broader history of colonization and empire. You said you stood on the shoulders of those who came be-fore you and critiqued Canada's colonial foundations, but you also sug-gested that change could only really happen if oppressed peoples, Indigenous and non-Indigenous, worked together. I hope people in the future will look at you the same way. But what would you say about set-

tler-colonialism today? Almost all of the issues the ows brought attention to still make news today. Mercury poisoning, for example. Louis, as
I rewrite this letter, I have a newspaper article in front of me from September 2019. It says that there is a second mercury dump site near Grassy
Narrows. The second new one since you passed away, in fact. The first
was reported in 2015 after a retired mill-worker said that he had been involved in dumping fifty drums of mercury in 1972. The Ontario government has not yet excavated the site. This new discovery was the result of
a tip from another former employee, who said this mixture of concrete
and mercury was placed into forty-five gallon drums and then buried in
a pit.[1] Of course, Louis, this isn't unique to First Nations communities
in Treaty #3. Poisoned water is found on hundreds of Indigenous communities across this country. And like you, others in those communities
have spent the better part of the last fifty years trying to get various levels
of government to rectify the situation.

Canada has a complicated relationship to its past. You brought this up
when referencing the similarities Indigenous peoples here share with
other colonized peoples. It was also a point Fred Kelly made when he met
with Black Power activists in Toronto and that Lee Maracle often made
as part of NARP. This country maintains a formal attachment to a past
empire through the figurehead of the Governor General, and also to a
current one to our south through culture and economic gain. Canada,
however, is not simply a victim of American imperialism. You drew attention to the way that Kenora was a hinterland and how, in the 1970s,
Toronto and Montreal, as our country's economic centres, oppressed the
peripheries. They took the trees and gave back jobs, but only for a short
time. Canada also downplays its complicity in imperial aggression and
has worked hard to disguise colonialisms within its borders. I wonder
what you thought when you heard that Prime Minister Stephen Harper,
speaking to reporters at a G-20 meeting in September 2009, said that
"Canada has no history of colonialism." Mainstream media outlets in
Canada seemed to ignore Harper's amnesia, but others did not. Shawn
Atleo, then National Chief of the Assembly of First Nations, replied that
not only did Canada have a colonial history, it lived a colonial present –
a point not lost outside this country. "Internationally," Atleo wrote,
"Canada has been scrutinized and harshly criticized for its treatment of

Indigenous peoples and failure to respect Aboriginal and Treaty rights."[2] Russel Lawrence Barsh writes that the narrative of peaceful coexistence between the Canadian state and Indigenous peoples is just moralizing state propaganda. This legend, he suggests, is that "Canada settled its territory peacefully ... while the United States fought many bloody Indian wars for greed and gold." "Canada," it is often repeated, "has been 'gentle tolerant, just and impartial' in its treatment of First Nations."[3]

Louis, as I finish this book, I keep returning to two pieces written about Indigenous protest in Kenora just after the Native People's Caravan ended. You were at the centre of both pieces, and each illustrates the enormous burden you and other Indigenous women and men have been forced to carry when you challenge settler-colonial power. One of these books is *Bended Elbow*, written by Eleanor Jacobson, a former nurse in Wabaseemoong. The first time I went to the Kenora Library to check it out, a librarian had to retrieve it from stacks closed to the public. I know you knew about this book, because you wanted it categorized as hate literature.[4] No kidding! Of the many dehumanizing portrayals of Indigenous folks that circulated in that era, whether in public, or as anthropologists' notes show, at dinner tables, this could have been one of the worst. Or, more likely, it was par for the course from your perspective. It traded on the well-worn stereotypes you and others worked hard not only to debunk but to treat as real sources of power that shaped the long history of dispossession and dehumanization.

Eleanor Jacobson took direct aim at you, Louis, urging readers to see Indigenous activists as pawns of a communist conspiracy – a trope almost as cliché as the others she trotted out. She claimed her book was Kenora speaking back at you. I hope it wasn't. In her follow-up volume, she even printed letters from "Indians" who she said supported her, one being Dick Wilson, the infamous tribal chairman of Pine Ridge Reservation made famous by Wounded Knee. Both volumes depict "Indians" in Kenora as lazy and drunk, less than human. I doubt she realized just how well she proved your argument about the material and discursive foundations of settler-colonialism.

But Louis, she was not the only writer speaking for Kenora. I wonder if you ever saw the second book I've been thinking about, a comic entitled *Red Power* that Clermont Duval wrote and illustrated in 1975.[5] Divided into two parts and published in both English and French, the story begins with the chiefs of the three largest "Indian reservations in Canada" sending a message to rendezvous at an unnamed lake. Upon arrival, they are guided through a forest to a hidden opening to a secret passage leading to a futuristic underground building. Shiny floors and a monorail train are part of this giant hall which is full of young Indians, giant totem poles, and eagle statues. Then the three chiefs, Mawouk, Mirko, and Fasca, meet the leader of this new Indian futurism: Chief Kenora.

That's you. I think he imagined you as Chief Kenora.

The new visitors learn that an elder named Carava is also part of Chief Kenora's underground, this fantastical place with rows upon row of incubators holding 40,000 Indigenous men and women ready for rebirth. As they emerge, Chief Kenora tells the three others that these newborns are complete humans, "endowed with a superior intelligence, free from jealousy and egoism." They are ready for the collective birth of a new nation. In Duval's comic, out of this massive rebirth comes one new character to join Carava and Chief Kenora, "the future chief of us all": Red Power.

Chief Kenora, Red Power, and Carava emerge from the underground and in a series dramatic battles with the Canadian military, liberate Indigenous communities across Canada. Louis, I understand why Duval thought you were a superhero who was going to become Canada's Che Guevara. In defiance of the kind of hatred embodied in the pages of *Bended Elbow*, this comic book told a different story. And as much as I want this second version to be the truth, it too misses the point. Just as you and others were not the villains that Eleanor Jacobson portrayed you as, neither were any of the activists of the period comicbook superheroes. You were complicated and imperfect; as you said many times, you were working to become a complete human being, but to be able to do that you needed to be free. Like you said in 1974:

All these things – with education system, the churches – are pushing our people. You know, everybody knows, that people have to be free to express human freedom. They have to laugh, they have to yell and they have to be free to move around. But when you push people into a group like that a lot of that expression turns inside. It's what

you call internal aggression. And as a result of that Indians live a
dangerous style of life. They fight each other, they drink a lot. And
the tendency of suicide is higher.[6]

As much as anything else, our flaws illustrate our humanity – a word
you invoked when speaking about liberation. I think one of the last
public appearances you made gives us insight into how you had come
to understand the past. Thirty-two years after making Anicinabe Park
symbolic beyond its borders, in late June 2007, you returned. You were
there for celebrations marking the first annual Aboriginal Day of Action,
a moment during which tens of thousands of Indigenous peoples and
their allies across Canada made demanded an end to continued injustices. All I have is a copy of the next day's newspaper saying you encouraged peaceful demonstration.

Your obituary also told us about your involvement in the Ojibway
Warrior Society. But what also caught my eye in that obituary was that
the writer called you a "philosopher." A philosopher. Such a truthful description. The way you spoke about human liberation betrays the notion
that post-1968, protest politics in North America were just fractured identity battles or that Indigenous political demands were narrowly conceived. When many Kenora residents wanted you thrown in jail, you tried
to relate to them by saying you understood how they faced their own difficult circumstances. Years before the occupation, those who marched
for Indian Rights identified the mill as a key example of the employment
discrimination Indigenous men faced in trying to find well-paying jobs
in Kenora. Years later, the Dryden mill was found to have polluted the
English-Wabigoon River with mercury pollutants, aided by a provincial
government which hid knowledge of the disaster from the people it impacted and who relied on that water system for food and employment.
You and other concerned people drew international attention to all of
this. The first visit by the Japanese researchers who brought much attention to mercury poisoning in the 1970s was recently commemorated by
a return trip to Grassy Narrows.[7] What it demonstrated is that people in
these communities still live daily with the effects of poisoned water.

Following the examples of activists before them, people in the community continually push back against this form of erasure. Young acti-

vists there have also staged blockades to protect the Whiskey Jack forest. In doing so they prevented Abitibi, the last corporation to run the Kenora mill, from clear-cutting the area in the early 2000s. What did you think of some of those protests? Are they different than those of the 1960s and 1970s?

Though your thoughts are only collected in a few small pamphlets and in a couple of interviews from the early seventies, they profoundly shaped the direction of this book. The way you spoke about decolonization globally made me want to learn more about how other Indigenous peoples made sense of their actions in the global sphere. The occupation and the caravan spoke a complicated language that understood the way that the local and global are intimately bound up with each other. Each of the chapters in this book attempted to illustrate how broader historical processes such as Third World decolonization, rights movements, racial regimes, and state surveillance all deeply shape how to make sense of the period between 1965 and 1974 in the Treaty #3 territory, especially Kenora.

Returning to Kenora is always a profoundly humbling experience, reminding me that there were people like you who exhibited profound imagination and courage against the crushing machine that is settler-colonization. Thinking and acting expansively, you embraced goals not yet attained. These are not fairytales about how resistance immediately creates a better world. This book shows that as people resist the very structures and attitudes that resolidify around them, the struggle becomes even more difficult. So much of the structural and cultural disempowerment from that moment still exists. But the way you and others worked to change the world around you then will forever guide my thinking about how to help create a just world today.

Notes

INTRODUCTION

1 "Kenora: A Town with a Bad Name," *Akwesasne Notes* 6.3 (1974): 19–20.
2 In this book is I use the following definition for the term "Indigenous": "to describe groups of people who maintain historical continuity with precolonial societies, and who consider themselves distinct from other societies that became dominant through conquest, occupation, settlement or other means. In Canada, it is a term used to collectively describe Inuit, First Nations and Métis." *Canadian Geographic Indigenous Peoples Atlas of Canada*, 67. When I use terms such as "Indian," "Aboriginal," "First Nations," or "Métis," I do so when the subjects of the book are using those terms to discuss their own identity and histories or when they are used as legal terms. I try not to change the phrasing Indigenous activists and writers used during the period. If they wrote about "Indian rights" or the "Ojibway nation," for example, I leave those terms as they are in an attempt to best represent the author's voice.
3 Coulthard, *Red Skin White Masks*, 6–7. See also, Harris, "How Did Colonialism Dispossess? Comments from an Edge of Empire"; Wolfe, *Settler-Colonialism and the Transformation of Anthropology*.
4 Logan McCallum and Perry, *Structures of Indifference*, 7.
5 I am using "Anishinaabe" most commonly in this book as a broad reference to the Ojibwe, Potawatomi, Odawa (Ottawa), Chippewa, Mississauga, Saulteaux, Nipissing, and Algonquin peoples. It was common in the period covered in this book for Anishinaabe and Indigenous activists in Treaty #3 area to use "Ojibway" as an umbrella term capturing culture, language, and

nation in the region. I leave "Ojibwa" or "Ojibway" in quotations to indicate specific use as best as possible. I use "Anishinaabemowin" at times in general reference to Ojibwe as a language. First Nations place names have been kept as they were referred to publicly in the period, with more recent Anishi-naabemowin naming in parentheses. For example, I reference the "White-dog First Nation" (Wabaseemoong) because activists from the period used "Whitedog" commonly in public communication and as part of their activism. If I am making a more contemporary reference, I will refer to "Wabaseemoong" (Whitedog). I also try to locate individuals by nation or by language when possible.

6 Logan McCallum and Perry, *Structures of Indifference*, 19.

7 Talaga, *Seven Fallen Feathers*, 3.

8 Communities of the Anishinaabe Nation represented by Grand Council Treaty #3 are: Animakee Wa Zhing, Asubpeeschoseewagong (Grassy Nar-rows), Buffalo Point, Couchiching, Iskatewizaagegan 39, Lac des Mille Lacs, Lac La Croix, Lac Seul, Migisi Sahgaigan (Eagle Lake), Mishkosiminiziibiing (Big Grassy), Mitaanjigamiing, Naicatchewenin (Northwest Bay), Naon-gashiing (Big Island), Naotkamegwanning (Whitefish bay), Nigigoonsi-minikaaning (Red Gut), Niisaachewan (Dalles), Northwest Angle 33, Onigaming (Sabaskong), Rainy River (Manitou Rapids), Sagkeeng (Fort Alexander), Saugeen, Seine River, Shoal Lake 40, Waabigoniiw Saaga'iganiiw (Wabigoon Lake), Wabaseemoong (White Dog), Wabauskang, Washagamis Bay, Wauzhushk Onigum (Rat Portage). See also: http://gct3.ca/our-nation/. The map included in this book marks only those local communities that are referenced most often throughout the following chapters.

9 See for example, Miller, *Compact, Contract, Covenant*, 167–71.

10 Cottam, "Federal/Provincial Disputes, Natural Resources and the Treaty #3 Ojibway, 1867–1924," 32.

11 Friesen, *The Canadian Prairies: A History*, 137.

12 Luby, "'The Department is Going Back on These Promises," 205, 207; see also Willow, *Strong Hearts, Native Lands*, 42.

13 Luby, "'The Department is Going Back on These Promises," 204.

14 Waisberg and Holzkamm, "'A Tendency to Discourage Them from Cultivat-ing,'" 182.

15 Willow, *Strong Hearts, Native Lands*, 47.

16 Ibid., 43.

17   Louis Cameron in *Ojibway Warrior Society in Occupied Anicinabe Park, Kenora, Ontario, August* 1974, 6.

18   Luby, "The Department Is Going Back on These Promises," 211–12.

19   Daschuk, *Clearing the Plains*, 127.

20   Walker, "Immigration Policy, Colonization, and the Development of a White Canada," 38.

21   Cooper, *Colonialism in Question*, 4.

22   Trouillot, *Silencing the Past*, 71.

23   Ibid., 72.

24   Cameron quoted in Burke, *Paper Tomahawks: From Red Tape to Red Power*.

25   Wightman and Wightman, *The Land Between*, 296. See also, Scott, "Northern Alienation," 235–48; and Weller, "Hinterland Politics."

26   Weller, "Hinterland Politics," 733.

27   Talaga, *Seven Fallen Feathers*, 35.

28   Denis, "Contact Theory in a Small Town Settler-Colonial Context," 220.

29   Ibid., 231–2.

30   Robinson, *Black Marxism*, 3; I turn to Robin D.G. Kelley often as a source to help me flesh out Robinson's ideas. See for example, Kelley, "What Did Cedric Robinson Mean by Racial Capitalism," *Boston Review*, 12 January 2017, accessed at bostonreview.net, and more recently Kelley, Amarigilio, and Wilson, "'Solidarity Is Not a Market Exchange,'" 159, 161–2; Pulido, "Flint, Environmental Racism, and Racial Capitalism."

31   Teigrob, *Warming Up to the Cold War*, 93, 96.

32   Goldberg, *The Threat of Race*, 10.

33   Ibid., 11.

34   Ibid., 12–13.

35   Ibid., 14.

36   Kelley, *Freedom Dreams*, 60; see also Tyson, *Radio Free Dixie*.

37   Ibid., 61–2.

38   Echols, *Shaky Ground*, 64.

39   Gosse, *Where the Boys Are*, 8; see also Varon, *Bringing the War Home*.

40   Rutherford et. al, "Introduction: The Global Sixties," 2–3.

41   Adams, *Prison of Grass*; Maracle, *Bobbi Lee*.

42   See for example, Austin, *Fear of a Black Nation*; Maynard, *Policing Black Lives*; Milligan, *Rebel Youth*; Mills, *The Empire Within*; Nelson, *Razing Africville*; Palmer, *Canada's 1960s*; Wright, "Between Nation and Empire."

43   Rutherford et. al, "Introduction: The Global Sixties," 3.

44   Hall, *The American Empire and the Fourth World*, 499.

45   Westad, *The Global Cold War*, 2.

46   Meren, "'Commend Me the Yak,'" 346.

47   Coulthard, *Red Skin, White Masks*, 4–6.

48   Trouillot, *Silencing the Past*, 26.

CHAPTER ONE

1   James Eayrs, "Canada's Black Fact: From Universities and Pullmans to Reservations and Igloos," *Toronto Star*, 28 February 1969, 6.

2   George Miller quoted in Ian Adams, "The Indians: An Abandoned and Dispossessed People," *Weekend Magazine*, 31 July 1965, 5.

3   Sokol, *There Goes My Everything*, 244.

4   Dudziak, *Cold War Civil Rights*, 233.

5   Rolston, "The Brothers on the Walls," 464. Also important is Prince, *Northern Ireland's '68*.

6   Curthoys, *Freedom Ride*. Curthoys emphasized this transnational influence in personal correspondence with me on 22 April 2009. See also Maynard, "Transcultural/Transnational Interaction and Influences on Aboriginal Australia," 198–9.

7   Churchill, "SUPA, Selma, and Stevenson," 34; "U of M Student Council Backs Fight for Rights," *Winnipeg Free Press*, 17 March 1965, 14.

8   "Ottawa Protests Continue," *Winnipeg Free Press*, 15 March 1965, 8.

9   Churchill, "SUPA, Selma, and Stevenson," 49.

10   F.N. Ferguson, "Help Indians First," *Toronto Star*, 13 March 1965, 6; L.E. Kaylor, "Look to Own Problem," *Toronto Star*, 18 March 1965, 6.

11   "Selma-Manquang-Ottawa," *Marxist Quarterly* 1, no. 13 (1965): 41–2.

12   Patricia Clarke, "Monthly Column," *United Church Observer* 27, no. 1 (1965): 8.

13   In 1876, *The Indian Act* became the legal framework which governed First Nations in Canada. Barrington Walker calls it a "foundational moment in how race was legally produced in Canada." It perpetuated the term "Indian," defining it by blood (biology) and the performance of "Indian culture." It was ordered through gender, defining as Indian "any male person reputed to belong to a particular band," as well as "the children or wife of such a per-

son." Indigenous women and their children lost their Indian status, and thus band membership, becoming involuntarily enfranchised (as Canadian citizens) when they married non-Indian men; see Walker, "Immigration Policy, Colonization, and the Development of a White Canada," 39–40. It was not until 1985, after nearly two decades of agitating by people such as Jeannette Corbiere Lavell and the Native Women's Association of Canada, that the "patrilineal bias," to use Audra Simpson's phrase, was amended through Bill C-31. These actions saw non-status Indigenous women "go head to head with their reserve or band council government, the state, and finally, international authorities ... to let them return, to raise their children, and to exercise their rights as Indians." See Simpson, *Mohawk Interruptus*, 56; Lawrence, *"Real" Indians and Others*, 50–6.

14 Adams, "The Indians," 2–6.

15 The Indian-Eskimo Association would later become the Canadian Association in Support of Native Peoples. It was a national organization meant to advance the status of Indigenous peoples in Canada, and stipulated that a quarter of its membership at all times had to be Indigenous.

16 "Chief Green Sees Need for Regional Indian Organization," *Kenora Daily Miner and News*, 14 January 1965, 1, 4.

17 "Women's Group Active, Indian Delegate Finds," *Kenora Daily Miner and News*, 20 January 1965, 1.

18 Miller, "Owen Glendower, Hotspur, and Canadian Indian Policy," 110.

19 Downey, *The Creators Game*, 132. Downey argued that one way that Indigenous people could circumvent such bans was sport. During sport days in residential schools kids were encouraged to dance and display regalia.

20 Miller, "Owen Glendower, Hotspur, and Canadian Indian Policy," 113.

21 "Women's Group Active, Indian Delegate Finds," 1.

22 Coates, *A Global History of Indigenous Peoples*, 237.

23 Austin, *Fear of a Black Nation*, 182.

24 Ibid., 183

25 "Indian Problem Termed Mainly a Human Problem – Shankowsky," *Kenora Daily Miner and News*, 6 February 1965, 3–4.

26 Fred Kelly, "Indian White Committee Plan November Conference in Kenora," *Kenora Daily Miner and News*, 29 October 1965, 1, 3.

27 "Indians Are Frustrated; Uprisings Sure to Follow," *Kenora Daily Miner and News*, 17 November 1965, 1.

28 Borovoy, *Uncivil Obedience*, 31–2.

29 Ibid., 30.

30 "Indians on March Protest Treatment," *Toronto Telegram*, 23 November 1965, 44; Perry Anglin, "March 4 Abreast, 400 Indians Protest Kenora 'White Bias,'" *Toronto Star*, 23 November 1965, 1, 2; "Unprecedented Display of Unity," *Indian Record* 29, no. 1 (January 1966): 3, 6.

31 Barbarash's commentary is taken from a radio program recorded in February 1974 to mark the tenth anniversary of *Indian Magazine* (which had been renamed *Our Native Land* in 1970). See http://archives.cbc.ca/society/native_issues/clips/15991 (last accessed 6 April 2010).

32 Adele Perry argues that in twentieth-century Canada, "cities were emphatically defined as non-indigenous space," a description that Indian Rights marchers were challenging through their words and their presence, both as marchers and in attendance at the town hall meeting. Perry, *Aqueduct Colonialism*, 25.

33 Kenora Town Council Re: Indian-Non Indian Relations, Indian White Committee, Kenora, Ont, 1965, RG 76-3-0-331, Ontario Human Rights Commission fonds, AO, Toronto, Ontario.

34 Ibid.

35 Ibid.

36 Logan McCallum, *Indigenous Women, Work, and History, 1940–1980*, 24.

37 Ibid., 80.

38 Kenora Town Council Re: Indian-Non Indian Relations.

39 Ibid.

40 "Protest by Canada's Indians Stirs Conscience," *The Times of London*, 7 December 1965, 11.

41 "The Shame of Our 'Mississippi' Indians," *Toronto Star*, 22 November 1965, 6.

42 Perry Anglin, "100 Kenora Indians Plan 'Selma' March," *Toronto Star*, 17 November 1965, 1, 4.

43 Palmer, *Canada's 1960s*, 398–9.

44 Walker, "Finding Jim Crow in Canada, 1767–1967," 81–98.

45 *House of Commons Debates*, First Session – Twenty Seventh Parliament 1966, 189.

46 Hill and Borovoy, who was Jewish, were blamed by the *Winnipeg Tribune* for creating the idea for the march in an article entitled "Negro and Jew Spear-

headed March of Indians," cited by Ian Adams in "Kenora One Year Later," *Maclean's*, February 1967, 31.

47 Re: Lake of the Woods Hotel, Indian White Committee, Kenora, Ont, 1965. RG 76-3-0-331, Ontario Human Rights Commission fonds, AO, Toronto, Ontario.

48 Wightman and Wightman, *The Land Between*, 289.

49 Re: Complaints Against Northern Ontario Tourist Establishment by American Negro Tourists, Ontario Report, Dr DG Hill, 1967, RG 76-3-0-631, Ontario Human Rights Commission fonds, AO, Toronto, Ontario.

50 Ibid.

51 Mackey, *The House of Difference*, 67.

52 Maynard, *Policing Black Lives*, 37–8.

53 E. Simmons, "The Lessons of Kenora," *Winnipeg Free Press*, 2 December 1965, 33.

54 Logan McCallum, *Indigenous Women, Work, and History, 1940–1980*, 81.

55 "We Have Bigotry All Right – But No Alabamas," *Maclean's Magazine*, 17 April 1965, 4.

56 "Council Demands Answers for Firing," *Winnipeg Free Press*, 3 December 1965, 8; Gene Lahache quoted in "Indians Rally around Kelly," *Winnipeg Free Press*, 1 December 1965, 1.

57 "New March Hinted: Kenora 'Luther King,' Indian Leader Fired," *Toronto Star*, 29 November 1965, 1, 2; Fred Kelly quoted in Tim Traynor, "Headlines Trumpet Kelly, Indians' Hero," *Winnipeg Free Press*, 10 December 1965, 10.

58 Charles Clark quoted in "Kenora Indian Says He Lost Job for Role in Protest March," *Globe and Mail*, 29 November 1965, 4.

59 Deloria, *Custer Died for Your Sins*, 169.

60 Ibid., 172.

61 Crow Dog, *Lakota Woman*, 77.

62 "The Role of the Ontario Human Rights Commission in Northern Ontario" OHRC, RG-76-3-0, AO, Toronto.

63 Until 1960, only "Indians" who lived on reserve but accepted taxation, lived off reserve, or were war veterans had been allowed the federal franchise. Provincially, "Indians" were without the franchise in New Brunswick and Prince Edward Island until 1963, and in Quebec until 1969.

64 Ellen Fairclough quoted in Bartlett, "Citizens Minus," 191–2.

65 Hall, *The American Empire*, 256.

66 Ibid., 255, 496.

67 Austin, *Fear of a Black Nation*, 45.

68 The English translation of the title was *The White Niggers of America*.

69 Austin, *Fear of a Black Nation*, 67.

70 Walker, *Race on Trial*, 4.

71 Goldberg, *The Threat of Race*, 4, 8.

72 Austin, *Fear of a Black Nation,* 48.

73 Sealy, "Canadianizing Blackness: Resisting the Political," 97–8.

74 Barsh, "Aboriginal Peoples and Canada's Conscience," 272.

75 Adams, "The Indians: An Abandoned and Dispossessed People."

76 Meeting of the Mayor's Indian Committee, 28 January 1966, RG-76-3-0, Ontario Human Rights Commission fonds, AO, Toronto, Ontario.

77 Ibid., 1.

78 Meeting of the Mayor's Indian Committee, 8 July 1966, 2, RG 76-3-0, Ontario Human Rights Commission fonds, AO, Toronto, Ontario.

79 Ibid., 3.

80 Sokol, *There Goes My Everything*, 85.

81 See for example, Coates, *A Global History of Indigenous Peoples*, 246.

82 Spence, "Cultural Globalization and the US Civil Rights Movement," 568.

83 Alexandra Paul, "New Era of First Nations Civil Rights Ushered In 50 Years Ago in Kenora," *Winnipeg Free Press*, 21 November 2015, http://www.winnipegfreepress.com/local/the-riots-that-werent-352513511.html.

CHAPTER TWO

1 Frederick Kelly, "Address to the Lakehead University Students," 24 February 1966, 1.

2 Ibid.

3 Rifkin, "The Transatlantic Indian Problem," 337.

4 Kelly, "Address," 2.

5 Ibid., 3.

6 Ibid., 5.

7 "Introduction," in *Resolving Conflicts: A Cross Cultural Approach*. Kenora, Ontario, 10 February–14 May 1967: 3.

8   Logan McCallum, *Indigenous Women, Work, and History, 1940–1980*, 72–3.

9   Meren, "'Commend Me the Yak,'" 346.

10 Bradley, "Decolonization, the Global South, and the Cold War, 1919–1962," 464.

11 Prashad, *The Darker Nations*, 6–11.

12 "JFK Address at UN General Assembly, 25 September 1961," Historic Speeches, John F. Kennedy Presidential Library and Museum, https://www.jfklibrary.org/Asset-Viewer/DOPIN64xJUGRKgdHJ9NfgQ.aspx.

13 Rist, *The History of Development*, 90.

14 Rostow, *The Stages of Economic Growth*.

15 Meren, *Commend Me the Yak*; Webster, "Foreign Policy, Diplomacy, and Decolonization," 166–7.

16 Webster, "Foreign Policy, Diplomacy, and Decolonization."

17 Hall, "The West and the Rest," 277.

18 Goldstein, "On the Internal Border," 26, 37–8.

19 Ibid., 27.

20 Ibid., 32.

21 Kelly, *Freedom Dreams*, 60–110; for the Latin American use of the "internal colony" thesis in the United States, see Ramón A. Gutiérrez, "Internal Colonialism," 281–95.

22 Miller, *Skyscrapers Hide the Heavens*, 223.

23 Lloyd, *Community Development in Canada*, 22.

24 "Social Justice for Canada's Indians," *Human Relations* 5.10 (December 1964): 1.

25 Meren, "'Commend Me the Yak,'" 350.

26 Ibid., 348.

27 Langford, "Jean Lagassé, Community Development, and the 'Indian and Métis Problem' in Manitoba in the 1950s and 1960s," 353.

28 Dyck and Lux, "Population Control in the 'Global North?'" 483.

29 Ibid., 483–4.

30 Young, *Third World in the First*, xii.

31 Patterson, *The Canadian Indian*.

32 Weaver, *Making Canadian Indian Policy*, 15.

33 Langford, "Jean Lagassé," 352.

34 Shewell, "'What Makes the Indian Tick?'" 137.

35 Ibid., 136.

36 Hawthorn, *A Survey of the Contemporary Indians of Canada: A Report on Economic, Political, Educational Needs and Policies.*

37 Shewell, "'Bitterness behind Every Smiling Face.'"

38 Langford, "Jean Lagassé," 356–8.

39 Goldstein, "On the Internal Border," 32.

40 Ibid., 33.

41 D'Arcy McNickle, "Definition of a Problem," in *Resolving Conflicts: A Cross Cultural Approach*. Kenora, Ontario, 10 February–14 May 1967: 9–10.

42 McNickle, "Definition of a Problem," 6–15. See also Parker, *Singing an Indian Song*; Cobb, "Talking the Language of the Larger World."

43 James Howard, "Indian Cultures: Their History and Contributions," in *Resolving Conflicts: A Cross Cultural Approach*, Kenora, Ontario, 10 February–14 May 1967: 17.

44 Howard, "Indian Cultures," 24.

45 Matthews, "Canada and Anglophone Africa," 105.

46 Lackenbrauer and Cooper, "The Achilles Heel of Canadian International Citizenship," 102. See also Lackenbrauer, *Battle Grounds*.

47 Mrs A.M. Hewitt, "Justice for the Eskimos!" *Maclean's*, 6 August 1966, 42.

48 Eleanor D. Ross, "Fellow Citizens," *Toronto Telegram*, 27 November 1965, 6.

49 E. Frank Litt, "Aid Foreigners? Why Not Indians?" *Toronto Star*, 9 September 1966, 6; E. Frank Litt, "Indian Problem," *Globe and Mail*, 9 September 1966, 6.

50 In 1965, at the urging of the US and Britain, Canada and Tanzania agreed to what Matthews called Canada's "most ambitious program of military assistance"; see Matthews, "Canada and Anglophone Africa," 110.

51 R. Keith Earl, "Indians First," *Toronto Telegram*, 30 November1965, 6.

52 Howard, "Indian Cultures: Their History and Contributions," 30.

53 Ibid., 25.

54 John Steinbring, "Ojibwa Culture: The Modern Situation and Problems," in *Resolving Conflicts: A Cross Cultural Approach*. Kenora, Ontario, 10 February–14 May 1967: 48, 51.

55 Steinbring, "Ojibwa Culture," 53.

56 Ibid., 67–8.

57 Ibid., 61.

58 Ibid., 70.

59 Dr Joan F. de Pena, "Contributions of Anthropology and Other Social Sciences in Method and Theory to Such Problems: Pertinent Concepts of Anthropology," in *Resolving Conflicts: A Cross Cultural Approach.* Kenora, Ontario, 10 February–14 May 1967, 112.

60 Ibid., 112.

61 E.S. Rogers, "Ojibwa Culture: The Traditional Culture History," in *Resolving Conflicts: A Cross Cultural Approach.* Kenora, Ontario, 10 February–14 May 1967, 40; J. Steinbring, "Ojibwa Culture," 65.

62 Nancy Oestreich-Lurie, "The Indian Moves to an Urban Setting," in *Resolving Conflicts: A Cross Cultural Approach.* Kenora, Ontario, 10 February–14 May 1967, 77.

63 Oestreich-Lurie, "The Indian Moves to an Urban Setting," 74.

64 Pickering, "Decolonizing Time Regimes," 88–9.

65 Ibid., 86.

66 Ibid., 87.

67 Deloria, "Counterculture Indians and the New Age," 161.

68 A.D. Asimi, "The Urban Setting," in *Resolving Conflicts: A Cross Cultural Approach*, Kenora, Ontario, 10 February–14 May 1967, 92.

69 Cole, *Ruth Landes*, 242.

70 In *The Ojibwa Woman*, Landes relied heavily on stories by Maggie Wilson, who lived in Manitou Falls and who Landes paid. Landes's biographer, Sally Cole, met the family of Maggie Wilson in August 1995 in an attempt to learn more about responses to Landes's book. Wilson's granddaughter told Cole that the stories were "gossip" and "should not have been written down." Wilson's great-granddaughter, who was a teacher in 1995, had similar feelings, even telling Cole that she removed the book from shelves when it arrived in Manitou Falls. For her part, Cole tried to convince the two women that Landes's research was feminist and that the difficulties of women in the 1930s were spoken through her work. It does not appear as though either of them was moved by the argument. Cole, *Ruth Landes*, 66–9. One source of controversy and subsequent anger over Landes's book was the anthropologist's failure to maintain the confidentiality of those negatively portrayed in Wilson's stories. See Lovisek, Holzkamm, and Waisburg, "Fatal Errors."

71 *The Ojibwa Woman*, Landes's most controversial Anishinaabe-focused research, was reprinted in 1971. *Ojibwa Religion and the Midéwiwin* was

written in the 1930s but published in 1968, while *Ojibwa Sociology* was already in publication when Landes spoke in Kenora in 1967. See Cole, *Ruth Landes*, 67.

72 Ruth Landes, "Techniques of Dealing with Cross-Cultural Problems," in *Resolving Conflicts: A Cross-Cultural Approach*. Kenora, Ontario, 10 February–14 May 1967, 149.

73 Steinbring, "Ojibwa Culture" 62.

74 Landes, "Techniques of Dealing with Cross-Cultural Problems," 155–6.

CHAPTER THREE

1 Canada, Robert Thompson, Question in the House of Commons, 17 October 1967, *House of Commons Debates*, Second Session – Twenty Seventh Parliament, vol. 3 (1967): 3170; "Cuba Beams Propaganda to Quebec," *Montreal Star*, 18 October 1967, 1; "Seditious Cuban Broadcasts Charged," *Montreal Gazette*, 18 October 1967, 1; Lewis Seale, "SC Charge: Cubans Inciting Quebec," *Globe and Mail*, 18 October 1967, 1; Stan Reid, "Cuban Radio 'Subversion' Amplified," *Edmonton Journal*, 19 October 1967, 14; Bob Cohen, "Subversion Charge Laid," *Ottawa Citizen*, 18 October 1967, 56.

2 Robert Thompson, Question in House of Commons, 22 November 1967, *House of Commons Debates*, Second Session – Twenty Seventh Parliament, vol., 3 (1967), 4565.

3 "Radio Havana Urging Revolts?" *Winnipeg Free Press*, 18 October 1967, 1.

4 As historian Cynthia Wright notes, "Many working-class people in Canada in this era still did not own televisions and it was Cuban radio, rather than North American media, that formed their sense of the Revolution." Wright, "Between Nation and Empire: The Fair Play for Cuba Committee and the Making of Canada-Cuba Solidarity in the Early 1960s," 100.

5 Wayne Edmonstone, "Cubans *Are* Interested in Quebec Separatists," *Toronto Star*, 14 November 1967, 7.

6 Hazlitt, "Is Cuban Radio Inciting Separatists?" 4.

7 "Vive Red Deer, Alberta, Libre!" *Montreal Star*, 19 October 1967, 8.

8 Gary Lautens, "Fidel! Our Indians Are Pretty with It – I Mean, Those Beads," *Toronto Star*, 1 November 1967, 4.

9 "New Empires," *Winnipeg Free Press*, 19 October 1967, 33.

10   Kersey, "The Havana Connection," 491; Kersey, *An Assumption of Sovereignty*, 182.

11   Quoted in Kersey, "The Havana Connection," 499; Buffalo Tiger and Kersey, *Buffalo Tiger*, 143.

12   Kersey, "The Havana Connection," 502.

13   Wallace "Mad Bear" Anderson, quoted in Steiner, *The New Indians*, 281, and in Hall, *The American Empire and the Fourth World*, 260. Steiner and Hall each mark the date of the celebrations as July 1958, which is incorrect. The date is correctly noted as July 1959 in Buffalo Tiger and Kersey Jr, *Buffalo Tiger*, 143.

14   Dunbar-Ortiz quoted in Chris Dixon, "The Opposite of Truth Is Forgetting: An Interview with Roxanne Dunbar-Ortiz," 50.

15   Lopez quoted in "No Evidence Yet for Claim Cuba Radios Subversion Here," *Montreal Gazette*, 21 October 1967, 4.

16   Hazlitt, "Is Cuban Radio Inciting Separatists?" 4; Bob Cohen, "Subversion Charge Laid," *Ottawa Citizen*, 18 October 1967, 57; "'Revolt' Charge Denied," *Winnipeg Free Press*, 18 October 1967, 8; Bob Cohen, "Paul Martin Accepts Denial of Broadcasts," *Ottawa Citizen*, 21 October 1967, 13. The allegations upset one reader enough that she wrote a letter stating she could not understand Thompson's "tirade." She was a regular listener to Radio Havana, and found that "their news contains much more detailed coverage of international affairs" than any media source in Canada. See Regina Modlich, "Cuban Radio Fine," *Toronto Star*, 20 November 1967, 6.

17   Joyce Fairbairn, "Cuba Denies Charge," *Winnipeg Free Press*, 20 October 1967, 23; Paul Martin, Response to the House of Commons, 19 October 1967, *House of Commons Debates*, Second Session – Twenty Seventh Parliament, vol. 3 (1967), 3264.

18   Fairbairn, "Cuba Denies Charge," 23; Bob Cohen, "Paul Martin Accepts Denial of Broadcasts," *Ottawa Citizen*, 21 October 1967, 13.

19   "On & Off the Record," *The Gazette*, 25 July 1967, 4.

20   Mills, *The Empire Within*, 38.

21   Griffith, "One Little, Two Little, Three Canadians," 172.

22   Dyck and Lux, "Population Control in the 'Global North'?" 505.

23   Ibid., 505–6.

24   Ibid., 506.

25 de Costa, "Snakes That Are Rainbow," 234.

26 Winant, *The World Is a Ghetto*, 2

27 de Rosa, "Studio One: Of Storytellers and Stories," 329.

28 Marchessault, "Reflections of the Dispossessed," 131–46.

29 Willie Dunn, "The Ballad of Crowfoot," viewable online at http://www.nfb. ca/film/ballad_of_crowfoot.

30 "Introduction: Forty Years Later … A Space for Challenge for Change/ Société nouvelle," 11.

31 Deloria, "Counterculture Indians and the New Age," 166.

32 Ibid., 164, 166.

33 Ellen Simmons, "A Campaign to Name Riel the Father of a Province," *Globe and Mail*, 15 March 1969, 8.

34 See, for example, "History's Pendulum Swings towards a Rebel," *Globe and Mail*, 6 September 1969, 8; "Bernard Turgeon Lives Louis Riel," *Toronto Star* 28 June 1969, 43; James Montagnes, "Our Orange 6 Cent Stamp Will Change to Black for Progress," *Toronto Star*, 29 November 1969, 16.

35 Miller, "From Riel to Métis," 41.

36 Owram, "The Myth of Louis Riel," 328; J.R. Miller makes almost the same observation, arguing that "in the 1960s Riel was adopted and patronized by white, middle-class student radicals who found him an acceptable substitute for the Cuban Revolution's Che Guevara." See Miller, *Skyscrapers Hide the Heavens*, 251. Decades later, the association between the two remains controversial, continuing to shape the historical memory of Riel. A recent entry in a Manitoba guidebook introduces Riel to the province's new visitors as a man of many identities, most recently as a "Métis Che Guevara." The *Encyclopedia of Saskatchewan* has as the introduction for an entry on Gabriel Dumont: "the name conjures up a host of images," including "the 19th-century Che Guevara passionately concerned with his people's self-governance." There are those who see the association negatively. Commentators who define Guevara as a murderer and a tyrant mobilize the image as a way to shape the memory of Riel as a traitor who twice took up arms against Canada. The association concerned commentator Cherie Dimaline. While not diminishing Riel's important contributions to Métis rights, she questions the meaning of his recent trendiness, a branding not unlike that of Che – though without the global reach, a "Che light," perhaps.

The branding represents a simplification, a failure to understand the complexities of Riel's life. For Dimaline, the Métis need "to stay true to Riel's memory, to pass down his stories and beliefs to their children and grandchildren around fires and in ceremonies. And we don't need a t-shirt to do that," see Cherie Dimaline, "Che Riel," *Métis Voyageur* (November/December 2004), 19.

37 Coulter, *The Crime of Louis Riel.*
38 "Spirit of Geronimo Inspires Red Power Growth," *Akwesasne Notes* 1, no. 7 (July 1969), 17.
39 "Perspective," *Globe and Mail*, 21 July 1969: 6; "Pardon for Riel Sought," *Winnipeg Free Press*, 9 July 1969, 24.
40 "Political 'Foofaraw' Unwanted," *Winnipeg Free Press*, 19 July 1969; Garth Stouffer, "Keystone Notebook: No Pardon for Riel," *Brandon Sun*, 6 November 1970, 2.
41 Stouffer, "Keystone Notebook"; George Dunsford, "Letter to Editor," *Globe and Mail*, 27 December 1970, 7.
42 "Professor Reveals 'Native Power' Drive: Indians Not Agitated by Cuba – Métis Leader," *Toronto Star*, 2 November 1967, 37.
43 "Commentary: George Manuel Looks at New Zealand," *The Indian News* (March 1971), 5.
44 McFarlane, *Brotherhood to Nationhood*, 162.
45 Ibid.
46 Ibid., 163–5.
47 Kelley, *Freedom Dreams*, 68.
48 Clem Chartier, "China through a Native Perspective," *New Breed* (October 1975), 5.
49 Ray Bobb, "Red China: Visit," *Native Peoples Struggle* (July 1975), 4.
50 Dunbar-Ortiz, *Blood on the Border*, 33.
51 "Maoris Get the Same," *Akwesasne Notes*, "Early Spring" 1975, 45.
52 "More News from Maori-land," *Akwesasne Notes*, "Early Spring" 1975, 47.
53 George-Kanentiio, *Iroquois on Fire*, 73.
54 Andrew G. Paschal, "Natural Allies: Afro-Americans, Indians Once Fought Side-by-Side," *Akwesasne Notes*, 1:8, 1969, 39.
55 Carmichael and Hamilton, *Black Power*, 6.
56 Baldwin, "In the Shadow of the Gun," 75.

57   Rap Brown, "H. Rap Brown, Free Huey Rally," sound recording, KPFA
     Berkeley, 2 February 1968.

58   Stokely Carmichael, "Stokely Carmichael, Free Huey Rally," sound record-
     ing, KPFA Berkeley, 2 February 1968.

59   Stokely Carmichael quoted in Austin, "All Roads Lead to Montreal," 525, and
     in Mills, *The Empire Within*, 103.

60   J.G. Diefenbaker, Question in the House of Commons, 28 October 1968,
     House of Commons Debates (first session – twenty-eighth parliament, vol 2.,
     1968): 2086.

61   Ibid.

62   Kostash, *Long Way from Home*, 164–5; Nielsen, "The Tragedy of Fred Hamp-
     ton," 8–9; Rae Flood, "A Black Panther in the Great White North," 23, 31–2;
     Palmer, *Canada's 1960s*, 400.

63   LaRocque, *When the Other Is Me*, 23.

64   Palmer, *Canada's 1960s*, 370, 405–07.

65   Maracle, *Bobbi Lee*, 135, 161.

66   Ibid.

67   Maracle, "Red Power Legacies and Lives," 360.

68   Ibid., 363.

69   Simmons, "In Tribute to Howard Adams," 7.

70   Tony Burman, "Métis Leader Forecasts Ugly Scene," *Montreal Star*, 2 July 2,
     1970, reprinted in *Akwesasne Notes* 2:5 (Sept 1970): 39.

71   Adams, *Prison of Grass*, 152; see also the autobiography, Adams, *Howard
     Adams*.

72   Adams, *Prison of Grass*, 11.

73   Ibid., 123.

74   Ibid., 16.

75   Ibid., 139.

76   Ibid., 167.

77   Said, "Traveling Theory Reconsidered," 438.

78   Adams, *Prison of Grass*, 167.

79   Ibid., 166.

80   Ibid., 167.

81   Sivanandan, "Jan Carew, Renaissance Man," and David Austin, "The Gentle
     Revolutionary: Jan Carew at 90."

82   AAPA News Letter, Box 44, OHRC RG 76-3-0-787, AO, Toronto, Ontario.

83 R. Watt, "Bigoted Carew," *Toronto Star*, 15 March 1968, 6.

84 Jan Carew, interview with the author, November 2007.

85 "Red Power in Canada," *Uhuru*, 26 September 1969, 3.

86 T.E. Berry, "The Political System and Minority Groups," *Contrast*, 31 March 1969, 14.

87 Gail Bruyere, "I Am an Indian," *Contrast*, June 1969.

88 "Indians, Black Power Form Alliance," *Toronto Star*, 22 February 1969, 3; Roy Dawkins, "Anniversary of the Assassination: U.S. Black Leader Malcolm X," *Contrast*, March 1969, 7.

89 "Negro, Indian, Assail Toronto's Uncle Toms," *Globe and Mail*, 22 February 1969, 2

90 Emory Douglas, the Black Panther Party's "Minister of Culture," and a person responsible for the unique style of Panther propaganda.

91 "Kathleen Cleaver Leads Rally," *Contrast*, 10 May 1969, 1, 4.

92 Bowlles, *The Indian: Assimilation, Integration or Separation?* 24–6.

93 Adams, *Tortured People*, 86.

94 "Violence, Oppression, and Action," *Take 30*, CBC television, 2 June 1969.

CHAPTER FOUR

1 Rapp, "The Doris Duke American Indian Oral History Program," 11.

2 According to Rapp, the program launched in 1966 at several universities across the United States, apparently as a form of tax shelter. Rapp suggests that the program came into fruition after a plan for Duke to buy monumental antiquities from Egypt fell through after Egyptian President Gamal Abdel Nasser demanded more money be paid than agreed upon. Duke was outraged, withdrew her offer, but still needed to find a tax shelter before 31 December 1966, so the Doris Duke American Indian Oral History program was established. Ibid., 18.

3 Ibid.," 20.

4 Ruffo, *Norval Morrisseau*, 166–8.

5 Lynn's Fieldnotes (Copy) – Daily Acct – 1973, "March 7, 1973." Doris Duke Indian Oral History Program, 1908–1995, Field Worker Reports: Lynn Kauffman, 1967–1973, Series No: 15/2/32 Box 29, University of Illinois-Champaign Archives: Liberal Arts and Sciences, Champaign, Illinois.

6 Ibid.

7 Lynn's Field Notes (Copy) – Daily Acct – 1973, "February 23, 1973."

8 Lynn's Field Notes (Copy) – Daily Acct – 1973, "February 24, 1973."

9 Lynn's Field Notes (Copy) – Daily Acct – 1973, "March 2, 1973."

10 Lynn's Field Notes (Copy) – Daily Acct – 1973, "February 25, 1973."

11 "Copy of Letter-Kenora Metis and Non-Status Indian Housing Assoc, Files," 28 December 1971, Violent Death Committee, RG 47-138, AO, Toronto.

12 Logan McCallum and Perry, *Structures of Indifference*, 14.

13 Razack, *Dying from Improvement*, 4.

14 Wolfe, *Settler-Colonialism and the Transformation of Anthropology.*

15 Logan McCallum and Perry, *Structures of Indifference*, 6

16 "Letter to Minister of Natural Resources, Leo Bernier from W. Errington, and R.F. Munford, October 20th, 1972." Violent Death Committee, RG 47-138, AO, Toronto.

17 Violent Death Committee, RG 47-138, AO, Toronto.

18 Talaga, *Seven Fallen Feathers*, 82–5.

19 John Yaremko, Solicitor General, to Rory McMillan, Chairman, Concerned Citizens' Committee, 29 June 1973, RG 33; 13.5; b223573, AO, Toronto.

20 Violent Death Committee, 19 October 1972, RG 47-13, AO, Toronto.

21 Razack, *Dying from Improvement*, 114.

22 Violent Death Committee, 19 October 1972, RG 47-13, AO, Toronto.

23 Shkilnyk, *A Poison Stronger than Love*, 20.

24 Ibid., 11–13.

25 Ibid., 30.

26 SS 86–88 of the 1876 Indian Act explicitly stated that one had to demonstrate the "character" of sobriety to be considered eligible for enfranchisement.

27 Thompson and Genosko, *Punched Drunk*, 135–6.

28 Ibid., 185.

29 Band Council Resolution, 4 June 1973, RG 33, 5G.21; b223702, AO, Toronto.

30 Letter, Roy McDonald to John Reid, 13 June 1973, RG 33, 5G.21; b223702, AO, Toronto.

31 Leo Bernier to Jean Chrétien, 9 July 1973, RG 33, 5G.21; b223702, AO, Toronto.

32 Islington Band Council, letter, Roy McDonald and Larry Boyd to Solicitor General John Yaremko, 16 August 1973, RG 33, 5G.21; b223702, AO, Toronto.

33 Dahn D. Higley to R.M. Warren, 22 August 1973, Minister of the Solicitor General, memorandum RG 33, 5G.21; b223702, AO, Toronto.

34 Elmer Bell to R.M. Warren, 29 August 1973, RG 33, 5G.21; b223702, AO, Toronto.

35 H.H. Graham to R.M. Warren, 28 August 1973, RG 33, 5G.21; b223702, AO, Toronto.

36 Jean Chrétien to Leo Bernier, 5 September 1973, RG 33, 5G.21; b223702, AO, Toronto.

37 R.M. Warren to Roy McDonald, 6 September 1973, RG 33, 5G.21; b223702, AO, Toronto.

38 R.M. Warren to A.H. Bird, 11 September 1973, RG 33, 5G.21; b223702, AO, Toronto.

39 Det. Sgt. M. Kulmatycki for Insp. W. Parfitt to Assist. Commissioner Field Division, Re: Suspected Arson – Islington Indian Reserve, White Dog, Ontario, District of Kenora, 29 Sept. 73, RG 33, 5G.21; b223702, AO, Toronto; memo, Frank L. Wilson to R.M. Warren, re: Incendiary Fires at the White-dog Indian Reserve, District of Kenora, 12 October 1973, RG 33, 5G.21; b223702, AO, Toronto.

40 Dubinsky, *Improper Advances*, 17.

41 Frank Wilson to R.M. Warren, 4 October 1973, RG 33, 5G.21; b223702, AO, Toronto.

42 Frank Wilson to R.M. Warren, 25 September 1973, RG 33, 5G.21; b223702, AO, Toronto.

43 Shkilnyk, *A Poison Stronger than Love*, 179.

44 Leo Bernier quoted in Robert Reguly, "Mercury or No Mercury, the Tourists Are Eating the Fish," *Toronto Star*, 8 June 1973, 9.

45 Shkilnyk, *A Poison Stronger than Love*, 11.

46 Ibid., 19.

47 Peter Kelly would publicly go by the name Tobasonakwut Kaagagewanak-web Peter Kinew (Kelly) later in life. I use Peter Kelly in this book because that is how he often identified himself publicly and in official Treaty #3 communications from 1972–75 when he was Grand Chief of Grand Council Treaty #3.

48 Violent Death Committee, 13 November 1972, RG 47-13, AO, Toronto.

49 Ministry of the Solicitor General, G. Coffin to R.M. Warren, "Violent Deaths Committee – Kenora," 21 September 1973. RG 33; 13.5; b223573, AO, Toronto.

50 Ministry of the Solicitor General, F.L. Wilson to R.M. Warren, "Violent

Deaths Committee – Kenora," 18 October 1973, RG 33; 13.5; b223573 AO, Toronto.

51 Ministry of the Solicitor General, R.M. Warren to F.L. Wilson, "Violent Deaths Committee – Kenora," 9 October 1973, RG 33; 13.5; b223573 AO, Toronto.

52 Violent Death Committee, F.D. Herman to W. Welldon, "Confidential," 21 August 1973, RG 47-138, AO, Toronto.

53 Violent Death Committee, W. Welldon to D.R. Martyn, "Re: Violent Death Committee," 6 September 1973, RG 47-138, AO, Toronto.

54 "Situation of Indian Students in Treaty #3 – Spring 1972," *Treaty #3 Council Fire "Special Education Issue*, June 1972, 2.

55 Cecilia Jeffrey Indian Residential School operated at Round Lake from 1929 until 1976. After it was shut down, the building was torn down and the land was eventually returned to Grand Council of Treaty #3. See Talaga, *Seven Fallen Feathers*, 64–5.

56 Lynn's Field Notes (Copy) – Daily Acct – 1973, "March 8, 1973."

57 Agnes Mills, "National Native Women's Conference, Saskatoon 22–24 March, Report," *Council Fire* (undated copy).

58 Dyck and Lux, "Population Control in the 'Global North?'" 488.

59 Luby, "From Milk-Medicine to Public (Re)Education Programs," 378.

60 Ibid, 379.

61 Ibid, 379; *Council Fire*, May 1973 (a copy of this issue was included in the Lynn Kauffman collection as well).

62 D'Arcus, "Protest, Scale, and Publicity," 719.

63 While some mainstream Indigenous publications distanced from AIM's confrontational methods, "a wave of Native support came from all across the U.S. and Canada," see Price, *Native Studies*, 228.

64 "Could It Happen Here?" *Winnipeg Free Press*, 15 March 1973.

65 Wally Dennison, "Indians Believed Heading for Wounded Knee," *Winnipeg Free Press*, 16 March 1973, 1, 5; "Wounded Knee Talks Will Resume: Canadian Indians Head for Area," *The Globe and Mail*, 16 March 1973, 10.

66 Tim Haverluck, "Dusk in Wounded Knee," *Winnipeg Free Press* 20 March 1973, 14.

67 "Memorandum to: Mr. R.M. Warren, Deputy Solicitor General, Re: Demonstration at Pigeon River, Canada and United States Border Crossing," 13 March 1973, Ontario Provincial Police, RG 33; 58.17; 6223701, AO Toronto.

68 Simpson, *Mohawk Interruptus*, 133.

69 Ibid., 115.

70 "Memorandum to: Mr. R.M. Warren, Deputy Solicitor General, Re: Demonstration at Pigeon River."

71 Memo to R.M. Warren, March 5, 1973; memo to R.M. Warren, 13 March 1973, Ontario Provincial Police, RG 33; 58-17-b223701, AO, Toronto.

72 Lynn's Field Notes (Copy) – Daily Acct – 1973, "March 15, 1973."

73 Lynn's Field Notes (Copy) – Daily Acct – 1973, "February 23, 1973."

74 "Memorandum To: Mr. R.M. Warren, Deputy Solicitor General, Re: Possible Civil Unrest Involving Indians – Kenora, March 20, 1973, File 304 Indian Policing, RG 33; 59.2; b223702, AO, Toronto. This was one of Bird's first acts as deputy commissioner, as he had only been promoted to the position on the day the CBC broadcasted the controversial interview. See "OPP Postings Announced by Yaremko," *The Globe and Mail*, 15 March 1973, 5.

75 "Memorandum To: Attn: Assistant Commissioner Field Division, Re: Possible Civil Unrest Involving Indians – Kenora, March 15, 1973." File 304 Indian Policing, RG 33; 59.2; b223702, AO, Toronto.

76 Ojibway Warrior Society, "Statement to Indian Affairs," 27 November 1973; Ojibway Warrior Society, "Statement to the Press," 27 November 1973; Don Colborne Private Papers, Thunder Bay, Ontario.

77 "Memorandum To: Mr C.E. Brannan, Deputy Solicitor General, RE: Indian Incident - November 29, 1973" File 304-11, RG 33; 58.17; 6223701, AO Toronto.

CHAPTER FIVE

1 Ojibway Nation Conference, "Promotional Poster," July 1974, Don Colborne Private Papers, Thunder Bay, Ontario.

2 *Ojibway Warrior Society in Occupied Anicinabe Park*, 14–15.

3 Ramos, "Divergent Paths," 53.

4 Coates, *A Global History of Indigenous Peoples*, 239.

5 Grand Council Treaty #3 Press release, 18 June 1974, Don Colborne Private Papers, Thunder Bay, Ontario.

6 Ojibway Warrior Society, Press Release, no date, Don Colborne Private Papers, Thunder Bay, Ontario.

7 Burton, *Journal of a Country Lawyer*, 199.

8 Peter Kelly, "Correspondence to Jim Davidson," 16 July 1974, Don Colborne Private Papers, Thunder Bay, Ontario.

9   Ojibway Nation Conference, "Promotional Poster."

10 Ron Seymour to Mayor Jim Davidson and Don Sweeney, Secretary Chamber of Commerce, "Ojibway Nation Conference Security," 17 July 1974, Don Colborne Private Papers, Thunder Bay, Ontario.; Louie Cameron to Peter Hare, District Supervisor, Department of Indian Affairs, 17 July 1974, Don Colborne Private Papers, Thunder Bay, Ontario.

11 "Ojibway Conference Gets under Way in Kenora," *Chronicle Journal* (Thunder Bay) 20 July 1974, 1.

12 Grand Council Treaty No. 3, "Theme of Conference" 18 June 1974. Don Colborne Private Papers, Thunder Bay, Ontario.

13 See Burton, *Journal of a Country Lawyer*, 215–17.

14 Dennis Banks quoted in, April Holland, "Native People Urged to Work Together," *Kenora Daily Miner and News* 22 July 1974, 1.

15 "Conference Orderly on the Weekend," *Kenora Daily Miner and News*, 22 July 1974, 14.

16 David Lee, "Armed Indians Seize Kenora Park, List Demands" *Winnipeg Free Press*, 23 July 1974, 1.

17 "Research Notes," Don Colborne Private Papers, Thunder Bay, Ontario.

18 *Ojibway Warriors Society in Occupied Anicinabe Park, Kenora, Ontario, August 1974*, 9.

19 Louis Cameron interviewed in Burke, *Paper Tomahawks*, 378–96.

20 The summer of 1974 in Northwestern Ontario was particularly dry. At the time of the occupation, forest fires were threatening a number of small communities including Vermillion Bay and Red Lake. See Atkins, "The River, the City, and the Yellow Line," 115–17.

21 Journalists often quoted Harvey Major when the media reported threats of violence by the ows. See "Armed Vigilantes Warned by Indians," *Montreal Gazette*, 26 July 1974, 16; "Indians Holding Park as Chiefs Meet," *Montreal Gazette*, July 25, 1975, 8; Ken Nelson, "Indian Talks Resume," *Kenora Daily Miner and News*, 26 July 1974, 1.

22 Hamilton, Ont. Resident, "Park Issue Not Important," *Kenora Daily Miner and News*, 1 August 1974, 4. In fact, the town police did threaten to arrest the Warriors for, among other things, breach of fire regulations; see "Status of Park Could Lead to Changes," *Kenora Daily Miner and News*, 24 July 1974, 1.

23 Lee, "Kill or Be Killed."

24 *Akwesasne Notes* (Early Summer 1974), 21; "Indian Issue Talks Underway,"
    Kenora Daily Miner and News, 25 July 1974, 1.

25 Clarence Dusang, "Sessions Held over Protest," *Kenora Daily Miner and
    News*, July 24, 1974, 1; David Lee, "Little Reaction to Takeover; Park Indians
    More Militant," *Winnipeg Free Press*, 24 July 1974, 1.

26 Pat Brennan, "'Let Indians Have the Park,' Kenora Mayor Opposes Force,"
    Toronto Star, 24 July 1974, 2.

27 "Indians Issue Talks Underway," 1.

28 Negotiating Committee of the Ojibway Warrior Society, "Meeting with
    Town Council, DIA and Provincial Representatives at the Fellowship Cen-
    tre," 24 July 1974, 3, Don Colborne Private Papers, Thunder Bay, Ontario.

29 Negotiating Committee of the Ojibway Warrior Society, "Meeting with
    Town Council, DIA and Provincial Representatives at the Fellowship
    Centre," 4.

30 "Armed Powwow," *Montreal Gazette*, 25 July 1974, 1.

31 *Winnipeg Free Press*, 24 July 1974, 21.

32 Conrad Hodinott, "Reporter Describes Indian Occupation," *Kenora Daily
    Miner and News*, 31 July 1974, 8.

33 Derik Hodgson, "Revolutionary Rhetoric, Indian Phrases Mix Tom-toms
    and Tough Talk at Kenora Campsite," *The Globe and Mail*, 6 August 1974, 2.

34 Anderson and Robertson, "The 'Bended Elbow' News, Kenora 1974," 428.

35 "An Unnecessary Occupation," *The Chronicle Journal*, 16 August 1974, 4.

36 Anderson and Robertson, "The 'Bended Elbow' News, Kenora 1974."

37 *Kenora Daily Miner and News*, 2 August 1974, 4.

38 Judy Parkes, "Anicinabe Park Group Example of Thrill Seekers," *Kenora
    Daily Miner and News*, 26 July 1974, 4; Pat Malashewski, "We Don't Owe
    Indians Anything," *Kenora Daily Miner and News*, 1 August 1974, 4; Pat
    Malashewski, "Indians," *Winnipeg Free Press*, August 3, 1974, 7; Hamilton,
    Ont. Resident,' "Park Issue Not Important," 4; M. Treleavan, "Taxpayers
    Shouldn't Support Indians," *Kenora Daily Miner and News*, 29 August
    1974, 4.

39 "Natives Don't Approve of Occupation" *Kenora Daily Miner and News*,
    26 July 1974, 11. Two days earlier the newspaper had claimed that the silence
    from Indigenous organizations was evidence that "the majority of Indian
    people in the Kenora area do not condone the actions of the Ojibwa

Warriors Society." See "Status of Park Could Change" *Kenora Daily Miner and News*, 24 July 1974, 1

40 Price, *Native Studies* 228; Len O. Hakenson, Director, Addiction Research Foundation, "Pow-wow Group Not Associated with Warriors," *Kenora Daily Miner and News*, 31 July 1974: 9; John Ward, "Possibility of Violence," *The Chronicle-Journal* (Thunder Bay), 2 August 1974, 3; "Union Ont. Indians Opposes Militancy," *The Chronicle-Journal* (Thunder Bay), 14 August 1974, 1.

41 See "Toronto Demonstrators Support Kenora Indians," *The Chronicle-Journal* (Thunder Bay, Ontario), 27 July 1974, 11; a copy of Bellecourt's speech can be found in "Kenora Uprising-August 1974," Box 3, File 50, CASNP, Trent University Archives, Peterborough, Ontario.

42 Francis, *The Imaginary Indian*, 167; Churchill, *The Ward Churchill Reader*, 194–8.

43 "Trouble at Anicinabe," *The Chronicle-Journal*, 25 July 1974, 4.

44 Les Whittington, "Ojibway Nation Rebelled against Injustices Steeped in Time," *The Gazette*, 20 August 1974, 7.

45 John Gallagher and Cy Gonick, "The Occupation of Anicinabe Park," *Canadian Dimension* 10, no. 5 (1974), 22, 35.

46 Wayne Edmonstone, "A Cure for Which There Is No Disease," *Canadian Dimension*, 10, no. 5 (1974), 33. Edmonstone originally wrote his comments for the *Toronto Sun*; they were reprinted in *Canadian Dimension*'s feature on Anicinabe Park.

47 Louis Cameron to Jim Davidson, "Request to Use Anicinabe Park for the Ojibway Nation Conference – July 19–22, 1974," 16 July 1974. Don Colborne Private Papers, Thunder Bay, Ontario.

48 Coulthard, *Red Skin, White Masks*, 13.

49 Ibid., 5.

50 Ibid., 6.

51 Native Study Group, "Land Is the Basis of a Nation," *Akwesasne Notes* (Late Summer, 1975), 46.

52 *Ojibway Warriors Society in Occupied Anicinabe Park*, 1.

53 Ibid., 2, 3.

54 *Native Peoples Struggle: An Organ of the Toronto Warrior Society* 1:1 (July 1975), Box 19, File 23, Canadian Liberation Movement fonds, McMaster University Archives, Hamilton, Ontario.

55 "Caravan 1974: Correspondence re Caravan from West to Ottawa, 1974."
    Box 2, File 16, CASNP, Trent University, Peterborough, Ontario.

56 Louis Cameron, quoted in David Fuller, "Indians Ready to Fight Society,"
    The Ubyssey, 4 October 1974: 16.

57 Louis Cameron, quoted in Ned Dmytryshyn, "An Interview with Louis
    Cameron," *Manitoban* (September 1974).

58 *Ojibway Warrior Society in Occupied Anicinabe Park*, 10.

59 Johnston, *Ojibway Heritage*, 83. Johnston was on a lecture tour about
    Midewiwin (and the book referenced above) during the summer and fall
    of 1974; Angel, *Preserving the Sacred*, 48.

60 Angel, *Preserving the Sacred*, 20.

61 Ibid., 122–3.

62 Louis Cameron quoted in Tom Harpur, "Kenora Indian Leader Says Rebel-
    lion Is Religious," *Toronto Star*, 7 September 1974, C04.

63 Cameron in Burke, *Paper Tomahawks*, 394.

64 Cameron, *Ojibway Warrior Society in Occupied Anicinabe Park*, 7–8.

65 Francis, *The Imaginary Indian*.

66 Mihesuah, *Indigenous American Women*, 164.

67 Louis Cameron, quoted in David Fuller, "Indians Ready to Fight Society" 16.

68 Young, *White Mythologies*, 24.

69 Radha, "Indian Symbolic Politics," 19–37.

70 Prashad, *The Darker Nations* 13.

71 Mills, *The Empire Within*, 176.

72 Ibid., 178.

73 Ross, *Fast Cars, Clean Bodies*, 158–9.

74 Springwood, "Gunscapes," 20–1.

75 Sayer, *Ghost Dancing the Law*, 91.

76 *Ojibway Warrior Society in Occupied Anicinabe Park*, 11

77 Cameron, in the *Indian Voice* (September 1974).

78 Lyle Ironstand in Burke, *Paper Tomahawks*, 365–6.

79 Chinchilla, "Nationalism, Feminism, and Revolution in Central America,"
    212–13.

80 Maracle, *I Am Woman*, 107.

81 Ibid., 99.

82 On the gendered division of labour in the Black Panther Party see Rhodes,
    Framing the Black Panthers, 107.

83 Harper, *Following the Red Path*, 27.

84 Lynn's Fieldnotes (Copy)-Daily Acct-1973, "March 26, 1973."

85 Ibid.

86 Mihesuah, *Indigenous American Women*, 163.

87 Cameron, *Ojibway Warrios Society at Occupied Anicinabe Park*, 4–6.

88 "Agreement Likely on Indian Dispute: Mayor to Release Details Later Today," *Kenora Daily Miner and News*, 2 August 1974, 1; "Hopes in Kenora Vanish; Indians Report No Deal!" *The Chronicle-Journal*, 3 August 1974, 1.

89 David Lee, "Mayor Is Contradicted: No Pact, Say Kenora Indians," *Winnipeg Free Press*, 3 August 1974, 1.

90 "Little Progress Seen at Joint Meeting," *Kenora Daily Miner and News*, 1 August 1974, 1; "Only Limited Success in Kenora Discussions," *The Chronicle-Journal* (Thunder Bay), 1 August 1974, 17.

91 Louis Cameron quoted in "Little Progress Seen at Joint Meeting," 1; and "Only Limited Success in Kenora Discussion," 17.

92 Grand Council Treaty #3, "Press Release," 4 August 1974, 2, Don Colborne Private Papers, Thunder Bay, Ontario.

93 "Council of Area Chiefs behind Kenora Militants," *The Chronical-Journal* (Thunder Bay), 6 August 1974, 3; "Chiefs Support Ojibways," *Winnipeg Free Press*, 6 August 1974: 7.

94 Ken Nelson, "Leader Vows He Won't Leave the Park," *Kenora Daily Miner and News*, 25 July 1974, 1.

95 Cameron quoted in Burke, *Paper Tomahawks*, 384.

96 *Ojibway Warrior Society in Occupied Anicinabe Park*, 21.

97 "Armed White 'Vigilantes' Provoke Standoff at Kenora," *The Chronicle-Journal*, 25 July 1974, 1; "Meeting July 25, Negotiating Committee, Town Council, DIA, Prov. Rep." Don Colborne Private Papers, Thunder Bay, Ontario.

98 "500 Kenora Citizens Hold Meeting, Demand Indians Drop Weapons," *The Chronicle-Journal* (Thunder Bay), 7 August 1974, 3.

99 Concerned citizen, "Where's All the Law and Order?" *Kenora Daily Miner and News*, 16 August 1974, 4.

100 David Lee, "Kenora Residents Ask End to Park Takeover," *Winnipeg Free Press*, 7 August 1974, 1, 5.

101 Jacobson quoted in "Citizens Want Indians Removed," *The Chronical-Journal*, 29 August 1974: 1.

102 Lee, "Kenora Residents Ask End to Park Takeover," 1, 5; Bruce Kirkland, "The
     Indian Occupation: Backlash Brewing by Kenora's Whites," *Toronto Star*, 24
     August 1974, B7; "Citizens' Committee Outlines Meeting," *Kenora Daily Miner
     and News*, 26 August 1974, 1; Ross Porter, "Groups Says No Law and Order Ex-
     ists," *Kenora Daily Miner and News*, 26 August 1974, 1; "Kenora Citizens Unite
     to Help End Park Occupation" *The Chronicle-Journal*, 24 August 1974, 1.

103 Tronnes, "Where Is John Wayne?" 535; see also Perry and Robyn, "Putting
     Anti-Indian Violence in Context," 590–624.

104 Tronnes, "Where Is John Wayne?" 536.

105 Marion Fawcett quoted in David Lee, "Kenora Residents Ask End to Park
     Takeover," 5; Dennis Braithwaite, "Obey the Law? Who's Going to Make
     Us?" *Toronto Star*, 4 September 1974, B6.

106 Tom Harpur, "Kenora Indian Leaders Say Rebellion Is Religious," *Toronto
     Star*, 7 September 1974, L4.

107 Dave Lee, "Kenora Search Started," *Winnipeg Free Press*, 8 August 1974, 1, 4;
     Katie FitzRandolph, "Park Occupation Gaining Support," *Winnipeg Free
     Press*, 3 August 1974, 1, 9.

108 "Arrest Warrants," Don Colborne Private Papers, Thunder Bay, Ontario;
     "Four Arrested at Kenora as Occupation Goes On" *The Chronicle-Journal*,
     14 August 1974, 21.

109 "Solidarity with the Ojibwa Struggle," Vancouver 1974–76, Box 1, File 16,
     Revolutionary Marxist Group, McMaster University, Hamilton, Ontario.

110 Angela Davis quoted in "Angela Racism," *Jail-break: High School Bulletin
     of the Revolutionary Marxist Group* (Nov–Dec 1974), 6.

111 Betty Polster, "Ad Hoc Group of Concern for Ojibway Indians (from yearly
     meeting 1974): Report on Activity to Date" in Canadian Association in
     Support of Native Peoples fonds, Box 2, File 16, "Caravan 1974: Correspon-
     dence," Trent University, Peterborough, Ontario.

112 "Local Crown Attorney Wants Banks on Scene," *Kenora Daily Miner and
     News*, 15 August 1974, 1. In his memoirs Burton recalls, in extensive and
     sometimes sensationalistic detail, the series of events which resulted in
     Banks leaving the Wounded Knee trial and being allowed into Canada to
     act as a mediator in Kenora.

113 Louis Cameron, quoted in "Militants Lay Down Arms," *Kenora Daily Miner
     and News*, 19 August 1974, 1; "Indians Lay Down Their Arms as Talks Resolve
     Park Siege," *Montreal Gazette*, 19 August 1974, 1.

114 James N. Davidson, Mayor's Office, 28 August 1974.

115 Letter co-signed by Douglas T. Wright, Deputy Provincial Secretary for Social Development and E.C. Burton, Crown Attorney, *Ministry of the Attorney General,* 29 August 1974, 2, Don Colborne Private Papers, Thunder Bay, Ontario.

116 "Anicinabe Park Assembly Charges Dropped for 21," *Winnipeg Free Press,* 30 April 1976.

117 Heather Robertson, "Shoot-Out at Anicinabe Park: Another Skirmish in a Long War," *Maclean's,* December 1974, 108.

CHAPTER SIX

1 "Native People's Caravan: The Demonstration," *Native People's Embassy,* November 1974, 9.

2 Jac MacDonald, "Native Activist out to Get Even; Cruelty in Schools, Social Injustice Led to Role as Cree Spokesman," *Edmonton Journal,* 12 November 1990, A7; housing is noted as a main demand by Purich, *Our Land,* 184 and Tennant, *Aboriginal Peoples and Politics,* 175.

3 Tennant, *Aboriginal Peoples and Politics,* 175

4 Hall, *The American Empire and the Fourth World,* 276.

5 Memo to George Brown, Assistant Director, Human Rights Committee, from Kathleen Fraser, 16 September 1974, CASNP, Trent University.

6 Harper, *Following the Red Path,* 9.

7 Ibid., 40.

8 Ibid., 13.

9 Memo to George Brown from Kathleen Fraser, 16 September 1974.

10 Long, "Culture, Ideology, and Militancy," 127.

11 Ken Basil quoted in Dave Ticoll and Stan Persky, "Welcome to Ottawa: The Native People's Caravan," *Canadian Dimension,* November 1974, 22.

12 Ticoll and Persky, "Welcome to Ottawa," 23.

13 Harper, *Following the Red Path,* 27.

14 "Re: Caravan Advance People," Box 2, CASNP, Trent University

15 Price, *Native Studies,* 237.

16 Telegram to Diane Mackay from Bill B. Stetson, Secretary Hamilton and District Labour Council, 24 September 1974 and Telegram to Diane McKay

and Ed Hunt, Recording Secretary UER and NWA local 504, Box 2, CASNP, Trent University.

17 Harper, *Following the Red Path.*

18 Telegram, 27 September 1974, Box 2, CASNP, Trent University.

19 "Cameron Denies Report," *Winnipeg Free Press*, 28 September 1974, 12; see also "Rebuttal," *The Toronto Native Times*, April 1975, 2.

20 "Re: Indian Caravan," 24 September 1974, George Manuel, Box 2, CASNP, Trent University,

21 "The Great Canadian Myth-Fit," *Akwesasne Notes* (Early Autumn, 1974): 20.

22 Louis Cameron quoted in James Burke, *Paper Tomahawks*, 391–3.

23 Harper, *Following the Red Path*, 57.

24 Ibid., 65.

25 Ticoll and Stan Persky, "Welcome to Ottawa."

26 Shane Parkhill, "Native People's Demands Met with Violence!" *The Young Worker* (October 1974), 3.

24 Purich, *Our Land*, 184.

28 Elbaum, *Revolution in the Air*, 3–4.

29 Mills, *The Empire Within*, 210, 271.

30 Clem Chartier, "China through a Native Person," *New Breed,* (October 1975), 5; Ray Bobb, "Red China: Visit," *Native People's Struggle*, July 1975, 4

31 Dunbar-Ortiz was in attendance and wrote about the meeting in *Blood on the Border*, 33.

32 Parkhill, "Natives People's Demands Met with Violence!" 3.

33 Ticoll and Persky, "Welcome to Ottawa," 19.

34 David Somerville, "Did Maoists Cause Ottawa Brawl?" *Toronto Sun* reprinted in *Indian Record* (November–December 1974), 8–9; "Communists Not Wanted," *Edmonton Sun* reprinted in *Indian Record* (November–December 1974), 16, and *The Native People*, 11 October 1974, 1, 3.

35 Tom Jackson, "Communists," *The Native People*, 4 October 1974, 1, 7.

36 Price, *Native Studies*, 237.

37 "Native Embassy: A Sad Farewell to a Building – The Work Goes On," *Akwesasne Notes* (Early Spring, 1975), 22.

38 "Newsletter – November 1974," *Native People's Embassy*, November 1974, 1–2.

39 Banks, *Ojibwa Warrior*, 266; Churchill and Vander Wall, *Agents of Repression*, 212.

40   Churchill and Vander Wall, *Agents of Repression*, 213.

41   Matthiessen, *In the Spirit of Crazy Horse*, 11.

42   Banks, *Ojibwa Warrior*, 267, 269, 271–2, 276; Baringer, *The Metanarrative of Suspicion in Late Twentieth-Century America*, 22.

43   Hendricks, *The Unquiet Grave*, 177–8. A key account of Durham's past is found in "The Many Faces of Doug Durham," *Akwesasne Notes* (Early Winter, 1975): 12–13.

44   Baringer, *The Metanarrative of Suspicion in Late Twentieth-Century America*, 41.

45   Hendricks, *The Unquiet Grave*, 189.

46   Harper, *Following the Red Path*, 74.

47   Louis Cameron quoted in "FBI Man Agitated Indians: Cameron," *Winnipeg Free Press*, 24 April 1975, 4.

48   Burton, *Journal of a Country Lawyer*, 226.

49   Tronnes, "Where Is John Wayne?" 539.

50   "Advisers to Indians a Spy, RCMP Learn," *Toronto Star*, 18 April 1975, A3; "Ottawa Did Not Know FBI Man in Canada," *Toronto Star*, 22 April 1975, B7.

51   US Senate, Committee on the Judiciary, Subcommittee on Internal Security (Eastland Subcommittee) *Revolutionary Activities within the United States: The American Indian Movement* (Washington, DC: Government Printing Office, 1976).

52   Ibid., 7, 66.

53   Ibid., 66.

54   Baringer, *The Metanarrative of Suspicion in Late Twentieth-Century America*, 27.

55   "Durham in the John Birch Society," *Akwesasne Notes* (Early Winter, 1975): 13.

56   Austin, *Fear of A Black Nation*, 148.

57   Whitaker, *Double Standard*, 329.

58   Austin, *Fear of a Black Nation*, 166–7; Hewitt, *Spying 101*, 146–58.

59   Austin, *Fear of A Black Nation*, 167.

60   Saskatoon Sub Division, 16 December 1974, RG 146, Library and Archives of Canada, Ottawa.

61   Hewitt, *Spying 101*, 158.

62   Ibid., 190–1.

63   Pender, "The Gaze on Clubs, Native Studies, and Teachers at Laurentian University," 113.

64 RCMP report quoted by Pender, "The Gaze on Clubs, Native Studies, and Teachers at Laurentian University, 1960s-1970s," 112.

65 "Barbra" quoted by Kinsman and Gentile, *The Canadian War on Queers*, 252.

66 Harper, *Following the Red Path*, 27.

67 Kinsman and Gentile, *The Canadian War on Queers*, 266.

68 Ibid., 280–6.

69 The Revolutionary Marxist Group was formed by people in the Waffle's "red circle," ex-members of the League for Socialist Action, and a variety of student activists; see Kinsman and Gentile, *The Canadian War on Queers*, 280.

70 Revolutionary Marxist Group, "Solidarity with the Ojibway Struggle," August 1974.

71 "The Future of the Native Movement." RMG *Red Forum*, Regina Branch, 29 January 1975, Revolutionary Marxist Group, 1974–1980, McMaster University Archives, Hamilton.

72 "The Future of the Native Movement," 29 January 1975.

73 "Anti-Racist Work, National Circular, June 1975," Box 3, File 33, "Racism, 1974–76," Revolutionary Marxist Group, 1947–1980, McMaster University Archives, Hamilton.

74 "Anti-Racist Balance Sheet, December 1975."

75 Ibid.

76 "Anti-Racist Work, National Circular, June 1975."

77 The Black Workers Alliance formed in January 1975 and disbanded by the end of the same year. According to Chris Harris, Rosie Douglas led the group, which "struggled for Black workers' rights in the workplace." See Harris, "Canadian Black Power, Organic Intellectuals and the War of Position in Toronto, 1967–75," 332.

78 "Anti-Racist Work, National Circular, June 1975," 10.

79 Austin, "All Roads Led to Montreal," 518, 520.

80 The Sir George Williams Affairs is also popularly known as the Sir George Williams Computer Incident. It took place in late January and early February 1969 at what is now Concordia University in Montreal. Caribbean students occupied the ninth-floor computer lab at the university to protest racist treatment from a faculty member. Police intervened on 11 February to end the occupation. As Sean Mills writes, the "events of February 1969 grew out of tension caused by racial injustice in Montreal and throughout the world." Mills, *The Empire Within*, 107.

81 For more on policing and surveillance of Black activists around Sir George
    Williams, see Austin, *Fear of a Black Nation*; Maynard, *Policing Black Lives*;
    and Mills, *The Empire Within*.

82 Ned Dmytryshyn, "Rosie Douglas on Racism: Black Leader to Speak," *Mani-
    toban*, 27 February 1975, 5; Alan Christie, "Immigration Paper Attacked as
    Racist," *Winnipeg Free Press*, 7 March 1975, 7. The five hundred attendees far
    outnumber the reported seventy-five who came out to see Douglas in Van-
    couver; see Paul Knox, "Racism Blamed on Capitalism 'Crisis,'" *Vancouver
    Sun*, 26 March 1975, 18.

83 "Rosie Douglas Speaks Out: Racism in Canada," *Manitoban*, 20 March 1975,
    4.

84 Ned Dmytryshyn, "Anti-racist Committee Formed," *Manitoban*, 14 March
    1975.

85 "The Committee Against the Deportation of 1500 Haitians, Racism, and
    Political Repression, Winnipeg, March 14, 1975," Box 3, File 33 "Racism
    1974–1976." Revolutionary Marxist Group, 1947–1980, McMaster University
    Archives, Hamilton.

86 Ibid.

87 "Roosevelt Bernard Douglas," 13 August 1975. Native Peoples Friendship
    Delegation, Vol 1, RG 146. Library and Archives of Canada, Ottawa.

88 "Certain RCMP Activities and the Question of Governmental Knowledge,"
    *Commission of Inquiry Concerning Certain Activities of the Royal Canadian
    Mounted Police* (McDonald Commission: Ottawa, 1981), 425.

89 Jon Ferry, "Suspected Hart Was Agent, Douglas Says," *Globe and Mail*,
    23 February 1978.

90 Warren Hart quoted in "Hart Ready to Testify," *Toronto Sun*, 24 February
    1978.

91 Conway, *Marshall Law*, 39, 48.

92 Austin, "All Roads Led to Montreal," 534; see also "Hart Hired by Space
    Research," *Globe and Mail*, 30 November 1978; Peter Moon, "RCMP Wants
    Charge Laid," *Globe and Mail*, 8 March 1980, B2; "Man Named as Informer
    for RCMP Employed by Arms Firm in Antigua," *Globe and Mail*, 30 Novem-
    ber 1978, 10.

93 "Ugly New Questions and an Old Stone Wall," *Globe and Mail*, 24 February
    1978.

94 "Attempt to Organize Radicals: RCMP 'Spy,'" *Toronto Sun*, 24 February 1978.

95 Ibid.; Robert MacDonald, "Hart Kept Cool in Metro Demo," *Toronto Sun*, 26 February 1978.

96 "Activist's Lawyer Says Probe Did Not Seek Explanation," *Globe and Mail*, 3 March 1980, 5.

97 Don Colborne quoted in Third Report, McDonald Commission, April 1981, 488.

98 Gary Cristall quoted in Third Report, McDonald Commission, April 1981, 489.

99 Phil Kinsman, "Commission to Rule on Indians' Demand," *Ottawa Journal*, 30 January 1980.

100 "Mounties Approved Training of Militant Indians: Hart," *Montreal Gazette*, 23 April 1980; "Spurned Offers of Arms, Training, Native Leaders say," *Globe and Mail*, 26 May 1980.

101 *The National Indian*, 2:6 (1979), see also Robert Sheppard, "Inspector's Suicide Has Shaken Force, Mounties Say," *Globe and Mail*, 7 May 1980, 11.

102 "Treatment of Informer Criticized," *Globe and Mail*, 6 June 1987, A2.

103 "Kelleher Won't Alter Decision to Pay Spy," *Globe and Mail*, 6 May 1987, A4.

104 Stewart Phillip quoted in Bill Curry "Forces' Terror Manual Lists Natives with Hezbollah," *Globe and Mail*, 31 March 2007, A1.

105 "Native People's Caravan: Foreign Agitators," *Native People's Embassy*, November 1974, 9.

CONCLUSION

1 David Bruser, "New Report of Mercury Dumping Probed Near First Nation," *Toronto Star*, 23 September 2019, A1, A8.

2 Atleo, "AFN National Chief Responds to Prime Minister's Statements on Colonialism," 1. October 2009, http://www.afn.ca/article.asp?id=4609.

3 Barsh, "Aboriginal People and Canada's Conscience," 272–3.

4 "Defend Louis Cameron," *New Breed*, 1975.

5 In the early 1970s, Duval was immersed in the vibrant world of Québécois comics. Michel Viau explains that "as in all artistic movements of the time, the trend [in comics] was to challenge and question society." ("Springtime of the Quebecois Comic Strip," Beyond the Funnies, 24 June 2002, accessed

18 June 2008, http://www.collectionscanada.gc.ca/bandes-dessinees/027002-7400-e.html, site defunct.)

6 Cameron, *Ojibway Warrior Society in Occupied Anicinabe Park*, 4–5.

7 See "Japanese and Native Victims Unite to Fight Mercury Pollution," *Toronto Native Times* 6.10 (October 1975), 1, 10.

Bibliography

ARCHIVAL AND LIBRARY COLLECTIONS

Archives of Ontario
   RG 33; 13.5; b223573
   RG 33; 58-17-b223701
   RG 33; 59.2; b223702
   RG 33, 5G.21; b223702
   RG 47-138
   RG-76-3-0
   RG-76-3-0-331
   RG 76-3-0-649
   RG 76-3-0-787
Library and Archives Canada
   RG 146
McMaster University Archives
   Revolutionary Marxist Group, 1947-1980
Trent University Archives
   Canadian Association in Support of Native Peoples
University of Illinois-Champaign Archives
   Doris Duke Indian Oral History Program, 1908–1995

PERSONAL PAPERS

Don Colborne, Thunder Bay, Ontario.

NEWSPAPERS AND PERIODICALS

Akwesasne Notes
Brandon Sun
Canadian Dimension
Contrast
Counterpunch
Edmonton Journal
Kenora Daily Miner and News
Forbes
Globe and Mail (Toronto)
Human Relations
Indian Record
Maclean's
The Manitoban (University of Manitoba)
Manitoba Free Press
Marxist Quarterly
Montreal Gazette
Montreal Star
Native Times
New Breed
New York Times
Ottawa Citizen
Ottawa Journal
Saturday Night
The Chronicle-Journal (Thunder Bay)
The Indian News
The Native People
Times of London
Toronto Star
Toronto Sun
Toronto Telegram
Ubyssey (University of British Columbia)
Uhuru
United Church Observer
Vancouver Sun

Weekend Magazine
Winnipeg Free Press
Young Worker

TELEVISION

"Violence, Oppression, and Action," *Take 30*, CBC television, aired 2 June 1969, see
http://archives.cbc.ca/society/poverty/clips/15387/.

RADIO/SOUND RECORDINGS

Indian Magazine, February 1974, http://archives.cbc.ca/society/native_issues/
clips/15991/.
Rap Brown, "H. Rap Brown, Free Huey Rally," sound recording, KPFA Berkeley,
2 February 1968.
Stokely Carmichael, "Stokely Carmichael, Free Huey Rally," sound recording,
KPFA Berkeley, 2 February 1968.

FILM

Willie Dunn, "The Ballad of Crowfoot," viewable online at http://www.nfb.ca
/film/ballad_of_crowfoot.

PARLIAMENTARY PAPERS AND GOVERNMENT COMMISSIONS

John Reid, *House of Commons Debates*, First Session – Twenty Seventh Parlia-
ment, vol. 1 (1966).
Robert Thompson, Question in the House of Commons, 17 October 1967, *House
of Commons Debates*, Second Session – Twenty Seventh Parliament, vol. 3 (1967).
Paul Martin, Response to the House of Commons, 19 October 1967, *House of
Commons Debates*, Second Session – Twenty Seventh Parliament, vol. 3 (1967).
J.G. Diefenbaker, Question in the House of Commons, 28 October 1968, *House of
Commons Debates*, First Session – Twenty Eighth Parliament, vol. 2 (1968).
Commission of Inquiry Concerning Certain Activities of the Royal Canadian
Mounted Police, McDonald Commission: Ottawa, 1981.

Revolutionary Activities within the United States: The American Indian Movement -Washington, U.S. Government Printing Office, 1976.

ARTICLES, BOOKS, AND PAMPHLETS

Adams, Howard. *Howard Adams: Otapawy! The Life of a Métis leader in His Own Words and Those of His Contemporaries.* Saskatoon, SK: Gabriel Dumont Institute, 2005.

– *Prison of Grass: Canada from a Native Point of View.* Saskatoon, SK: Fifth House, [1974] 1989.

– *Tortured People: The Politics of Colonization (Revised Edition).* Penticton, BC: Theytus Books, 1999.

Anderson, Benedict. *Imagined Communities: Reflections on the Origin and Spread of Nationalism.* London: Verso, revised edition, 2006.

Anderson, Mark and Carmen Robertson. "The 'Bended Elbow' News, Kenora 1974: How a Small-Town Newspaper Promoted Colonization." *American Indian Quarterly,* 31, no.3 (2007): 410–40.

Angel, Michael. *Preserving the Sacred: Historical Perspectives on the Ojibwa Midewiwin.* Winnipeg: University of Manitoba Press, 2002.

Atkins, Sean. "The River, the City, and the Yellow Line: Reimagining Associative Landscapes in Post-War Northwestern Ontario." *Native Studies Review* 17, no. 2 (2008): 115–41.

Austin, David. "All Roads Lead to Montreal: Black Power, the Caribbean, and the Black Radical Tradition in Canada." *Journal of African American History* 94, no. 2 (2007): 516–39.

– *Fear of a Black Nation: Race, Sex and Security in Sixties Montreal.* Toronto: Between the Lines, 2013.

– "The Gentle Revolutionary: Jan Carew at 90." *Guyanese Online,* 28 September 2010. http://guyaneseonline.wordpress.com/2010/09/28/.

Bageant, Joe. *Deer Hunting with Jesus: Dispatches from America's Class War.* New York: Three Rivers Press, 2007.

Baldwin, Bridgette. "In the Shadow of the Gun: The Black Panther Party, the Ninth Amendment, and Discourses of Self-Defense." In *In Search of the Black Panther Party,* edited by Jama Lazerow and Yohuru Williams, 67–96. Durham, NC: Duke University Press, 2006.

Barsh, Russel Lawrence. "Aboriginal Peoples and Canada's Conscience." In *Hidden* in Plain Sight: Contributions of Aboriginal Peoples to Canadian Identity and Culture, edited by Cora J. Voyageur, David R. Newhouse, and Dan Beavon, 270–91, Toronto: University of Toronto Press, 2005.

Bartlett, R.H. "Citizens Minus: Indians and the Right to Vote." Saskatchewan Law Review 44, no.2 (1979–80): 163–94.

Baum, Bruce. The Rise and Fall of the Caucasian Race: A Political History of Racial Identity. New York: NYU Press, 2006.

Borovoy, A. Alan. Uncivil Obedience: The Tactics and Tales of a Democratic Agitator. Toronto: Lester Publishing, 1991.

Bowles, R.P et. al., eds. The Indian: Assimilation, Integration or Separation? Scarborough, ON: Prentice Hall, 1972.

Bradley, Mark Philip. "Decolonization, the Global South, and the Cold War, 1919–1962." In The Cold War. Volume 1: Origins, edited by Melvyn P. Leffler and Odd Arne Westad, 464–85. Cambridge: Cambridge University Press, 2010.

Buffalo Tiger and Harry A. Kersey Jr. Buffalo Tiger: A Life in the Everglades. Lincoln: University of Nebraska Press, 2002.

Burke, James. Paper Tomahawks: From Red Tape to Red Power. Winnipeg, MB: Queenston House Publishing, 1976.

Burton, E.C. Journal of a Country Lawyer: Crime, Sin and Damn Good Fun. Surrey, BC: Hancock House, 1995.

Carmichael, Stokely, and Charles V. Hamilton. Black Power: The Politics of Liberation in America. New York: Vintage Books, 1967.

Carter, Sarah. The Importance of Being Monogamous: Marriage and Nation Building in Western Canada in 1915. Athabasca, AB: Athabasca University Press, 2008.

Cermakian, Jean. "Canada's Role in the Foreign Aid Programmes to the Developing Nations: A Geographical Appraisal." Cahiers de géographie du Québec 12, no. 26 (1968): 543–66.

"Certain RCMP Activities and the Question of Governmental Knowledge," Commission of Inquiry Concerning Certain Activities of the Royal Canadian Mounted Police Macdonald Commission: Ottawa, 1981.

Chinchilla, Norma Stoltz. "Nationalism, Feminism, and Revolution in Central America." In Feminist Nationalism, edited by Lois A. West, 201–19. New York: Routledge, 1997.

Churchill, David. "SUPA, Selma, and Stevenson: The Politics of Solidarity in Mid-1960s Toronto." Journal of Canadian Studies 44, no.2 (2010): 32–69.

Churchill, Ward. The Ward Churchill Reader. New York: Routledge, 2003.

Coates, Ken S. *A Global History of Indigenous Peoples: Struggle and Survival.* New York: Palgrave-Macmillan, 2004.

Cobb, Daniel M. "Talking the Language of the Larger World: Politics in Cold War (Native) America." In *Beyond Red Power: New Perspectives on American Indian Politics and Activism,* edited by Daniel M. Cobb and Loretta Fowlers, 161–77. Santa Fe, NM: School for Advanced Research Press, 2007.

Cole, Sally. *Ruth Landes: A Life in Anthropology.* Lincoln: University of Nebraska Press, 2003.

Conway, Marshall Eddie. *Marshall Law: The Life and Times of a Baltimore Black Panther.* Oakland, CA: AK Press, 2011.

Cooper, Afua. *The Hanging of Angélique: The Untold Story of Canadian Slavery and the Burning of Old Montreal.* Toronto: Harper Collins, 2006.

Cooper, Frederick. *Colonialism in Question: Theory, Knowledge, History.* Berkeley: University of California Press, 2005.

de Costa, Ravi. "Snakes That Are Rainbows: Indigenous Worldviews and the Constitution of Autonomy." In *Empires and Autonomy: Moments in the History of Globalization,* edited by Stephen M. Streeter, John C. Weaver, and William D. Coleman, 232–46. Vancouver: UBC Press, 2009.

Cottam, Barry S. "Federal/Provincial Disputes, Natural Resources and the Treaty #3 Ojibway, 1867–1924." PhD diss., University of Ottawa, 1994.

Coulter, John. *The Crime of Louis Riel.* Toronto: Playwrights Co-op, 1976.

Coulthard, Glen Sean. *Red Skin, White Masks: Rejecting the Colonial Politics of Recognition.* Minneapolis: University of Minnesota Press, 2014.

Crow Dog, Mary. *Lakota Woman.* New York: Harper Perennial, 1990.

Curthoys, Ann. *Freedom Ride: A Freedom Rider Remembers.* Crows Nest, NSW: Allen and Unwin, 2002.

D'Arcus, Bruce. "Protest, Scale, and Publicity: The FBI and the H. Rap Brown Act." *Antipode* 35, no.4 (2003): 718–41.

Daschuk, James. *Clearing the Plains: Disease, Politics of Starvation, and the Loss of Aboriginal Life.* Regina, SK: University of Regina Press, 2013.

Deloria, Philip. "Counterculture Indians and the New Age." In *Imagine Nation: The American Counterculture of the 1960s and '70s,* edited by Peter Braunstein and Michael William Doyle, 159–88. New York: Routledge, 2002.

Deloria Jr, Vine. *Custer Died for Your Sins: An Indian Manifesto.* Norman: University of Oklahoma Press, 1988 [1969].

Denis, Jeffrey S. "Contact Theory in a Small-Town Settler-Colonial Context: The

Reproduction of Laissez-Faire Racism in Indigenous-White Canadian Relations." *American Sociological Review* 80, no.1 (2015): 218–42.

Dimaline, Cherie. "Che Riel." *Métis Voyageur*. November/December 2004.

Dixon, Chris. "The Opposite of Truth Is Forgetting: An Interview with Roxanne Dunbar-Ortiz." *Upping the Anti* 6 (April, 2008). https://uppingtheanti.org/jour nal/article/06-the-opposite-of-truth-is-forgetting.

Downey, Allan. *The Creator's Game: Lacrosse, Identity, and Indigenous Nationhood.* Vancouver: UBC Press, 2018.

Dubinsky, Karen. *Improper Advances: Rape and Heterosexual Conflict in Ontario, 1880–1929.* Chicago: University of Chicago Press, 1993.

Dubinsky, Karen, et al., eds. *New World Coming: The Sixties and the Shaping of Global Consciousness.* Toronto: Between the Lines, 2009.

Dudziak, Mary L. *Cold War Civil Rights: Race and the Image of American Democracy.* Princeton, NH: Princeton University Press, 2000.

Dunbar-Ortiz, Roxanne. *Blood on the Border: A Memoir of the Contra War.* Cambridge: South End Press, 2005.

Dyck, Erika, and Maureen Lux. "Population Control in the 'Global North'? Canada's Response to Indigenous Reproductive Rights and Neo-Eugenics." *The Canadian Historical Review* 97, no.4 (December 2016): 481–512.

Echols, Alice. *Shaky Ground: The Sixties and Its Aftershocks.* New York: Columbia University Press, 2002.

Fidler, Richard. *RCMP: The Real Subversives.* Toronto: Vanguard Publications, 1978.

Flood, Dawn Rae. "A Black Panther in the Great White North: Fred Hampton Visits Saskatchewan, 1969." *Journal for the Study of Radicalism* 8, no.2 (2014): 21–49.

Francis, Daniel. *The Imaginary Indian: The Image of the Indian in Canadian Culture.* Vancouver, BC: Arsenal Pulp Press, 1992.

Friesen, Gerald. *The Canadian Prairies: A History.* Toronto: University of Toronto Press, 1987.

Fruehling Springwood, Charles. "Gunscapes: Toward a Global Geography of the Firearm." In *Open Fire: Understanding Global Gun Cultures,* edited by Charles Fruehling Springwood. 15–27. New York: Berg Publishers, 2007.

George-Kanentiio, Douglas M. *Iroquois on Fire: A Voice from Mohawk Nation.* Lincoln: University of Nebraska Press, 2008.

Goldberg, David Theo. *The Threat of Race: Reflections on Racial Neoliberalism.* Malden, MA: Wiley-Blackwell, 2009.

Goldstein, Alyosha. "On the Internal Border: Colonial Difference, the Cold War, and the Locations of 'Underdevelopment.'" *Comparative Studies in Society and History* 50, no. 1 (January 2008): 26–56.

Gosse, Van. *Where the Boys Are: Cuba, Cold War America and the Making of the New Left*. New York: Verso, 1993.

Griffith, Jane. "One Little, Two Little, Three Canadians: The Indians of Canada Pavilion and Public Pedagogy, Expo 1967." *Journal of Canadian Studies/Revue d'études canadiennes* (Spring 2015): 171–204.

Gutiérrez, Ramón A. "Internal Colonialism: An American Theory of Race." *Du Bois Review* 1, no.2 (2004): 281–95.

Hall, Anthony J. *The American Empire and the Fourth World*. Montreal and Kingston: McGill-Queen's University Press, 2003.

Hall, Stuart. "The West and the Rest: Discourse and Power," In *Formations of Modernity*, edited by Stuart Hall and Bram Gieben, 275–331. Cambridge, MA: Polity Press, 1992.

Harper, Vern. *Following the Red Path: The Native Peoples Caravan 1974*. Toronto: NC Press Limited, 1979.

Harris, Chris. "Canadian Black Power, Organic Intellectuals and the War of Position in Toronto, 1967–75." In *The Sixties in Canada: A Turbulent and Creative Decade*, edited by M. Athena Palaeologu, 324–39. Montreal: Black Rose Press, 2009.

Harris, Cole. "How Did Colonialism Dispossess? Comments from an Edge of Empire," *Annals of the Association of American Geographers* 94, no.1 (2004): 165–82.

Hawthorn, H.B. *A Survey of the Contemporary Indians of Canada: A Report on Economic, Political, Educational Needs and Policies*, Indian Affairs Branch: Ottawa, 1966.

Hendricks, Steve. *The Unquiet Grave: The FBI and the Struggle for the Soul of Indian Country*. New York: Thunder's Mouth Press, 2006.

Hewitt, Steve. *Spying 101: The RCMP's Secret Activities at Canadian Universities, 1917–1997*. Toronto: University of Toronto Press, 2002.

Ho, Fred. "Kickin' the White Man's Ass: Black Power, Aesthetics, and the Asian Martial Arts." In *AfroAsian Encounters: Culture, History, Politics* edited by Heike Raphael-Hernandez and Shannon Steen, 295–312. New York: NYU Press, 2006.

Jackson, Justin. "Kissinger's Kidnapper: Eqbal Ahmad, the U.S. New Left, and the Transnational Romance of Revolutionary War." *Journal for the Study of Radicalism* 4, no.1 (Spring 2010): 75–119.

Jhappan, C. Radha. "Indian Symbolic Politics: The Double-Edged Sword of Publicity." *Canadian Ethnic Studies* 22, no.3 (1990): 19–37.

Johnston, Basil. *Ojibway Heritage: The Ceremonies, Rituals, Songs, Dances, Prayers and Legends of the Ojibway.* Toronto: McClelland and Stewart, 1976.

Kelley, Robin D.G. *Freedom Dreams: The Black Radical Imagination.* Boston, MA: Beacon Press, 2002.

– "What Did Cedric Robinson Mean by Racial Capitalism?" *Boston Review* (January 2017).

Kelley, Robin D.G, Jack Amariglio, and Lucas Wilson. "'Solidarity Is Not a Market Exchange': An RM Interview with Robin D.G. Kelley, Part 2." *Rethinking Marxism* 31, no.2 (2019): 152–72.

Kelm, Mary-Ellen. *Colonizing Bodies: Aboriginal Health and Healing in British Columbia 1900–1950.* Vancouver: UBC Press, 1998.

Kersey, Harry A. *An Assumption of Sovereignty: Social and Political Transformation among the Florida Seminoles, 1953–1979.* Lincoln: University of Nebraska Press, 1996.

– "The Havana Connection: Buffalo Tiger, Fidel Castro, and the Origin of Miccosukee Tribal Sovereignty, 1959–1962." *American Indian Quarterly* 25, no.4 (Fall 2001): 491–507.

Kinsman, Gary, and Patrizia Gentile. *The Canadian War on Queers: National Security as Sexual Regulation.* Vancouver: UBC Press, 2010.

Kostash, Myrna. *Long Way from Home: The Story of the Sixties Generation.* Toronto: J. Lorimer, 1980.

Kuhlken, Robert. "Settin' the Woods on Fire: Rural Incendiarism as Protest." *Geographical Review* 89, no. 3 (1999): 343–63.

Lackenbrauer, P. Whitney. *Battle Grounds: The Canadian Military and Aboriginal Lands.* Vancouver: UBC Press, 2007.

Lackenbrauer, P. Whitney, and Andrew F. Cooper. "The Achilles Heel of Canadian International Citizenship: Indigenous Diplomacies and State Responses." *Canadian Foreign Policy* 13, no. 3 (2007): 99–119.

Langford, Will. "Jean Lagassé, Community Development, and the 'Indian and Métis Problem' in Manitoba in the 1950s and 1960s." *Canadian Historical Review* 97, no.3 (September 2016): 346–76.

LaRocque, Emma. *When the Other Is Me: Native Resistance Discourse 1850–1990.* Winnipeg: University of Manitoba Press, 2010.

Lawrence, Bonita. *"Real" Indians and Others: Mixed-Blood Urban Native Peoples and Indigenous Nationhood.* Vancouver: UBC Press, 2004.

Logan McCallum, Mary Jane. *Indigenous Women, Work, and History 1940–1980.* Winnipeg: University of Manitoba Press, 2014.

Logan McCallum, Mary Jane, and Adele Perry. *Structures of Indifference: An Indigenous Life and Death in a Canadian City.* Winnipeg: University of Manitoba Press, 2018.

Long, David. "Culture, Ideology, and Militancy: The Movement of Native Indians in Canada, 1969–1991." In *Organizing Dissent: Contemporary Social Movements in Theory and Practice,* edited by W.K. Carroll, 151–170. Toronto, ON: Garamond Press: 1992.

Lovisek, Joan A., Tim E. Holzkamm, and Leo G. Waisburg. "Fatal Errors: Ruth Landes and the Creation of the 'Atomistic Ojibwa.'" *Anthropologica* 39, no. 1/2, (1997): 134–45.

Lloyd, Antony John. *Community Development in Canada.* Ottawa: Canadian Research Centre for Anthropology, 1967.

Luby, Brittany "'The department is going back on these promises': An Examination of Anishinaabe and Crown Understandings of Treaty." *Canadian Journal of Native Studies* 30, no. 2 (2010): 203–28

– "From Milk-Medicine to Public (Re)Education Programs: An Examination of Anishinabek Mothers' Responses to Hydroelectric Flooding in the Treaty #3 District, 1900–1975." *CBMH/BCHM* 32, no. 2 (2015): 363–89.

Mackey, Eva. *The House of Difference: Cultural Politics and National Identity in Canada.* London: Routledge, 1999.

Maracle, Lee. *Bobbi Lee: Indian Rebel.* Toronto: Women's Press, 1990.

– *I Am Woman: A Native Perspective on Sociology and Feminism.* Vancouver: Press Gang, 1996.

– "Red Power Legacies and Lives: An Interview by Scott Rutherford." In *New World Coming: The Sixties and the Shaping of Global Consciousness,* edited by Dubinsky et.al, 358–67. Toronto: Between the Lines, 2009.

Marchessault, Janine. "Reflections on the Dispossessed: Video and the 'Challenge for Change' Experiment." *Screen* 36, no. 2 (1995): 131–46.

Matthews, Robert O. "Canada and Anglophone Africa." In *Canada and the Third World,* edited by Peyton V. Lyon and Tareq Y. Ismael, 60–132. Toronto, ON: Macmillan, 1976.

Maynard, John. "Transcultural/transnational Interaction and Influences on Aboriginal Australia." In *Connected Worlds: History in Transnational Perspective*, edited by Ann Curthoys and Marilyn Lake, 195–208. Canberra: ANU E Press, 2005.

Maynard, Robyn. *Policing Black Lives: State Violence in Canada from Slavery to the Present*. Halifax & Winnipeg: Fernwood Publishing, 2017.

McFarlane, Peter. *Brotherhood to Nationhood: George Manuel and the Making of the Modern Indian Movement*. Toronto: Between the Lines, 1993.

Meren, David. "'Commend Me the Yak': The Colombo Plan, the Inuit of Ungava, and 'Developing' Canada's North." *Histoire sociale/Social history* 50, no. 102 (November 2017): 343–70.

Mihesuah, Devon Abbott. *Indigenous American Women: Decolonization, Empowerment, Activism*. Lincoln: University of Nebraska Press, 2003.

Miller, J.R. *Compact, Contract, Covenant: Aboriginal Treaty-making in Canada*. Toronto: University of Toronto Press, 2013.

– "From Riel to Métis." In *Reflections on Native-Newcomer Relations: Selected Essays*, edited by J.R. Miller, 37–60. Toronto: University of Toronto, 2004.

– "Owen Glendower, Hotspur, and Canadian Indian Policy." In *Reflections on Native-Newcomer Relations*, edited by J.R. Miller, 107–39. Toronto: University of Toronto Press, 2004.

– *Skyscrapers Hide the Heavens: A History of Indian-White Relations in Canada*. Toronto: University of Toronto Press, 1991.

Milligan, Ian. *Rebel Youth: 1960s Labour Unrest, Young Workers, and New Leftists in English Canada*. Vancouver: UBC Press, 2015

Mills, Sean. *The Empire Within: Postcolonial Thought and Political Activism in Sixties Montreal*. Montreal and Kingston: McGill-Queen's University Press, 2010.

Native People's Embassy, November 1974.

Nelson, Jennifer. *Razing Africville: A Geography of Racism*. Toronto: University of Toronto Press, 2008.

Ojibway Warrior Society in Occupied Anicinabe Park, Kenora, Ontario, August 1974. Toronto: Better Reads Collective, 1974.

Owram, Douglas. "The Myth of Louis Riel," *The Canadian Historical Review* 63, no.3 (September 1982), 315–36.

Palmer, Bryan D. *Canada's 1960s: The Ironies of Identity in a Rebellious Era*. Toronto: University of Toronto Press, 2009.

Parker, Dorothy R. *Singing an Indian Song: A Biography of D'Arcy McNickle*. Lincoln: University of Nebraska Press, 1992.

Patterson, Palmer. *The Canadian Indian: A History since 1500*. Don Mills, ON: Collier-Macmillan, 1972.

Pender, Terry. "The Gaze on Clubs, Native Studies, and Teachers at Laurentian University, 1960s-1970s." In *Whose National Security: Canadian State Surveillance and the Creation of Enemies*, edited by Gary Kinsman, Dieter K. Buse, and Mercedes Steedman, 110–20. Toronto: Between the Lines, 2000.

Perry, Adele. *Aqueduct Colonialism: Colonialism, Resources, and the Histories We Remember*. Winnipeg, MA: ARP Books, 2016.

– *On the Edge of Empire: Gender, Race and the Making of British Columbia, 1849–1871*. Toronto: University of Toronto Press, 2001.

Perry, Barbara and Linda Robyn. "Putting Anti-Indian Violence in Context: The Case of the Great Lakes Chippewas of Wisconsin." *American Indian Quarterly* 29, no. 3&4 (2005): 590–624.

Pickering, Kathleen. "Decolonizing Time Regimes: Lakota Conceptions of Work, Economy, and Society." *American Anthropologist* 106, no.1 (2004): 85–97.

Prashad, Vijay. *The Darker Nations: A People's History of the Third World*. New York: New Press, 2007.

Price, John. *Native Studies: American and Canadian Indians*. Toronto: McGraw-Hill Ryerson, 1978.

Prince, Simon. *Northern Ireland's '68: Civil Rights, Global Revolt and the Origins of the Troubles*. Dublin: Irish Academic Press, 2007.

Pulido, Laura. "Flint, Environmental Racism, and Racial Capitalism." *Capitalism, Nature, Socialism* 27, no.3 (2016): 1–16.

Purich, Donald. *Our Land: Native Rights in Canada in Canada*. Toronto: James Lorimer, 1986.

Ramos, Howard. "Divergent Paths: Aboriginal Mobilization in Canada, 1951–2000." Ph.D. diss., McGill University, 2004.

Rapp, Dianna. "The Doris Duke American Indian Oral History Program: Gathering the "Raw Material of History." *Journal of the Southwest* 47, no. 1 (2005): 11–28.

Razack, Sherene. *Dying from Improvement: Inquests and Inquiries into Indigenous Deaths in Custody*. Toronto: University of Toronto Press, 2015.

Rhodes, Jane. *Framing the Black Panthers: The Spectacular Rise of a Black Power Icon*. New York: New Press, 2007.

Rifkin, Mark. "The Transatlantic Indian Problem." *American Literary History* 24, no. 2 (2012): 337–55.

Rist, Gilbert. *The History of Development: From Western Origins to Global Faith.* 3rd ed. New York: Zed Books, [1997] 2008.

Robinson, Cedric. *Black Marxism: The Making of the Black Radical Tradition.* 2nd ed. Chapel Hill: The University of North Carolina Press, [1983] 2000.

Rolston, Bill. "'The Brothers on the Walls': International Solidarity and Irish Political Murals." *Journal of Black Studies* 39, no. 3 (2009): 446–70.

Ross, Kristin. *May 1968: And Its Afterlives.* Chicago, IL: University of Chicago Press, 2002.

Rostow, Walt Whitman. *The Stages of Economic Growth: A Non-Communist Manifesto.* Cambridge: Cambridge Univeristy Press, 1960.

Ruffo, Armand Garnet. *Norval Morrisseau: Man Changing into Thunderbird.* Madeira Park, BC: Douglas and McIntyre, 2014.

Rutherford, Scott. "Canada's Other Red Scare: Indigenous Anti-colonialism and the Anicinabe Park Occupation." In *The Hidden 1970s: Histories of Radicalism,* edited by Dan Berger, 77–96. Rutgers, NJ: Rutgers University Press, 2010.

– "'We Have Bigotry All Right – But No Alabamas': Racism and Aboriginal Protest in Canada during the 1960s." *The American Indian Quarterly* 41, no. 2 (2017): 158–79.

Rutherford, Scott, Sean Mills, Susan Lord, Catherine Krull, and Karen Dubinsky. "Introduction: The Global Sixties." In *New World Coming: The Sixties and the Shaping of Global Consciousness,* edited by Karen Dubinsky, et al., 1–6. Toronto: Between the Lines, 2009.

Said, Edward. "Traveling Theory Reconsidered." In *Reflections on Exile and Other Essays,* 436–52. Cambridge, MA: Harvard University Press, 2000.

Sayer, John William. *Ghost Dancing the Law: The Wounded Knee Trials.* Cambridge, MA: Harvard University Press, 1997.

Scott, Don. "Northern Alienation." In *Government and Politics of Ontario,* edited by Donald C. MacDonald, 235–48. Toronto: Macmillan, 1975.

Sealy, David. "'Canadianizing' Blackness: Resisting the Political." In *Rude: Contemporary Black Canadian Cultural Criticism,* edited by Rinaldo Walcott, 87–108. Toronto: Insomniac Press, 2000.

Shewell, Hugh. "'Bitterness behind Every Smiling Face': Community Development and Canada's First Nations, 1954–1968." *The Canadian History Review* 83, no.1 (2002): 58–83.

– "'What Makes the Indian Tick?' The Influence of Social Sciences on Canada's Indian Policy, 1947–1964." *Histoire sociale/Social History* 34, no 67 (2001): 133–67.

Shkilnyk, Anastasia M. *A Poison Stronger than Love: The Destruction of an Ojibwa Community*. New Haven, CT: Yale University Press, 1985.

Simmons, Deborah. "In Tribute to Howard Adams." *Studies in Political Economy: A Socialist Review* (2002): 5–12.

Simpson, Audra. *Mohawk Interruptus: Political Life across the Borders of Settler States*. Durham and London: Duke University Press, 2014.

Sivanandan, A. "Jan Carew, Renaissance Man." *Race & Class* 43, no.3 (2002): 1–2.

Smith, Andrea. *Conquest: Sexual Violence and American Indian Genocide*. Cambridge: South End Press, 2005.

Sokol, Jason. *There Goes My Everything: White Southerners in the Age of Civil Rights, 1945–75*. New York: Alfred A. Knopf, 2006.

Spence, Steve. "Cultural Globalization and the US Civil Rights Movement." *Public Culture* 23, no. 3 (Fall 2011): 551–72.

Steiner, Stan. *The New Indians*. New York: Harper Colophon Books, 1968.

Stewart, Michelle. "The Indian Film Crews of Challenge for Change: Representation and the State." *Canadian Journal of Film Studies* 16, no.2 (2007): 49–81.

Talaga, Tanya. *Seven Fallen Feathers: Racism, Death, and Hard Truths in a Northern City*. Toronto: House of Anansi Press, 2017.

Teigrob, Robert. *Warming Up to the Cold War: Canada and the United States' Coalition of the Willing, from Hiroshima to Korea*. Toronto: University of Toronto Press, 2009.

Thompson, Scott, and Gary Genosko. *Punched Drunk: Alcohol, Surveillance, and the LCBO, 1922–75*. Winnipeg and Halifax: Fernwood, 2009.

Tennant, Paul. *Aboriginal Peoples and Politics: The Indian Land Question in British Columbia, 1849–1989*. Vancouver: UBC Press, 1990.

Tronnes, Libby. "'Where Is John Wayne?': The Menominee Warriors Society, Indian Militancy, and Social Unrest during the Alexian Brothers Novitiate Takeover." *American Indian Quarterly* 26, no. 4 (Autumn 2002): 526–58.

Trouillot, Michel-Rolph. *Silencing the Past: Power and the Production of History*. Boston, MA: Beacon Press, 1995.

Tyson, Timothy. *Radio Free Dixie: Robert F. Williams and the Roots of Black Power*. Chapel Hill: University of North Carolina Press, 2001

US Senate, Committee on the Judiciary, Subcommittee on Internal Security (Eastland Subcommittee) *Revolutionary Activities within the United States: The American Indian Movement*. Washington, DC: US Government Printing Office, 1976

Varon, Jeremy. *Bringing the War Home: The Weather Underground, the Red Army Faction, and Revolutionary Violence in the Sixties and Seventies.* Berkeley: University of California Press, 2004.

Waisberg, Leo G., and Tim E. Holzkamm, "'A Tendency to Discourage Them from Cultivating': Ojibwa Agriculture and Indian Affairs Administration in Northwestern Ontario." *Ethnohistory* 40, no. 2 (1993): 175–211.

Walker, Barrington. "Finding Jim Crow in Canada, 1767–1967." In *A History of Human Rights in Canada: Essential Issues,* edited by J. Miron, 81–98. Toronto: Canadian Scholars Press, 2009.

– "Immigration Policy, Colonization, and the Development of a White Canada," In *Canada and the Third World: Overlapping Histories*, edited by Karen Dubinsky, Sean Mills, and Scott Rutherford, 37–59. Toronto: University of Toronto Press, 2016.

– *Race on Trial: Black Defendants in Ontario's Criminal Courts, 1858–1958.* Toronto: University of Toronto Press, 2010.

Weaver, Sally. *Making Canadian Indian Policy: The Hidden Agenda 1968–70.* Toronto: University of Toronto Press, 1981.

Webster, David. "Foreign Policy, Diplomacy, and Decolonization." In *Canada and the Third World: Overlapping Histories*, edited by Karen Dubinsky, Sean Mills, and Scott Rutherford, 155–92. Toronto: University of Toronto Press, 2016.

Weller, G.R. "Hinterland Politics: The Case of Northwestern Ontario." *Canadian Journal of Political Science* 10, no.4 (December 1977): 727–54.

Westad, Odd Arne. *The Global Cold War: Third World Interventions and the Making of Our Times.* Cambridge: Cambridge University Press, 2007.

Whitaker, Reg. *Double Standard: The Secret History of Canadian Immigration.* Toronto: Lester and Orpen Dennys, 1987.

White, Aaronette M. "All the Men Are Fighting for Freedom, All the Women Are Mourning Their Men, But Some of Us Carried Guns: A Race-Gendered Analysis of Fanon's Psychological Perspectives of War," *Signs: Journal of Women in Culture and Society* 32, no. 4 (2007): 857–84.

Wightman, Robert, and Nancy M. Wightman. *The Land Between: Northwestern Ontario Resource Development, 1800s to the 1990s.* Toronto: University of Toronto Press, 1997.

Willow, J. *Strong Hearts, Native Lands: Anti-Clearcutting Activism in Grassy Narrows First Nation.* Winnipeg: University of Manitoba Press, 2012.

Winant, Howard. *The World Is a Ghetto: Race and Democracy since World War II.* New York: Basic Books, 2001.

Wolfe, Patrick. *Settler-Colonialism and the Transformation of Anthropology: The Politics and Poetics of an Ethnographic Event.* London: Cassell, 1996.

Wright, Cynthia. "Between Nation and Empire: The Fair Play for Cuba Committee and the Making of Canada-Cuba Solidarity in the Early 1960s." In *Our Place in the Sun: Canada and Cuba in the Castro Era*, edited by Robert Wright and Lana Wylie, 96–120. Toronto: University of Toronto Press, 2009.

Young, Elspeth. *Third World in the First: Development and Indigenous Peoples.* London: Routledge, 1995.

Young, Robert J.C. *White Mythologies: Writing History and the West* (Second Edition). New York: Routledge, 2004 [1990].

Index